# THE MAKING OF FOREIGN POLICY IN IRAQ

# THE MAKING OF FOREIGN POLICY IN IRAQ

## Political Factions and the Ruling Elite

Zana Gulmohamad

**I.B. TAURIS**
LONDON • NEW YORK • OXFORD • NEW DELHI • SYDNEY

I.B. TAURIS
Bloomsbury Publishing Plc
50 Bedford Square, London, WC1B 3DP, UK
1385 Broadway, New York, NY 10018, USA
29 Earlsfort Terrace, Dublin 2, Ireland

BLOOMSBURY, I.B. TAURIS and the I.B. Tauris logo are trademarks of
Bloomsbury Publishing Plc

First published in Great Britain 2021
This paperback edition published in 2022

Copyright © Zana Gulmohamad, 2021

Zana Gulmohamad has asserted his right under the Copyright, Designs and
Patents Act, 1988, to be identified as Author of this work.

For legal purposes the Acknowledgements on p. viii constitute an extension
of this copyright page.

Series cover design: Adriana Brioso
Cover image © Iraqi Prime Minister Office/Getty Images

All rights reserved. No part of this publication may be reproduced or
transmitted in any form or by any means, electronic or mechanical,
including photocopying, recording, or any information storage or retrieval
system, without prior permission in writing from the publishers.

Bloomsbury Publishing Plc does not have any control over, or responsibility for, any
third-party websites referred to or in this book. All internet addresses given in this
book were correct at the time of going to press. The author and publisher regret any
inconvenience caused if addresses have changed or sites have ceased to exist, but can
accept no responsibility for any such changes.

A catalogue record for this book is available from the British Library.

A catalog record for this book is available from the Library of Congress.

ISBN: HB: 978-1-8386-0497-4
PB: 978-0-7556-3751-5
ePDF: 978-1-8386-0498-1
eBook: 978-1-8386-0499-8

Typeset by Newgen KnowledgeWorks Pvt. Ltd., Chennai, India

To find out more about our authors and books visit www.bloomsbury.com
and sign up for our newsletters.

*For my family*

# CONTENTS

| | |
|---|---|
| Acknowledgements | viii |
| List of abbreviations | ix |

INTRODUCTION: A BRIEF HISTORY — 1

Chapter 1
MAJOR DOMESTIC ACTORS IN FOREIGN POLICY POST SADDAM — 9

Chapter 2
THE FEDERAL GOVERNMENT'S CORE EXECUTIVE BODIES IN
FOREIGN POLICY MAKING — 35

Chapter 3
THE KURDISTAN REGIONAL GOVERNMENT'S FOREIGN RELATIONS
AND FOREIGN POLICY — 75

Chapter 4
THE FEDERAL GOVERNMENT'S KEY FOREIGN POLICY PRIORITIES — 105

Chapter 5
REGIONAL INTERFERENCES AND INFLUENCES ON IRAQ'S FOREIGN
POLICY POST SADDAM — 123

CONCLUSION: THE CLOSING OF THE SAGA OF IRAQ'S
FOREIGN POLICIES — 151

| | |
|---|---|
| Notes | 157 |
| References | 159 |
| Index | 193 |

# ACKNOWLEDGEMENTS

This book has been a journey, which would have been arduous without the support of family and friends. My father, Dr Khasraw, has alleviated life's hurdles that consequently eased the path of work and research. My wife Suzanna's support during the research and writing of the manuscript was limitless, and I appreciate her reading the manuscript several times. The smiles of my children brought joy into my office. In February 2013, I began my doctoral research at the Department of Politics and International Relations at the University of Sheffield of which this monograph is the result, and I am grateful for the latter's programme that equipped me with the skills to successfully complete my PhD. The advice of my PhD supervisor, Professor Andrew Taylor, was generous and rigorous, and I learned from him not only as a researcher but also as a teacher. A few days after completing my doctoral research in January 2018, the effort to convert it into a book with further development and some modifications started. I greatly appreciate the enthusiasm and insights of Dr Sophie Rudland, the senior editor for Middle East and Islamic Studies at I.B. Tauris, in the development of this research since the beginning. I am thankful to all the interviewees for their time and contributions, which enriched the research. Help from friends, too numerous to name, has been unforgettable during the research and the fieldwork, particularly at the time of travel to Iraq and the Kurdistan Region of Iraq as well as across the UK and Europe. Others I would like to thank for their support include Dr Lisa Stampnitzky, my second PhD supervisor, Sarah Cooke, Dr Rhiannon Vickers and Dr David McCourt. The comments of Professor Charles Tripp and Professor Jonathan Joseph were invaluable. I would like to express my gratitude to the librarians at the University of Sheffield for providing access to resources at the university and also facilitating access to the British Library. Finally, I am thankful to the anonymous reviewers associated with I.B.Tauris who reviewed the manuscript and provided very constructive feedback.

## ABBREVIATIONS

| | |
|---|---|
| AAH | Asa'ib Ahl al-Haq |
| AKP | Adalet ve Kalkinma Partisi (Justice and Development Party) |
| AQI | Al-Qaeda in Iraq |
| CTG | Counter Terrorism Group (Kurdish, PUK) |
| EU | European Union |
| EUP | European Union Parliament |
| FDI | Foreign Direct Investment |
| GCC | Gulf Cooperation Council |
| IA | Iraqi Army |
| IAF | Iraqi Accord Front |
| ICR | Iraqi Council of Representatives |
| I-CTS | Iraqi Counter Terrorism Service |
| IED | Improvised Explosive Device |
| IGC | Iraqi Governing Council |
| IIG | Iraqi Interim Government |
| IIP | Iraqi Islamic Party |
| I-MOFA | Iraqi Ministry of Foreign Affairs |
| I-MONS | The Iraqi Ministry of National Security |
| INA | Iraqi National Accord |
| IRGC-QF | Iranian Revolutionary Guards Corps – Quds Force |
| IS | Islamic State of Iraq and al-Sham 'Levant' al-Dawla al-Islamiya fi al-Iraq wa al-Sham (Daesh) |
| ISCI | Islamic Supreme Council of Iraq |
| ISF | Iraqi Security Forces |
| ITG | Iraqi Transitional Government |
| JAM | Jaish al-Mahdi |
| KDP | Kurdistan Democratic Party |
| KNA | Kurdistan National Assembly |
| KNC | Kurdistan National Council |
| KP | Kurdistan Parliament |
| KRG | Kurdistan Regional Government of Iraq |
| KR-I | Kurdistan Region of Iraq |
| KRP | Kurdistan Region's Presidency |
| KRSC | Kurdistan Region Security Council |
| KSA | Kingdom of Saudi Arabia |
| MCNS | Ministerial Committee for National Security |
| MIT | Millî İstihbarat Teşkilatı (Turkey's National Intelligence Organization) |
| MNSTC-I | Multi-National Security Transition Command – Iraq |
| NATO | North Atlantic Treaty Organization |

| | |
|---|---|
| NTM-I | NATO Training Mission – Iraq |
| OPEC | Organization of the Petroleum Exporting Countries |
| PCNS | Political Council on National Security |
| PKK | Kurdish Workers Party |
| PL | Presidency Law of Kurdistan Region of Iraq |
| PMF | Popular Mobilization Forces (*al-Hashd al-Sha'abi*) |
| PUK | Patriotic Union of Kurdistan |
| PYD | Democratic Union Party |
| SLC | State of Law Coalition |
| SOFA | Status of Forces Agreement |
| TAL | Transitional Administrative Law |
| UIA | United Iraqi Alliance |

# INTRODUCTION: A BRIEF HISTORY

The nascent and weak political institutions in Iraq post 2003 led many to question the existence and process of its foreign policy making. After Saddam's regime was toppled by the US-led coalition, Iraq's political elites and factions and – to a certain degree and during confined periods – the United States and neighbouring states have shaped its foreign policy making and orientations. The first decade post Saddam witnessed the ascent of the Kurdistan Regional Government of Iraq (KRG) amid the insecurity in Baghdad, and the effectiveness of the federal government of Iraq in policymaking was questioned. Division in foreign policy messages emanated from Iraq, and factionalism and nepotism at all levels of governance escalated particularly during the tenure of Prime Minister Nouri al-Maliki, who had authoritarian tendencies. These factors and the rise of Islamic State (IS) brought the integrity and survival of Iraq's polity to the edge of the abyss. Today its foreign relations and foreign policy have been revitalized but still face domestic and external challenges.

Iraq's foreign policy (*al-Siyasa al-Kharijiyia al-Iraqyia*) has been a contested and limited area of study partly because of the intricate, unstable and fragmented political landscape that has moulded Iraq's policymaking since the state's creation in the 1920s. This book offers unique insights and details about the previously under-researched subject of Iraq's foreign policy making post Saddam. In addition to a brief analysis of Iraq's foreign policy before 2003, the book's focus stretches from the post 2003 period to the middle of 2019. The main question I address is: how is foreign policy made in Iraq? Post Saddam, Iraq's foreign policy became a more complex process; Iraq has been going through a transformational phase where more actors domestically and externally are involved in policymaking. I investigate the making of foreign policy by examining which elites, political forces, key figures and core executive bodies have been involved in conducting foreign relations and shaping Iraq's incoherent foreign policies post 2003. What are their roles and priorities, and who has superiority in foreign policy making? In this book, I map out the actors that contribute to Iraq's foreign policy making: the prime minister, the president, the foreign minister, the Speaker of the Iraqi Council of Representatives (ICR) as well as political factions, bureaucratic bodies and prominent charismatic individuals, such as the highest religious Shia reference *al-Marjaia* in Iraq Grand Ayatollah Sayyid Ali al-Husseini al-Sistani and a populist

Shia political figure and cleric Muqtada al-Sadr. The process of the Iraqi federal government's and the KRG's foreign policies and their imperatives or priorities and the neighbouring states' influences on them are thoroughly explained. By examining Iraqi factions' and elites' contribution to foreign policy making I demonstrate how bureaucratic institutions and policymaking have become politicalized and to some degree securitized.

To have an in-depth insight into Iraq's splintered policies I also explain why the KRG needs foreign policy. How is the KRG's foreign policy made, and who makes it? Do the KRG's foreign relations and foreign policy diverge from Baghdad's? In 1992 rival Kurdish factions in the Kurdistan Region of Iraq (KR-I) slowly began to build governmental and bureaucratic bodies that paved the way for the KRG's de facto foreign policy making post 2003. The KRG's foreign relations and foreign policy underline the second major centre of power and the official split in foreign policy making between the federal government and the KRG. After the Kurdish referendum, the lack of support from the international community and Baghdad's punitive measures have weakened (contracted) the KRG's foreign relations and foreign policy.

Iraq's weak state institutions and strong neighbours' interests in Iraq led me to investigate how these neighbouring states interfere in and influence its foreign policy making and which are the most influential. In addition to the United States' immediate takeover of Iraq after toppling Saddam, and its waning control of Iraq's policymaking, Iraq's neighbours (Iran, Turkey, the Kingdom of Saudi Arabia (KSA) and Syria (before the civil war)) have influenced and interfered in its internal affairs, and consequently in its bilateral relationships. I intend to focus more on neighbouring states than on the United States' foreign policy towards the Middle East, including Iraq; however, the relationships and perspectives of the United States and Iraqi actors, including elites and factions, are discussed throughout.

This is the first comprehensive study of how foreign policy was made in Iraq post 2003 until the middle of 2019 that contains perspectives from key decision-makers who are from various political, ethnic and religious backgrounds. Their viewpoints highlight and enrich the analysis of previously unexplored areas of the process of decision-making and help to unpack the complexity of key domestic and external actors' involvement. For four years I travelled across Europe and Iraq to conduct field work and interviews to address the main issues in foreign policy making. I interviewed more than forty elites, including political figures, ministers, diplomats and opposition politicians, in Iraq and the KR-I. Analysis of Arabic and Kurdish academic and non-academic literature and other documents unavailable in English further enriched this endeavour.

In the following chapters I examine the nexus between elites, factions, domestic politics, geopolitics and international relations in the context of foreign policy making in Iraq. The book's first chapter meticulously analyses the main political factions, including their elites as well as prominent non-bureaucratic figures' de facto external ties, primitive foreign affairs agendas and involvement in foreign policy making. The following two chapters explain core executive bodies that make the official foreign policies of the federal government of Baghdad and the

KRG, respectively. They map relevant institutions in foreign policy and illustrate elites' rivalries and compromises in foreign policy making and bring in the Iraqi constitution and laws within these parameters. In this context, I also explore the competition and schisms in foreign policy making between the federal government and the KRG's elites and political factions. Thereafter, the fourth chapter identifies the contested foreign policy priorities as imperatives that have materialized post 2003. The book ends its journey with the final chapter on neighbouring states' influences on and interferences in Iraq's politics and foreign policy making. This venture starts with a concise analysis of foreign policy since the establishment of the Iraqi state in the 1920s.

## A brief historical account of Iraqi foreign policy

### The epoch of Iraq's monarchy

Since the time of the Hashemite Kingdom of Iraq (*Al-Mamlakah al-Iraqiyya al-Hashimiyah*), foreign relations and foreign policy decisions were made by key executives (elites) who controlled the government and executed policy. Powerful key elites encouraged factionalism among officials and questioned their loyalty (Tripp, 2007, 75). They pursued their narrow interests based on their perceptions of the external environment, including influences, interferences and infiltration into the mechanism of foreign policy making by non-Iraqi or external forces (great powers at that time, particularly Great Britain).

Various interpretations and brands of political identities have been contested and reflected in Iraq's foreign policies; for example, Iraq's Arab identity and its unique character as a political community (inclusive of Arabs, Kurds and other minorities) as well as emerging subnational identities such as Kurdistani for Iraqi Kurds. However, elites' interests and perceptions and their own brand of identity and rivalries have overshadowed policymaking. These factors have shaped Iraqi foreign policy since the state's birth in the 1920s and throughout the twentieth century (Dawisha, 2002, 117) and are in play even today.

Historians and political analysts who follow Iraq and its foreign policy saga take into consideration a number of areas, including the creation of the state by foreign powers and its continued subjection to external manipulation and control and the fractious nature of its domestic power structure, as foreign policy constraints (Marr, 2004, 181). The weakness of Iraq's state institutions is reflected in its feebleness in international relations as is the case of many Third World countries, particularly those that have incoherent ethnic and religious components and artificial borders and/or border vulnerability. These factors led to the lack of autonomous (181), strategic, effective, coherent and/or consistent foreign policy. Although the flow of oil revenue in the mid-twentieth century was a contentious issue domestically and internationally (viz. between Iraqis and colonial powers), eventually the revenues provided Iraqi rulers with the capability to centralize power and press their interests in foreign affairs. Iraq's policymakers were unable to balance the aforementioned complex domestic and international factors that shape foreign policy making and outcomes.

The British designed the Kingdom of Iraq's political system and installed King Faisal I; the coronation took place in Baghdad on 23 August 1921 following a closely supervised bogus plebiscite that resulted in 96 per cent voting in favour of King Faisal (Podeh, 2010, 185). On 13 October 1932, Iraq became a sovereign state with a monarchy designed by Britain – the Hashemite Kingdom of Iraq – and was admitted to the League of Nations. This was one of the earliest achievements of King Faisal I and his government's foreign policy. However, there was no internal consensus between various Iraqi components on the state structure. The non-Arab population, particularly the Kurds, sought international protection and the securing of their rights while admitting Iraq to the League of Nations. The British influence on the monarchy's foreign policy continued formally through the 1930 Anglo-Iraqi alliance treaty, and British advisors were in the ministries and informally influenced the monarchy's elites (Tripp, 2008, 72; Marr, 2010, 22; Dougherty and Ghareeb, 2013, 78). Iraq's domestic politics faced upheaval and turbulence where factions with differing views about Iraq's political identities were competing to grasp power. Great powers were driving these dynamics directly and indirectly, and a considerable number of the ruling elites favoured the British while others opposed them. Between 1936 and 1941 the country experienced seven military coups (Anderson and Stansfield, 2004, 18), catalysed by the interests of domestic and external powers. Rashid Ali al-Gaylani and his factions were a prime example of anti-British leaning; they supported the pro-Axis powers and pan-Arabism. This was in contrast to Nuri al-Said, who was pro-British. Both Al-Gaylani and al-Said assumed high executive positions, including the post of prime minister. The pro-British camp managed to control most periods of Iraq's foreign policy trajectory until 1958. This was not without challenges from the opposing camp which successfully seized power for a period of time.

Milestones of the foreign policy of the Hashemite Kingdom of Iraq included being founding members of the Arab League and the United Nations in 1945. One of the key foreign policy makers for several cabinets during the monarchy was Prime Minister Nuri al-Said. Al-Said envisioned foreign policy interests with the West, Iran and Turkey (projected in the Baghdad Pact in 1955). He did not advocate for pan-Arabism because he believed that it was divisive (Tripp, 2008, 134 and 135; Marr, 2010, 23). The ascendance of pan-Arabism in the Arab Middle East, particularly the strand of Gamal Abdel Nasser and his followers, challenged the monarchy's elites in foreign policy making. For example, Nasser viewed the Baghdad Pact (which was disliked by the Union of Soviet Socialist Republic (USSR)) as a threat to his pan-Arabism movements and his leadership, and this drew him and Nuri into increasing rivalry (Ahmad, 2017, 117). During this period, Iraq's foreign policy was constrained by the earlier defeat of Arab armies at the hands of the Jewish state in 1949; anti-colonialist and pro-Palestine sentiments in Iraq's society and within the political and military class; and the rise of socialist thought and the Iraqi Communist Party in Iraq. These factors continued into the new era of Iraq following the overthrow of the monarchy on 14 July 1958; for some it is known as the 14 July Revolution (*Thawrat/Harakat 14 Tammuz*) and others call it (*Inqilab*) Iraqi coup d'etat led by Abd al-Karim Qasim and his associate Adul al-Salam Arif. The political system in Iraq from 1921 to 1958 allowed for the multiplicity of political opinions and orientations where opposition parties and parliament members had rigorous debates and some space for political freedom. However, the policymaking process was controlled by the Palace and the Cabinet (Dawisha, 2005, 29). Thus, foreign policy executives (elites) had the main say in policymaking.

The Kurds felt alienated, and their aspiration for autonomy was marginalized. They moved closer to Iraqi anti-monarchy forces (communists, pan-Arabists, anti-regime liberals) and were involved in a series of revolts against the monarchy; the last one in 1945 was crushed (Baram, 1991, 7; Rubin, 2007, 356). Baghdad government's international agreements, such as the Baghdad Pact and Saadabat in 1937 (the latter involved Iran, Iraq, Turkey and Afghanistan), included parts that suppressed Kurdish cross-border movements in Iraq, Iran and Turkey as the regional powers were anxious about the rise of Kurdish armed factions and revolts. One of the Kingdom of Iraq's foreign policy priorities was preventing Kurdish movements challenging Baghdad with the support of external powers who shared similar interests. The aforementioned understandings were disrupted when the monarchy was toppled in 1958 (Gunter, 1992, 7).

*Iraq's volatile transformation and foreign policy since 1958*

The military coup of 1958, spearheaded by the Free Officers (*Tantheem Th'ubat al-Wataneen/al-Ahrar*) and led by Abd al-Karim Qasim, toppled the monarchy and brought about the birth of the Republic of Iraq. The multiparty politics and free parliamentary life ceased to exist. From 1958 until 2003 Iraq was ruled by Arab nationalist republicans with various degrees of authoritarian tendencies – a radical example was Saddam Hussein. The first prime minister of the Republic of Iraq (*Al-Jumhuriya al-I'raqiya*) was General Abd al-Karim Qasim (held most executive powers), who centralized power and pursued the consolidation of Iraq's sovereign powers and withdrew from the Baghdad Pact. Qasim viewed this as a departure from the Hashemite kingdom being a client state for Britain, which maintained a military base and supplied the Iraqi Army (IA) with weapons. He pursued the destruction of Iraq's old political elites and aimed to prevent external interference in Iraq's affairs. He shied away from overt identification with Arab nationalism in both domestic and foreign policy (Rubin, 2007, 353). Qasim ruled as an Iraqi first (consolidating sovereignty and its vision of national or *watani* interests) and then as a nationalist leader cautiously leaning towards Arabism at a time when Arab nationalism and pan-Arabism were at their most potent across the Arab world. The rivalry between him and the pan-Arabist leader Gamal Abdel Nasser shaped Iraq's foreign policy; Qasim rejected joining the pan-Arabism bandwagon and undermined the United Arab Republic (a union between Egypt and Syria as one state in 1958–61; Syria seceded but Egypt retained the official name until 1971) led by Nasser. His Iraqi first foreign policy, unlike the monarchy, did not result in rapprochement with non-Arab states in the Middle East (Dawisha, 2002, 127; Tonini, 2007, 232; Tripp, 2007, 158). Iraq turned to the USSR for economic and diplomatic support and foreign and military aid. Qasim's lack of sympathy for communist ideology and the close ties between the USSR and Nasser's Egypt restrained him from projecting the USSR as a strategic ally of Iraq (Tripp, 2007, 158). However, Qasim's restored relationship with the USSR, lifting of the ban on the Iraqi Communist Party and suppression of pro-Western parties antagonized the United States (Gunter, 1992, 8). In addition to the deterioration of relationships with Iran over Shatt al-A'rab and Iran's Khuzestan, Qasim's claim on Kuwait as part of Iraqi territory resulted in Arab diplomatic tensions with Iraq. Thus, Qasim's foreign policy isolated Baghdad regionally.

Qasim had a populist style of governance, was depicted as a relatively tolerant leader and had some reform policies. However, his regime controlled the media and suppressed critics, expanded its loyalist network and gradually centralized power in one populist figure that was a cult of personality (Tripp, 2007, 162; Dawisha, 2009, 191). These legacies worsened and continued until 2003. The culmination of Iraq's political factions and armed officers against Qasim led to a bloody coup in 1963, which resulted in his demise. The Ba'ath Party's role in the coup and their ascendance into the political theatre shaped the direction of Iraq's foreign policy, namely, the advocacy of pan-Arabism. This was despite the fact that a Ba'athist did not hold the top position of president until 1968. The Presidency between 1963 and 1968 was held by Abdul al-Salam Arif and his brother Abdul Rahham Arif (Dawisha, 2009, 183 and 184). During Abdul al-Salam Arif's regime Iraq moved closer to the Arab world and to Gamal Abdel Nasser (with whom he held talks on unification with Egypt), and he paid lip service to pan-Arabism and unity with Egypt and Syria. This was because Arif pursued consolidation of power and there was Iraqi domestic political divergence over the unity.

Between 1958 and 1968 the Kurds and Shia were out of favour with decision-making circles and had mixed feelings about the consolidation of power in Baghdad. During this period rivalries among elites dominated the Iraqi political scene; Arab nationalists (who sought to strengthen Iraqi sovereignty) competed with those with pan-Arabism sentiments. Arab nationalists and the Kurds had brief conciliatory (negotiations) periods and truces, but it always ended in armed confrontation. The Kurdish political leaders were in contact with regional and international powers who had common objectives against Baghdad. For example, during the monarchy and then Qasim's era, Egyptian president Nasser cautiously supported the Kurds on a number of occasions and even met Jalal Talabani in 1963; he stated that the Kurds' demands were not excessive (Gunter, 1992, 7).

The 1968 coupe – called by its proponents as the 17 July Revolution (*Thawrat 17 Tammuz*) – was led by Ba'athists against Arif's regime. Ahmad Hassan Bakr and Saddam Hussein triumphed, and the Ba'athist era continued until 2003. This period was characterized by a more brutal continuation of the concentration of power and authority than former Iraqi republican regimes. Voices of dissent and opposition forces were systematically and gruesomely suppressed.

Elites, whether Ba'athist, pan-Arabist and/or nationalist anti-colonialist revolutionary figures, had a great degree of agency to pursue their interests, yet the Cold War played a significant role in shaping their domestic mobilization and foreign relations trajectories. They took sides according to their interests, whether materialistic and/or ideological. For example, Qasim unsuccessfully tried to control the Iraqi Petroleum Company (IPC) and produced laws such as Law 80 to limit its expansion. Although Qasim rhetorically attacked the IPC as a Western foreign entity dominated by the American, British, French and Dutch, he needed the oil revenues to fund his government, mainly the military forces. Iraq lacked technical expertise, and Qasim was concerned that Western buyers would boycott the oil as they did when Iran's Mossadeq nationalized the oil industry in the 1950s. It was not until 1 June 1972 that the Ba'athist government nationalized the IPC, which was gradually replaced by the Iraqi National Oil Company (INOC). The INOC received investment and technical support from the USSR (Brown, 1979, 108, 110 and 119).

Saddam's brutality and manipulation of political tools and resources in domestic and foreign affairs during the weak President Ahmad Hassam Baker's tenure (from 1968 to 1979) paved the way for his overshadowing of the president. Since 1979, when Saddam Hussein rose to the top in Iraq as president, he personalized power and determined Iraq's foreign policy decisions. Saddam's risky miscalculations and externalization of aggressive and violent methods in the hope they would serve his interests abroad squandered Iraq's power regionally and internationally. His repeatedly imprudent calculations, whether against Ayatollah Khomeini or President Bush (senior and junior), isolated Iraq, and it became a pariah state on the international scene. In many ways Saddam's absolutism in foreign policy asserts realism's prism that success in international politics is determined by the use of force and power (Hinnebusch, 2003, 112, 119, 120 and 152). His foreign policy partly reflected the challenges that had shaped Iraqi foreign policy since 1958 (Tonini, 2005, 123). Iraq's foreign policies have been shaped by the constraints under which Iraqi leaders must operate and the policy choices they make in their own cognitive environment (Stansfield, 2010a, 1395).

The Ba'athist's foreign policy approach when they seized power was uncompromising and trenchant and their slogans were anti-imperialist and anti-Zionist. For example, Iraq allied itself with the Arab states and factions of the Palestine Liberation Organisation. Iraq's Ba'athists rejected Resolution 242 in 1967 and other attempts to find a peaceful solution, such as the Rogers plan put forward by the United States in 1969, which was accepted by Israel, Egypt, Jordan and the USSR. Between the Algeria Agreement in 1975 and the Iran-Iraq War (1980-8) Iraqi foreign policy took two paths: first a mixture of amendments and revitalizing of relationships with potential allies and belligerency towards rivals; second an amalgamation of extreme verbal militancy, Arab nationalist and socialist rhetoric and practical caution towards the Arab-Israeli conflict (Sluglett and Sluglett, 2001, 132, 141, 201). Many Arab states and some countries in the Global North viewed Iraq's war with Iran as a bulwark against the Islamic Shia revolution of Ayatollahs in Iran. However, Iraq's invasion of Kuwait changed many of the external powers' perceptions and they began to view Saddam as a threat to the region's stability. Had some Western and non-Western actors not intervened to aid Iraq during the Iran-Iraq War to build its military capabilities Saddam would have been unseated (Makiya, 1989, 119). Iraq's weapons of mass destruction (WMD) became a notable issue during its invasion of Kuwait. Saddam's self-destructive errors in foreign policy turned the West and many in the region against Iraq, isolating it on an unprecedented level regionally and internationally. Furthermore, the US president George W. Bush labelled Saddam as a state promoter and sponsor of terrorism and characterized his Iraq as an axis of evil (Nagan and Hammer, 2004, 406). Although Saddam had nothing to do with the 9/11 plot and al-Qaeda, his regime had relations with some violent groups and sponsored assassinations and terrorist operations targeting Western and Israeli interests. For example, Wadie Haddad's Palestinian group was responsible for the hijacking of an Air France jet and Lufthansa jet at the end of the 1970s. Haddad was poisoned by Israeli Mossad in Baghdad. Another example is Abu Nidal's Iraq-based Palestinian group that carried out airport massacres in Rome and Vienna in 1985 before he died in Baghdad (Reidel, 2016). Iraq's foreign policy was made by the dictator; his entourage and inner circle aided him in shaping it according to his desire and wishes. Nonetheless, domestic and external factors shaped Saddam's decision-making. He usually acted impulsively and unwisely. Qasim's reinforced authoritarian structure in Iraqi politics remained in place until Saddam's fall in 2003 (Tonini, 2005, 141). A discontinuity in Iraq's foreign policy post Saddam is seen in the rise of different elites and factions in governance and shaping of polity and in the absence of absolute centralization of power in policymaking.

# Chapter 1

## MAJOR DOMESTIC ACTORS IN FOREIGN POLICY POST SADDAM

Iraq's foreign policy making is shaped by the conflicting and overlapping interests of the elites and their political factions, which occupy the decision-making process and the Iraqi political scene. The competition, division and external ties of Iraqi political forces (Shia, Arab Sunnis and Kurds) and their attempt to influence policymaking have contributed to the incoherent and weak foreign policy. In this chapter, I will examine how the visions and approaches of the political factions and key figures directly and indirectly contribute to Iraq's intricate and fragmented foreign policy making. The complexities are reflected in self-interest, political diversity between key figures and major factions, their exercise of external relations and their vying for influence over the federal government. According to former Iraqi deputy prime minister Dr Barham Salih: 'The real foreign policy of Iraq was conducted through the bilateral arrangements of Shia political parties, Arab Sunni political parties, and Kurdish political parties with the Iranians, the Turks, the Arabs [Arab world]' (author's interview with Salih, 2014). Shia, Arab Sunni and those who are purportedly cross-sectarian political figures and forces have been involved in conducting foreign relations. There have been some tendencies between various ethnic sectarian factions and figures to cooperate, which plays into the hands of factions and elites. The factions and their leaders' lack of detailed and committed foreign policy plans have left Iraq's foreign policy at the mercy of their interests and regional calculations.

The visions, agenda and ties of the political factions and key prominent leaders extend beyond Iraq's sovereign borders. Lukman Faily, Iraq's former ambassador to the United States, pointed out the differences between key influential figures and political factions, including those inside and outside the government, which make it difficult for diplomats to present a clear picture externally (author's interview with Faily, 2016). Labeed Abbawi, Iraq's former undersecretary at the Iraqi Ministry of Foreign Affairs (I-MOFA), said: 'Iraq's diplomatic ties with the outside world have become politicalized and political groups, especially Islamic parties, have an influence on how the country conducts foreign relations' (Rudaw, 2017a). Post 2003, Islamic parties have more influence on Iraqi foreign policy than the non-religion-based parties. According to Hussein Sinjari (a Kurdish Yazidi), Iraqi ambassador to Romania and formerly to Portugal, 'Iraq has a foreign policy but there is not coherence in Iraqi foreign policy ... Therefore, foreign countries will not take us seriously or with respect ... Iraq's different religious and ethnic groups make it difficult for a coherent foreign policy' (author's interview with Sinjari, 2015).

Various political factions via their ethnic, religious, political, ideological and personal differences and their competition for resources and power have contributed to an incoherent foreign policy. Dhafer al-A'ni, member of Parliament in the Iraqi Council of Representatives (ICR) and in the Foreign Relations Committee (FRC), stated:

> There are multiple or numerous levels of Iraqi foreign policy ... Firstly it is based on ethnic or sectarian foreign policies; Shiite, Sunnis and Kurdish foreign policies ... Secondly there are different foreign policies from decision makers' level, such as the President, Prime Minister, and Minister of Foreign Affairs where each have their own perspective and they are not compatible ... Thirdly, there are foreign policies that emanate from various political parties, which are different from each other; for example, the external relations of the Patriotic Union of Kurdistan are different from those of the Kurdistan Democratic Party. (Author's interview with al-A'ni, 2014)

These levels are interconnected, and there is room for cooperation between decision-makers to cut deals that reflect their personal and/or partisan interests. Therefore, policymaking is orientated by the agendas of the factions and elites as well as the increasing role of the influence of key figures such as Iraq's highest religious reference *al-Marjaia* in Najaf.

## Iraqi Shia factions and figures

### The Islamic Da'wa Party

The Islamic Da'wa Party (*Hizb al-Da'wa al-Islamiyya*) was the major ruling political party involved in formulating Iraq's foreign policy in the post-Saddam era until Iraq's parliamentary election in May 2018 where Da'wa lost the prime minister's post. The party's leaders had a pre-eminent role in conducting Iraq's foreign relations and drawing up its policy. From 2005 to 2018, figures in the Da'wa Party held the top executive position of prime minister: Ibrahim al-Jaafari (now leading his own party), Nouri al-Maliki and Haider al-Abadi (resigned from all positions in the party in May 2019). Following the 2005 election in Iraq, the Da'wa Party emerged as a compromising faction in order to maintain the fragile Shia unity (Hasan, 2018). From then until 2014, the party managed to manoeuvre other Shia factions at the elections and, to a degree, displayed secular and Iraqi nationalist tendencies, despite its Shia Islamic background.

Da'wa's origins lie in a Shia Islamic political party created in 1957 in the holy city of Najaf. Muhammad Baqr al-Sadr, inspired by the ideas of the *Wilayat al-Ummah* doctrine (the rule of community or people) (Latif, 2008), was the architect of the oldest currently active Iraqi Shia Islamist party in modern history.[1] Hasan Shubbar, one of the founding members of the party, credited the idea of founding the Da'wa Party to Talib al-Rifa'i, a prominent jurist who contributed through his network and activities to the party's establishment. Mahdi al-Hakim, the son of Grand Ayatollah Muhsin al-Hakim, also shaped the party; he managed to separate the religious establishment in Najaf from the party to protect both entities (Alaaldin, 2017, 52 and 55).

The party that began as a clandestine network became known outside Iraq, and members were often exiled or executed as a result of Saddam's persecution. Some of those who escaped were exposed to different ideas, cultures and education; some became less conservative than others. Da'wa's ideological roots were a revolt against secular Arab nationalism and socialism in favour of the formation of an Islamic state in Iraq (Mamouri, 2018). The party was inspired and influenced by the ideas of the Muslim Brotherhood's ideologue Sayyid Qutb and according to Shubbar Da'wa followed in the footsteps of Hizbu al-Tahrir in Jordan and the Muslim Brotherhood in Egypt (Alaaldin, 2017, 51; Mamouri, 2018). The Da'wa Party has experienced major ideological, theological and political transformations and internal political differences – the party lacks cohesiveness to this day – that have resulted in the splintering of figures and groups, such as former foreign minister al-Jaafari in 2008. Dai (2008) argues that the Da'wa Party experienced three major shifts before 2003.[2] Eventually, this factionalism moulded the party's flexible formula, which blends Iraqi nationalism with a Shia Islamic doctrine while attempting to formulate an independent policy. Islamic Shia theology matters in Da'wa politics; currently, the party and a large number of its members adhere to Sistani's doctrine rather than the Iranian Khomeini's. Post 2003, pragmatism has mattered in the parties' political attitudes and within the government. Sadiq al-Rikabi, a prominent Da'wa member in the ICR, said:

> The centre of Shia Islam is in Najaf rather than Qom. As Iraqis, we believe we are the real and historical leaders of the Shia rather than the Iranians, but maybe the West accuses us of following Iran for political reasons. Iran welcomes these accusations so they can use the Shia of Iraq as another card on the table in their dealings with the West. (Qtd in Sirri et al., 2013)

Al-Rikabi's views represent the pragmatic attitude of Da'wa senior officials. Although the party is indirectly influenced by Najaf's Hawza, some key figures (such as al-Maliki) and members in the party have close ties with Iran. Salim Hussni, a senior leader and Da'wa Party historian, said: 'Iran deals with and has a close rapport with part of the Da'wa Party, known as al-Maliki's group' (Fayad, 2011). Hussni acknowledged the close relationship between Iran and the Da'wa Party but asserted some differences between them: the Iranians have had closer historical relationships with other parties, such as the Islamic Supreme Council of Iraq (ISCI) (Fayad, 2011) and its splinter, Badr.

In 2013, the Da'wa Party's electoral manifesto briefly pointed to foreign policy and focused on three main areas: first, promoting economy, trade and tourism as a policy of economic cooperation and regional interdependence and a tool of peace, by increasing Iraq's oil production and GDP growth; second, promoting a moderate interpretation of religion and countering violence and sectarianism; and third, not repeating Saddam's mistakes in foreign affairs, instead supporting international peace and security while protecting Iraq's borders and sovereignty (Chatham House, 2013). The Da'wa Party portrays itself as defending Iraqi national interests. However, when the party's leaders assumed office, its priorities were rearranged and focused on restoring foreign relations, security and the economy.

The Da'wa Party's domestic and international opponents accuse it of aligning with Iran and failing to build ties with Gulf countries because of sectarian prejudice (Sirri et al., 2013). Although the party has been relatively sympathetic towards Iranian interests, it has been pragmatic in its approach to collaborating with the United States during its occupation (Van Veen et al., 2017, 48 and 49). In practice, the divisions between the Da'wa Party's key members are reflected in their approaches to foreign policy, which are mirrored in their personal, ideological, geopolitical and international perspectives. Its two main wings, which surfaced in 2014, were those of al-Maliki and al-Abadi, which offered different approaches to Iraq's foreign affairs. The latter was considered to be more open to Western engagement in Iraq. A third group within the Da'wa Party had the potential to emerge when neither al-Maliki nor al-Abadi succeeded in assuming office (Hasan, 2018). Al-Maliki has been the party leader three times: elected in 2007 (replacing former prime minister al-Jaafari) and re-elected in 2009, 2013 and 2019 as secretary general of the party. He gained considerable but not unanimous support from his party (Al-Mada Press, 2013a). Al-Maliki's approach involved controlling the party to expand his personal leverage over the government. Regardless of his authoritarian tendencies and the party's fragmentation, the party supported al-Maliki when he was prime minister and, to a certain extent, backed al-Abadi's stance on foreign affairs – particularly on supporting the Shia masses regionally.

The fragmentation in the Da'wa Party is reflected in its foreign relations. This can be seen in a group within the party shifting its support from al-Maliki to al-Abadi in 2014. A few days before Prime Minister al-Maliki's resignation, a number of Da'wa Party members visited Iran to persuade Iranian decision-makers not to support al-Maliki (Geranmayeh, 2014). However, Iran continued supporting al-Maliki in other positions and also his allies' Shia militias.

The United Iraqi Alliance (UIA) was formed in 2005 with assistance from Iran and was the most powerful Shia political coalition, consisting of Da'wa and nineteen other Shia Islamic parties. In its 2004 programme manifesto, it promised to adopt an independent foreign policy, continue to be part of the Arab League and the organization of the Islamic Conference and focus on internal security and welfare – without referring to any particular details (Cole, 2004a). The UIA has brought the Da'wa Party to power since 2005. In the 2010 Iraqi elections, Da'wa led in formulating the State of Law Coalition (SLC), which included a section regarding foreign policy in its programme. It praised al-Maliki's first government's achievements in foreign relations, stating:

> We were able to make great achievements in Iraq's foreign relations with world states. This was mirrored in the opening of 86 diplomatic missions from Arab and foreign states in Iraq. Eighty-five Iraqi representations in the form of consulates and embassies exist in 35 states around the world. We are seeking to increase these numbers to develop our international relations. (Al-Jaredah, 2010)

The SLC's electoral manifesto emphasizes that: foreign policy has to be under the authority of the central government; Iraq should have bilateral security agreements and cooperation with its neighbours to control the borders and fight terrorism; and Iraq's previous problems that were created by Saddam's regime need to be solved and strategic relationships formed with states such as Egypt, Jordan, Turkey and Iran (Al-Jaredah, 2010). Al-Maliki's second term witnessed very limited progress in Iraq's relationships with its neighbours (excluding Iran), and tensions re-emerged. For example, the marginalization of Iraqi Arab Sunnis and the persecution of their elites reflected on Iraq's foreign relations with its neighbours and the wider region.

Led by the Da'wa Party, the SLC's campaign for the 2014 elections again had similar foreign policy objectives to the parties within the SLC; but differences within the Da'wa Party surfaced over al-Maliki's approach in governance. These were especially prominent when al-Maliki was sidelined for the post of prime minister in 2014 and al-Abadi took office. Al-Maliki's wing and Prime Minister al-Abadi's opposing elements in the party, as well as in the SLC, tried to influence foreign policy. In October 2015, a number of members of the SLC formally requested that Prime Minister al-Abadi invite Russian military intervention (via airstrikes) in Iraq against Daesh. Al-Maliki promoted this, while al-Abadi ignored it. This demonstrates the different approaches within the Da'wa Party to foreign policy.

Since the Iraqi parliamentary election of 2018, the party became further divided as the two Da'wa leaders al-Maliki and al-Abadi campaigned on different political electoral platforms, the SLC and *Itilaf al-Nasr* (Victory), respectively. On 31 May 2019, al-Abadi resigned from the Da'wa Party and cemented his Nasr coalition – a significant move that heralded pro-Iran leaders' domination of Da'wa, namely, al-Maliki.

The Da'wa Party has reached out abroad to build relationships with the Iraqi diaspora and represent their vision through clusters of its members and supporters (Segell, 2005, 226). However, beyond their media engagements and religious, cultural and sociopolitical gatherings and activities, there have not been extensive endeavours to expand or support the party's cause abroad. In short, the new era of the party began post 2003, when it transformed from opposition party to one of the leading ruling parties in Iraq. Therefore, it has been relatively realistic in its foreign policy approach. The Da'wa Party has a close relationship with Iran and a pragmatic one with the United States in order to reap the benefits of such an association. The party's leaders, such as al-Maliki, utilized the government's facilities and resources to build a network of patronage and even reached out to external powers.

### The Sadrist Movement (al-Tayyar al-Sadri) and Muqtada al-Sadr

Post 2003, Muqtada al-Sadr, an Iraqi-born cleric, has drawn global attention, and since May 2018, when he won the Iraqi parliamentary election with fifty-four seats for the Sairoon coalition, he has been considered the most powerful figure on the Iraqi political scene. He enjoys popular support from a considerable segment of Shias, as he appears to be a defender of rights and services for poor Shia communities in neglected Shia areas (Tripp, 2007, 280). Muqtada is unpredictable, and his somewhat radical attitude as well as populist and strident rhetoric is blended with Iraqi nationalism and Shia Islamism (Lukitz, 2011, 66). He inherited his father Ayatollah Mohammad Sadiq al-Sadr's movement and the doctrine of Shia activism (Ehrenbery et al., 2010, 317). Like his father, he believes in *al-Hawza al-Natiqa*, according to which a cleric can be politically involved with and outspoken on politics and governance (Gulmohamad, 2020, 284). He has led the resurrection of the movement since 2003.

Muqtada's actions post 2003 resulted in further fracturing the Shia house; instability threatened the nascent political process, particularly until his self-exile to Iran in 2008. Upon his return his populist politics remained. Muqtada's loyalists followed his militant populism and resistance to the US occupation, as he called for fighting the US-led forces (Ehrenbery et al., 2010, 317). His move against the US-led occupation was mainly through his followers and Jaysh al-Mahdi (JAM), which emerged in 2003 and gained a reputation for ruthlessness and predatory criminality. The Sadrist Movement's political leadership is known as *al-Khatt al-Sadri*, the Sadrist line (a sociopolitical religious network within the movement that is linked with the al-Sadr family) (Doyle, 2018, 42 and 43). Some US officials in Baghdad perceived him as a 'mafia don' and a 'dangerous fire brand' (Lukitz, 2011, 66). Newly appointed Iraqi officials in Baghdad and the major Shia political factions shunned Muqtada, which resulted in his marginalization from decision-making for a period of time. However, Muqtada's movement entered electoral politics after 2005, as they feared being sidelined in the new politics and polity of Iraq. Muqtada proved his popularity when the Sadrist Movement won thirty seats in December 2005. In 2008, *Time* magazine listed him in the top 100 in the 'leaders and revolutionaries' category. Although Muqtada joined the UIA and took part in the coalition government, his radical and controversial statements on foreign policy were neither represented nor articulated by the Iraqi government's key agents in foreign relations. Muqtada's ability to mobilize the masses allowed him to influence policymaking. His anti-establishment, anti-corruption and allegedly anti-foreign interference slogans coupled with Iraqi Shiite discontent and frustration with the political class and the shaky position of Prime Minister Haider al-Abadi paved the way for his supporters and their associates to storm the ICR and the Council of Ministers in 2016. One of the masses' chants was 'Iran

Barra Barra' (out out Iran). This represented a turning point in Muqtada's external relations that could have translated to tangible policies but rather showed some sort of independence from Iran. It demonstrated Muqtada's ability to threaten the establishment and gave him the opportunity to shape the thinking of Baghdad's top decision-makers during al-Abadi's tenure.

Historically and even today, the relationship between Iran and Muqtada is complex, fluctuating and not as close as that of the Badr Organization, ISCI or the Islamic Da'wa Party. Post Saddam, Iran and Muqtada had common interests against the United States. Between 2006 and 2007, Muqtada received some assistance from Iran. For example, JAM fighters went to Iran for training (Juneau, 2015, 129), and sometimes Muqtada took advice from the Iranians (Baram, 2011, 119; al-Tamimi, 2014). Al-Maliki's government and the US-led coalition forces clashed with Muqtada's militias; he was defeated in 2004 and again in 2008. In the meantime, his militia was fractured, and in 2008 he went to Qum in Iran for around three years for religious studies. The relationship between Muqtada and Iran is characterized by mutual distrust; ulama (religious scholars) in Iran have become uneasy about the cult of personality surrounding the young cleric (Baram, 2011, 120). Al-Sadr's family remained in Iraq because Muqtada's father emphasized Iraqi nationalism, Arabism and tribalism as defining attributes for the Iraqi Shia.

Al-Sadr opposed the idea of Iranian clerics ruling Iraqi Shia and the Hawza in Najaf (Katzman, 2010; Krohley, 2014). Muqtada also posed a challenge to Iranian allies in Iraq, for instance, ISCI and the Da'wa Party, and he largely disbanded JAM – which Iran played a key role in fracturing – in 2008. Iranian interference led by the Iranian Revolutionary Guards Corps (IRGC) resulted in the establishment of multiple splinter groups, such as Asa'ib Ahl al-Haq (AAH) in 2006. Many of Muqtada's destabilizing actions were not under Iran's control; rather, they disrupted Iran's agendas and interests in Iraq.

In 2014, the Sadrist's own bloc (the Ahrar Alliance, the Elites Gathering and the National Partnership Gathering) won thirty-four seats in the ICR. In al-Abadi's cabinet, the Ahrar bloc temporarily obtained the position of deputy prime minister, and Baha al-Araji was appointed. The most influential movement in the Sadrists was Ahrar, and all the parties and their key figures adhered to Muqtada's instructions in domestic and foreign affairs issues. The foreign policy position in al-Ahrar's 2014 electoral programme differed from that of ISCI and Da'wa. Although it included some of the shared principles of the other programmes, it also stated that Iraq should reject and confront superpowers' hegemony and the country's occupation by foreign states (including the United States), demonstrating its firm position towards the United States.

Muqtada has transformed from someone who vehemently rejected the entire political system, to a sceptical participant therein, to someone who wanted to change or radically reform it, to recently cooperating with elites across the ethnic sectarian divide; he pushes bureaucrats to assume government posts. Muqtada has attempted to defy decision-makers on issues concerning both domestic and foreign policy. Although his movement had ministerial portfolios outside of foreign affairs in the cabinets of 2006, 2010 and 2014, he tried to influence foreign policy via his popular movement and masses of supporters. For example, Muqtada fiercely rejected the strategic agreement with the United States and used his weekly Friday sermons to mobilize thousands onto the streets against the agreement (Cordesman et al., 2008). He objected to the modified Status of Forces Agreement (SOFA) and demanded the withdrawal of US troops before the end of 2011. At that time Muqtada was considered a tactless interventionist in state, political and foreign affairs. The few years he spent in Iran, as well as his announcement of withdrawal from politics in February 2014 (which lasted only a few months), have shown him to be a highly unpredictable figure.

Muqtada has a rigid, centralized vision for Iraq. Although he is against a federal or decentralized Iraq, and has rejected the new Iraqi constitution (Marr, 2007; Al-Ali, 2014, 100), he has utilized the articles of the constitution for political purposes; for example, Muqtada's office stated that 'Iraqi Kurdistan's referendum is unconstitutional' and 'the Kurds should adhere to the Iraqi constitution' (CNN Arabic, 2017; Rudaw, 2017b). He has staunchly and consistently expressed his stance against US involvement in Iraq both during and after the occupation. One of his key statements after 2011 (when he came back from Qum) was about corrupt officials, the failed political system and the interference of external powers (regional and Western states) in Iraq. He called to fight or eject these powers from Iraq. Muqtada said: 'We reject the presence of the US army in Iraq and we view it as an occupying force' (France 24, 2015). This stance contrasts with Iraq's official foreign policy towards the United States. Muqtada claims that many (if not all) Iraqi elites and political factions are, or will become, clients of the United States and/or regional powers.

On Syria, however, his views waver: he initially claimed to have sympathy for the Syrian rebels but later argued that they were contributing to the destruction of Syria. For a period of time he favoured maintaining the Assad regime, as he claimed Assad opposes the United States and Israel (Al-Arab, 2011; France 24, 2015). However, he later asked Assad to resign and relinquish power (*New Arab*, 2017). This position could be partially attributed to Muqtada's rival pro-Iranian factions in Iraq becoming increasingly powerful. And while some Sadrists joined the Shia jihad in Syria – including individuals from his rebranded militia *Saraya al-Salam* (Peace Brigades), alongside Iraqi pro-Iran Shia militias and the Syrian regime – Muqtada did not fully support the campaign to rally Shia fighters to join the civil war in Syria (Smyth, 2015). Muqtada also deprecates the Saudi-led war in Yemen: 'We cannot accept the Saudi-led intervention in Yemen on any terms' (France 24, 2015). His written declaration not only states he is outraged by the execution of Shia cleric Nimr al-Nimr by the Kingdom of Saudi Arabia (KSA) but also claims the KSA's actions were backed by the United States, Israel and the UK (Ali Ma' al-Haq, 2017; al-Masalah, 2016). Muqtada's stance is more or less compatible with the Shia-led government's official statements towards the war in Yemen. Although there is no natural animosity between Muqtada and Turkey, and Turkey congratulated him on his success in the parliamentary elections of May 2018, Muqtada is incensed by Turkey's intervention in Iraq. This was in line with Iraq's rejection of Turkish military presence. Nonetheless, since 2017, Muqtada al-Sadr has invigorated his foreign relations. For example, he visited the KSA, the United Arab Emirates (UAE), Kuwait and Jordan and met with the top decision-makers in the aforementioned countries to counterbalance Iranian influence in Iraq; present himself as a reconciliatory figure among the Shia leaders in Iraq; and get closer to the Arab world. Although these visits were not as a representative of the Iraqi government, he demonstrated that it is paramount to have a cordial relationship with the Arab states free of Iranian influence. Muqtada often visits Iran for religious purposes and occasionally to meet key Iranian figures. However, his position contradicts Iraq's bilateral relationship with the United States and the West in general, as he is fiercely anti-West. Although Muqtada al-Sadr projects independent foreign relations, his distance from Iran is tactical and fluctuates. Muqtada's transformation from a confrontational figure in foreign affairs to being relatively pragmatic, yet unpredictable has given him the opportunity and leeway to shape policies that suit his goals.

*The Islamic Supreme Council of Iraq*

The ISCI (*al-Majlis al-A'ala al-Islami al-'Iraqi*) is a leading Shia political force that has become part of Iraq's political architecture; nevertheless it has slowly declined in strength and popularity due to the loss of charismatic leaders, fragmentation, splintering of factions and figures as well as its murky ideological direction. ISCI was renamed in 2007; it was formerly known as the Supreme Council for the Islamic Revolution in Iraq (SCIRI, *al-Majlis al-Ala lil-thawra al-Islamiya fil Iraq*) which was founded in Iran in 1982 by Baqir and Abdul Aziz al-Hakim, the sons of the Iraqi Ayatollah (Juneau, 2015, 109). After decades of al-Hakim family's leadership, ISCI is no longer led by the family, and its new leader is Sheikh Humam Hamoudi. In July 2017, ISCI's former leader Sayyid A'mmar al-Hakim (the founder's nephew) split from ISCI and created his own political party, *Tayyar al-Hikma al-Watani* (the National Wisdom Movement), that could be considered a somewhat more moderate faction within Shia politics; it has become a popular movement among segments of young Iraqi Shia. ISCI was created, funded and equipped by the Iranian Revolutionary Guard Corps (IRGC) as an umbrella for the Shia resistance to fight Saddam's regime in the 1980s via its military wing, the Badr Corps. Its first chief was the Iraqi-born Ayatollah Mohamad Hashemi Shahroudi, who went on to become advisor to the Iranian Supreme Leader Khamenei (Brennan et al., 2013).

SCIRI was intended to be a coalition of Shia Islamic parties and briefly included part of the Da'wa Party (Shanahan, 2004; Kadhim, 2017). Its spiritual leader Ayatollah Muhammad Baqir al-Hakim went to Iran in 1980. He had close ties with and followed Ayatollah Khomeini's doctrine of *Wilayat al-Faqih*, although his interpretations of some details of its jurist council selection and qualities slightly differed (Cleave, 2007, 59, 60 and 61). ISCI's former leader A'mmar al-Hakim and a number of ISCI's senior members have ties with Khamenei (Brennan et al., 2013). Post Saddam, ISCI supported the new political system in Iraq and endorsed the idea of federalism (Juneau, 2015, 109). It has demonstrated some pragmatism in the new Iraq, and the United States paved the way for its engagement just before the invasion. However, ISCI had dual policies before the split of Badr: it was engaged in state building and had a sectarian militia (Visser, 2012, 101). It has been involved in all phases of government since the Iraqi Governing Council and has held numerous governmental portfolios. Da'wa and ISCI have benefited from the state's resources, and the latter has also gained revenues from the Shia shrines in the south.

ISCI promotes Islamic Shiism and relies on its Shia grassroots. Post Saddam, and particularly after the assassination of Ayatollah Mohammed Baqir al-Hakim – its supreme leader – in Najaf on 29 August 2003, ISCI has lacked a clear ideological position and struggled to convey a clear message on religious ideological loyalties to Iraqis and the outside world. On the surface, it distanced itself from Iranian doctrines and symbolically aligned itself with Ayatollah al-Sistani's doctrine in Najaf (Visser, 2012, 102). This became clearer after it modified its name in 2007 and its armed wing, the pro-Iran Badr Organization, split from ISCI in 2012. On the one hand, ISCI had a historic opportunity to influence the new Iraq; on the other hand, being too close to the occupying forces reduced its popularity (Corboz, 2015, 155). Therefore, it denounced the occupation and requested the acceleration of the transition to Iraqi rule (158).

The party seized the opportunity to participate in the new political process, and Abdul Aziz al-Hakim built a relationship with George W. Bush (Cordesman and Khazai, 2014, 156). Al-Hakim was briefly appointed head of the Iraqi Governing Council (IGC); he managed to balance Iranian and US interests, and distanced the party from Khomeini's doctrine. Abdul Aziz al-Hakim succeeded in forming and heading the powerful Iraqi Shia alliance (UIA). He supported energizing foreign relations and received many foreign delegations. He died in August 2009; the young cleric and politician A'mmar al-Hakim, the son of Baqir, succeeded him. ISCI faced difficulties in regaining its place and strength, and fragmentation emerged between the moderate young leader and conservative senior members. Nonetheless, A'mmar gradually managed to become a popular figure in the Iraqi Shia house.

ISCI had officials in the government who influenced policies. For example, Adil Abdl al-Mahdi, former first vice president and former minister of finance and oil, enjoyed excellent relations with the Kurds, particularly the Talabanis. He left ISCI in 2017 and as an independent and compromising figure between Shia factions became prime minister in 2018. Despite Iran's close ties with and influence on ISCI, A'mmar al-Hakim has had a somewhat strained relationship with Iran, partially due to his initial rejection of al-Maliki's second-term selection in 2010 (Eisenstadt et al., 2011). However, ISCI views Iran as a strategic ally for Iraq. In 2010, the electoral manifesto of the UIA – a leading party in ISCI, alongside sixteen other parties – stated it would develop Iraqi relationships with both the Arab and Muslim world and international community on the principles of mutual interests and peaceful neighbours, would not interfere in domestic affairs and would respect international conventions. In addition, it stated it would support the Palestinians and not have an official relationship with Israel (Buratha News, 2014).

In 2014, ISCI's manifesto on the party's foreign policy agenda promised it would, first, have good relations with the international community and respect for all international conventions, such as human rights conventions; second, cooperate with international organizations, such as the UN; and third, engage in cultural and economic cooperation (Iraqi Parliament Info, 2016). ISCI's programme is not significantly different from that of the Da'wa Party; both lack details about their position on foreign policy.

ISCI's former leader A'mmar al-Hakim has received considerable international attention and visits from foreign leaders and diplomats, officials and UN and EU delegations. These visits are mainly to discuss domestic politics and ISCI's role in Iraq. A'mmar al-Hakim was trying to turn over a new leaf with respect to relations with regional powers, particularly the Sunni states. He visited Qatar, Kuwait and Turkey several times and met with their officials. He visited the KSA in 2010, where he met the now deceased King Abdullah Aziz, and Amman in 2015, where he met King Abdullah II. Allegedly, these visits were to improve bilateral relationships between the countries and to show the reconciled face of Iraqi Shias; but they had an internal dimension too – to reconstruct the party's ties with regional powers and strengthen al-Hakim's domestic status politically as a regional Shia Islamist peacemaker. However, the senior members of ISCI disapproved of his bringing the youth into the party's inner circle and his open and independent foreign relations vision (*Al-Journal*, 2017; Sattar, 2017). Al-Hakim's actions officially represented his position and a segment of the Shia community, not the federal government of Iraq – although his former party has been part of the coalition government. His behaviour towards and speeches to foreign entities project his attempt to contribute to Iraqi foreign relations and seek personal, partisan and Iraqi interests.

ISCI showed some pragmatism in its foreign relations and policy views that did not significantly contradict Prime Minister al-Abadi's foreign relations trajectory. Also, similarly to other Iraqi political parties, it has representation offices for public relations. Its role in external relations can be seen outside governmental institutions' foreign relations; it relied on its political weight, the status and family name of its former leader (A'mmar al-Hakim) and the party's government officials. During the rise of Daesh, ISCI acted in a similar fashion to the other Shia Islamic factions (excluding the ruling Da'wa Party). It responded to the call of Hawza's leader to engage with the masses of volunteers and thus created several militias. This can be portrayed as part of the militarization of the Iraqi Shia factions. ISCI's three main militias are Liwa Saraya A'shuwra, Liwa al-Muntadhir and Saraya Ansar al-A'qeeda. These are loyal to various leaders within ISCI. The militias have debated taking sides since ISCI's former leader, A'mmar al-Hakim, split due to the continuous friction between himself and senior ISCI members. A'mmar al-Hakim continues to be proactive in foreign relations, indicating the space the weak state of Iraq provides for powerful non-bureaucratic actors to have external ties.

The Syrian Civil War, the Saudi-led war in Yemen and instability in Iraq have strained the development of relationships of both ISCI and A'mmar al-Hakim with regional powers. For example, in May 2015, al-Hakim announced that the Saudi-led military intervention was not the right course of action in Yemen and would have dangerous consequences; in October 2015, he supported the intelligence cooperation between Baghdad, Russia, Iran and Assad's regime (Al-Rafidain, 2015; Al-Sharqiya, 2015). The party's foreign relations have shown solidarity with Shia issues and parties in the region. For example, in March 2016, ISCI strongly denounced the Arab League's categorization of the Lebanese Hezbollah as a terrorist organization and praised its heroic role in the region (al-Ahed News, 2016; Masrawy, 2016). ISCI's position is similar to that of the Shia-led government, which has not given support but has rather expressed reservations and denounced the statement of the Arab League (Hashisho, 2016). However, A'mmar al-Hakim acknowledged the importance of the US-led global coalition in fighting Daesh (Al-Rai, 2016). This contradicts the Badr Organization's rejection of US involvement in Iraq which currently has a closer relationship with ISCI without its former leader A'mmar al-Hakim, who is now the leader of *al-Hikma*. ISCI became a member in the Fatah alliance led by Badr (majority pro-Iran coalition), and it gained just three seats in 2018 compared to twenty-nine in 2014 as al-Muwatin Citizen Alliance led by ISCI. Since A'mmar's split the party's popularity has dwindled and moved closer to the pro-Iran political camp.

*Grand Ayatollah al-Sayyid al-Husseini Ali al-Sistani*

Post 2003, Iraq's policymaking has been shaped by the most powerful non-bureaucratic figure Grand Ayatollah Ali al-Sistani who is the highest religious authority for the Shiite in Iraq and some Shia populations around the world. He holds substantial political power in Iraq among the Shia community and indirectly in the Shia-led government – without holding any official governmental position. Al-Sistani remained in Iraq during Saddam's rule and maintained a low profile (Cordesman and Ramos, 2008). In the wake of Saddam's fall, al-Sistani did not call his followers to fight the US-led occupied forces; rather, he embraced the democratic process. However, he has condemned the US occupation in Iraq and blamed the United States for its tragedies (Sistani, 2006; Cordesman and Ramos, 2008; Riggs, 2012, 308). The Shias call al-Sistani's approach *al-Hawza al-Samita* or al-Sakita (silent Hawza or seminary); he follows what is known as the 'quietist school' (which calls for non-interference in governance) and the role of the *marjaia e-taqleed* (source of emulation) and has increasingly become engaged in political affairs (Rahimi, 2007). Al-Sistani 'supports the *Wilayat al-Insan w Shahadat al-Anbiya*, which grants responsibilities to human beings for an individual's actions' (Sayad Jawad al-Khoei, qtd by the American University of Iraq–Sulaimani, 2016). He has adopted the *Wilayat al-Insan w Shahadat al-Anbiya* as well as the *Wilayat al-Ummah*. These doctrines result in civilian governance with religious guidance, which have been established since 2003 in Iraq. Al-Sistani leads the theory of 'civil state' that his mentor Ayatollah Abu al-Qasim al-Khoei adopted. Jawad al-Khoei, Ayatollah al-Khoei's grandson, said that al-Sistani does not ask for an Islamic State; rather, he is endorsing a civil state in Iraq – a state based on a democratic process with a clear line between religious institutions and state bodies (Mamouri, 2018). These doctrines and theories are compatible with each other but contradict Iran's model (Khomeini's doctrine).

Besides other *marjaia*s in Iraq and beyond, al-Sistani is considered the head of all main Shiite clerics in the Shiite orthodox establishment, known as *Hawza al-Ilmiya wa al-Madrasa al-Taqlidia* in Najaf. The most prominent of these are Ayatollah Mohammad Saeed al-Hakim, Ayatollah Sheikh Mohammad Ishaq al-Fayyad and Ayatollah Sheikh Bashir al-Najafi (Rosen, 2006, 24; Lukitz, 2011, 71; Jamal al-Din, 2015). These clerics do not adhere to Khomeini's model *Wilayat al-Faqih* (the rule of the jurisconsult, or clerical rule); rather, the senior Iraqi-based clerics expect to be consulted and to provide advice to politicians, which can be understood by a phrase al-Sistani used to justify their involvement in politics: *Irshad wa tawjeeh* (guidance and direction) (Norton, 2011; Gvosdev, 2016, 254).

Post 2003, many have considered al-Sistani to be one of the major pillars in Iraq's state-building project. Post Saddam, al-Sistani shifted his role in politics from engagement to temporary reservation (he distanced himself from day-to-day political matters). Iraqis and outsiders alike see him as a peacemaker, mediator and stabilizer of the various Iraqi factions. In 2013, Turkey's prime minister Davutoglu called him 'safety valve' of Iraq and a 'global man of peace' (Cordesman and Khazai, 2014, 149). Although al-Sistani holds no government powers, he influenced the new Iraqi officials – and, gradually, US foreign policy – in favour of Iraq.[3] This is despite the United States' initial underestimation of his leverage over Iraqis and the political process.

Al-Sistani's statements and responses were heard not only by his followers in the Shia Islamic world, including Lebanon and Shias in Arab Gulf States, but also globally. Under the occupation, al-Sistani put pressure[4] on the United States, the head of the Coalition Provisional Authority (CPA; Paul Bremer), the IGC and the UN presence in Iraq regarding drafting the constitution, national elections and accelerating the process of transferring power and sovereignty to elected Iraqis (Bobrow, 2008, 24, 25 and 29). The end result was that al-Sistani proved his impact on the foundation of Iraqi state building. His credibility and ability to mobilize the Shia masses demonstrated his influence on both Iraqis and external powers, particularly the United States. Al-Sistani's interaction with international powers, organizations and occupiers (through intermediates) has indeed contributed significantly to the political process. In 2008, he had a remarkable impact on the negotiation process of the SOFA between the United States and the Iraqi government. He rejected the first draft of the pact (Geneva Center for the Democratic Control of Armed Forces, 2009). However, after talks with the then prime minister al-Maliki, Abdul Aziz al-Hakim (ISCI) and Iraq's national security advisor Muwafaq al-Rubaie, he laid out four conditions for accepting it (Cordesman and Ramos, 2008; Gvosdev, 2016, 260).[5] Sky, a political advisor to the United States in Iraq, stated it was important to get the agreement through the ICR with enough support so that al-Sistani would not issue a fatwa against it (2015, 265). Therefore, al-Sistani has clearly influenced Iraq's bilateral relationship with the United States.

Al-Sistani has engaged in some domestic issues with a regional dimension and vice versa. Regarding the Syrian Civil War, in May 2013, he refused to issue a fatwa to support Iraqis going to Syria for Shiite jihad. Clerics close to al-Sistani considered Shias travelling to fight in Syria as 'disobedient' (Smyth, 2015) – but this did not restrain some Iraqi Shias from joining pro-Iran Iraqi Shia militias operating in Syria. There is competition between al-Sistani and the Iranian supreme leader (Khamenei) in Iraq, in respect to political and security areas. Al-Maliki was ousted (his removal backed by al-Sistani) and al-Abadi took power (allied with and supported by al-Sistani), but he was tacitly challenged by Iraqi pro-Iran Shia militias.

Al-Sistani tries to avoid the rivalries between Iran and other regional states, such as the KSA. In contrast to Khamenei, he also tries to ease the tensions between Shia populations and their Sunni rulers. For example, al-Sistani called for dialogue between the Bahraini Shiites and the ruling al-Khalifa family whereas Khamenei harshly criticized the latter. In 2015, al-Sistani had a grand meeting with Shia clerics from the Arab Gulf States and asked them to interact positively with all parties in their home countries (al-Haddad, 2014; Mamouri, 2018). He has not spoken out against the KSA, Arab Gulf States or Sunni Salafism. Al-Sistani encouraged the Shias in those states to engage in the political system and not to support any kind of revolutionary attitude. He also tries to play the role of mediator between the Shia populations and their rulers in Arab states (Washington Institute, 2017). Moreover, al-Sistani does not support the actions of Iran's proxies and/or clients in the region, including Lebanon's Hezbollah (Mamouri, 2018).

Al-Sistani seeks to play a conciliatory role on a regional level. For instance, he called on Baghdad to improve relations with the KSA and backed the limited efforts that had been taking place. Al-Sistani expressed sorrow over the execution of the Shia cleric Sheikh Nimr al-Nimr (Reuters, 2016). His letter was compatible with Prime Minister al-Abadi's statement, which did not support the execution; Baghdad managed not to cut diplomatic ties. This issue and other regional tensions have not affected al-Sistani's strategic behaviour to improve relations regionally and with Arab and Gulf states. Arab Gulf States, including the KSA, recognized the importance of al-Sistani and his followers in improving bilateral relations and for regional stability; for instance, in 2018, the KSA announced its intention to open a consulate in Najaf.

With the rise of Daesh, al-Sistani issued a fatwa – *Wajab al-Jihad al-Kafai* – to defend Iraq, urging all able men to take arms and volunteer in the Iraqi Security Forces (ISF). However, Iran has exploited the fatwa through pro-Iran Iraqi actors in Iraq, which led to the rise of the Popular Mobilization Forces (PMF) and its pro-Iran factions. Al-Sistani and his supporters, led by Prime Minister al-Abadi, created armed groups of al-Hashd al-Sistani within the PMF, but they are not loyal to Tehran. This illustrates the competition between pro-Sistani and pro-Iran militias in Iraq. Hashd al-Sistani or pro-Hawza volunteer militias that emerged after al-Sistani's fatwa in 2014 answer to Najaf's religious establishment and are linked to pro-Sistani institutions; these include *A'tabat al-A'basya, A'taba al-Alawiyya al-Muqadasa* and *A'taba al-Hussaniya al-Muqadasa*.

Al-Sistani's statements and fatwas constitute turning points that influence domestic and foreign policy issues that many Iraqi Shias perceive as divine law. In foreign affairs with a domestic dimension, al-Sistani's statements also included support for al-Abadi's government for condemning Turkey's military deployment close to Mosul. Al-Sistani rejected the US Congress's proposed bill to directly arm the Kurds and Sunnis to fight Daesh (Sistani, 2015). The Kurds and some Sunni political factions welcomed the US bill proposal and boycotted the ICR vote in which the ICR's Shia factions rejected the US proposal (al-Hashimi, 2015; Salih, 2015).

Post Saddam, al-Sistani has been the highest source of political legitimacy in the country, and he strongly asserts Iraq's identity despite being born in Mashhad, Iran (Khadim, 2012). Iraqi officials have drawn al-Sistani even further into Iraq's foreign affairs to provide them with validity. In November 2014, President Fuad Masum, and the Speaker of the ICR, Salem al-Jabouri, met al-Sistani before their visit to the KSA (Baghdad Akhbaria, 2014; Mamouri, 2014). Al-Sistani's statements reflect his increasing engagement in politics, and if his statements are in line with the Iraqi government's foreign policy, then they provide legitimacy for policymakers' attitudes. His decision to accept or refuse a meeting appears to be shaped by a delicate calculation of complex circumstances and consequences that considers the significance of the status of *marjaia* in Najaf as well as attempting to convey an unbiased stance leaning towards an Iraqi first position.

Al-Sistani has developed a global network of offices and individual representations (*wakils*) that his mentor, Ayatollah al-Khoei, started. There are more than six hundred representations in Iraq and around one thousand the world over (Katzman, 2006; Norton, 2011, 132; Washington Institute, 2017). Besides al-Sistani's representations, offices, institutes pertaining to culture and religious affairs and those that provide humanitarian aid in Iraq, his establishment also has affiliations in the Middle East and beyond. His representatives and the institutes are actively engaged in different levels of public relations and project the *marjia* (a religious reference) image globally. These representations and institutes in Iraq and globally advocate al-Sistani's stance and positions, both religiously and politically. In addition to al-Sistani's status in Iraq and beyond as well as admiration for him among the masses, it is impossible for any policymaker to ignore him. He has substantial influence on Iraq's politics and foreign affairs, but he can be reserved and refrains from interfering. Therefore, his engagement in politics is inconsistent as intervention depends on whether he deems it necessary to intercede.

*The rise of the Shia militias as political hawks*

The Shia militias have become increasingly prominent and influential political forces; they have external ties and try to interfere in and influence Baghdad's foreign policy making. The pro-Iran Badr Organization and AAH have powerful political bodies, too, and receive somewhat popular support from Iraqi Shia communities – particularly since the war on Daesh and the creation of the PMF (an umbrella for dozens of Shia militias and now part of the government's apparatus). In al-Abadi's government, Badr controlled the Interior Ministry; the former ministers Qasim Mohammad Jalal al-Araji and Mohamad al-Ghabban were from Badr. It has obtained substantial military hardware from Iraq and the Iranian regime. Badr and AAH, alongside dozens of pro-Iran Shia militias, are not only equipped and funded by the IRGC but are also ideologically aligned with Khamenei and receive their instructions from Tehran. Yet, Badr is incohesive (between the hawkish ultraconservative and conservative wings) and some figures within it try to formulate some of their policies without going back to Iran.

Pro-Iran Iraqi Shia political forces with powerful militias are hostile to the West, Turkey and the KSA. The Shia militias are not politically monolithic; other militias follow Iraq-based religious figures, such as those affiliated to al-Sistani and al-Sadr. Not all pro-Iran militias have influence on Iraq's politics and foreign policy. The success of the pro-Iran *Fatah* alliance (e.g. Badr, AAH and ISCI) in May 2018 in the Iraqi parliamentary election as the second largest winner by forty-eight seats represents the scale of their political power. Besides their seats in the ICR between 2014 and 2018, when AAH had one seat (as of May 2018 it had fifteen) and Badr twenty-two, they exert influence over the Iraqi government through their armed groups and members of Parliament, al-Maliki, ministerial portfolio and interferences in the government and public sector. The pro-Iran Shia militias have a defiant stance on some of the federal government's foreign policy issues, try to redirect foreign policy towards their and Iran's interests and conduct their own de facto foreign relations.

Pro-Iran Iraqi Shia militias have threatened the KSA, Qatar and the Bahraini monarchies as well as Turkey and the United States in numerous statements. They have demanded that the Iraqi government sever its relationship with a number of them, for example, after the execution of Nimr al-Nimr. AAH has, for example, threatened the KSA. The PMF spokesperson and the militias threatened to attack Turkish troops if they participated and did not withdraw from the vicinity of Mosul (Reuters, 2015; Rudaw, 2016). Although the federal government and the ICR have a firm stance towards Turkey, the pro-Iran Shia militias make radical statements in foreign affairs. They are working to distance Iraq from the United States, the West and the Sunni Arab Gulf monarchies, particularly the KSA and the UAE. Meanwhile, the pro-Iran militia leaders have expressed their support for close ties with Russia. AAH and Badr leaders back Russian involvement because they believe the US-led coalition is not serious in its military campaign against Daesh. There is close military cooperation (in Iraq and Syria against Sunni rebels) and strategic ties between pro-Iran Iraqi Shia militias such as AAH and Lebanon's Hezbollah without the federal government's involvement.

Amid the rise of IS, the meltdown of ISF, the fall of a third of Iraq and threat to Baghdad, the birth of the PMF was triggered by Ayatollah al-Sistani's religious edict of the duty of jihad called the *fatwa Wajib Jihad al-Kafai*. The fatwa, read by his spokesperson Abdul Mahdi al-Karbalai on 13 June 2014, called upon 'all able-bodied Iraqis to defend the country and to volunteer in the security forces' and declared the war against Islamic State (IS) as a sacred defence *Difa' Muqadas* (Sistani, 2014; Gulmohamad, 2020, 259).

Since the rise of Daesh, the PMF has also tried to infiltrate and influence foreign policy agencies. It influences Iraqi foreign policy as it interferes in the I-MOFA; it asked Minister al-Jaafari to include members of the PMF in his foreign delegation (Qanat al-Tasi'a, 2016). Ahmad al-Asadi, the spokesperson of the PMF, was a key presenter at an I-MOFA meeting chaired by Foreign Minister al-Jaafari in 2016. One of the main purposes of the conference was to indicate that all Iraqi diplomats should openly support the PMF (I-MOFA, 2016a).

The pro-Iran militias seek to influence the Iraqi government by flaunting their power (armed groups) against the government if the latter acts against them or Iran. Although the pro-Iran militias' interference in foreign affairs has shown an image of Iraq's foreign policy that is further tilted towards Iran, the former prime minister al-Abadi and Prime Minister al-Mahdi have tried to manage Shia militias' influence. Nonetheless, this was a challenging task as a third of Iraq was under IS and the Shia militias played a critical role. After liberating most Iraqi territories, the competition between some Iraqi actors, including those in government, and pro-Iran militias escalated.

To summarize, the Shia coalitions or blocs are fragile. They merge and split depending on fluctuating interests, such as obtaining government posts. These coalitions do not have a coherent foreign policy programme; they have been predominantly formed between political parties and figures from the same sect, yet recently there have been some across ideological and sectarian alliances mainly to attract voters in order to have a bigger share in the government. There are some differences between the factions in the coalition regarding their political agendas, both domestically and externally. Therefore, their foreign policy perspectives vary and even clash. Nonetheless, the state has been projected as having a Shia-leaning government in its foreign affairs.

## Iraqi Arab Sunni factions

### Iraqi National Accord

The Iraqi National Accord (INA; *al-Itilaf al-Watani al-'Iraqi*) is an Iraqi nationalist and secular political party that was founded in 1990 and led by Ayad Allawi, a secular Shia who is leading a non-sectarian platform but leans towards Arab Sunnis with a progressive agenda. Since its inception, it has had solid ties with the West, Turkey and Sunni Arab states, especially the KSA. The INA had links with some intelligence agencies, mainly the CIA and MI6 (Prados, 2006, 600; Allawi, 2007, 52). It was composed of secularists, defectors from the military, intelligence and security forces and former Ba'athists. A strategic aspect of Allawi's political platform is his support for Sunni grievances amid the rise of Shia politics in Iraq. Post 2003, Allawi obtained a seat in the IGC. The latter disbanded and nominated Allawi as interim prime minister, with the backing of the United States (Alkifaey, 2015, 469). During Allawi's premiership, Iran and Iraq's bilateral governmental relationship experienced tension, particularly when the Iraqi interior minister

Falah Hassan al-Naqib and the defence minister Hazem Sha'alan under Allawi accused Iran of exporting terrorists (Ayman, 2004; Rafat, 2004). Several times during his premiership Allawi admitted there were problems with Iran (Mahdi, 2004); for example, he agreed with the KSA's accusations of Iranian interference by saying: 'I think that what brother Saud al-Faisal, Saudi Minister of Foreign Affairs, said [about Iran's interference] was not based on illusion' (Glenewinkel, 2004). As he distanced himself from Iran, he obtained political support from the United States, the UK and the KSA. This period witnessed Allawi's open-door policy towards the Arab states. He called to Iraqis to 'take a clear stance that projects Iraq's Arab and Islamic relationship' (Glenewinkel, 2004).

Part of the INA Charter focuses on foreign policy and points to four related issues: first, the adoption of a foreign policy based on non-aggression, dialogue and the respect of international law; second, the creation of an environment that enhances the relationship and cooperation between Arab and foreign countries; third, the development of friendly relations with Islamic countries that serve mutual interests; and fourth, the formation of a new Iraq that respects the UN Charter, seeks to comply with all its resolutions and cooperates with other members to keep security and peace in the world (Al-Bab, 2015). The principles of the INA Charter reflect the importance of respecting the international community and the significance of the Arab world to Iraq. In theory, its foreign policy programme – which is not unique among major mainstream political parties – aims to help Iraq regain its place, both regionally and internationally. Indeed, Allawi and his political party, bloc and supporters have lobbied in Washington, DC. In 2003 and 2004, an Iraqi doctor living in London paid US$340,000 to Preston Gates Ellis (a lobbying firm) to promote and elevate Allawi's profile in Washington, DC. In 2007, news emerged that Allawi had paid US$300,000 to the Barbour Griffith and Rogers firm to lobby on his behalf as he, his party and the Sunnis were sidelined from power (ABC News, 2007). One of the firm's strategies was to promote Allawi as an alternative to al-Maliki in the US capital (CNN, 2007). On 27 August 2008, Allawi said, 'I want to save Iraq and the mission of the United States ... I am trying to stop the deterioration, violence, and reverse the course to non-sectarianism in Iraq' (CNN, 2008).

The weak state of Iraq paved the way for the party and its leader to forge external relationships, including obtaining financial aid and funds, from states such as the KSA (Daragahi, 2014). In 2009, Allawi formed the Iraqi National Movement (*al-Haraka al-Wataniya Al-Iraqiya*) known as *al-Iraqiya*, which includes mostly Sunni key figures and factions; however, it was the major secular, moderate, non-sectarian political movement in Iraq. It was a powerful alliance and included strong political personalities. Regional Sunni states, such as the KSA, UAE, Turkey and Qatar, explicitly supported the formation of *al-Iraqiya* (Stein, 2014, 25). Allawi and other leaders of *al-Iraqiya* lobbied regionally by meeting with some of the regional state leaders to promote and support the political campaign. Allawi visited KSA and Turkey, where he met King Abdullah and Abdullah Gul, respectively. Allawi rejected the Shia-led government's accusations of *al-Iraqiya* being a client of regional Arab Sunni states and Turkey, as well as its foreign policy agenda of trying to destabilize Iraq. In contrast, *al-Iraqiya* said its primary objectives were to improve relationships regionally with Turkey and consolidate ties with the Arab world (Ma'd, 2009).

*Al-Iraqiya* won in the 2010 election, after which its leaders continued to lobby regional and international powers to influence other Iraqi powers to give it the opportunity to form the government. However, this attempt failed. Salih al-Mutalaq, a leader in *al-Iraqiya*, said in an interview in 2010: 'If *al-Iraqiya* had been given the chance to form the government, Iraq's external relations with countries around us would be different [better], Iranian influence would be limited' (Al-Jazeera English, 2010). In this phase, the major Iraqi political elites and factions welcomed the involvement of the US president and vice president with the elites of the major political parties in finalizing the formation of the government. Meanwhile, Iran unified the fractured Shia factions to form the government, and al-Maliki, with the support of the Iranians, outmanoeuvred Allawi (Dawisha, 2012). Despite Allawi's appointment as head of the new Council of Strategic Policies – a paper organization created to give him a post with a vague mandate and powers – he was sidelined from decision-making, and in 2011 he resigned from the body. Meanwhile, the INA and Allawi continue to have a close relationship with regional Sunni states and fiercely criticize Iran's interference. The *al-Iraqiya* bloc hired Sanitas, a Washington, DC public affairs firm, to illustrate al-Maliki's increasingly authoritarian attitude (Mardini, 2012). This showed Allawi's eagerness to return to power and his party's strategic interests in receiving political support from Washington, DC.

After *al-Iraqiya* split into several coalitions, Allawi formed the *al-Wataniya* bloc, which is far less popular or powerful than *al-Iraqiya* was. The *al-Wataniya* coalition's manifesto for the 2014 election campaign stated: 'Iraq had conducted an illogical contradictory foreign policy by creating trouble with the regional states' (al-Watani, 2016). This statement is partly correct: Iraq did indeed have a contradictory foreign policy, but this was also because the elites, government and society were fragmented. Iraq had extremely weak institutions, and elites and partisan interests overshadowed the state. Chapter 9 of *al-Wataniya*'s manifesto focused on foreign policy; it indicated that Iraq should play a more important role in the Arab League, the UN and the Organization of Islamic Cooperation, and that Iraq should be a stabilizing and developing factor in the region, respecting other countries, nurturing mutual interests, fighting terrorism and following a policy of non-interference (al-Watani, 2016). Allawi's regional position does not support Iran's proxies or their staunch ally Lebanon's Hezbollah as he views them as destabilizing actors (Al-Sumaria, 2019).

*Al-Wataniya*'s programme has shown its repeated objective to be closer with the Arab world, but included criticism of al-Maliki's foreign policy. In 2014, Allawi won twenty-one seats in the ICR, compared to ninety-one in 2010. This placed it in a poor position; nonetheless, Allawi became vice president. However, with respect to foreign policy and regional calculations, its stance did not alter. After Prime Minister al-Abadi abolished vice president positions, which were later restored by Iraq's Supreme Court, Allawi continued to criticize the government's foreign policies, particularly Iraq's close ties with Iran. During the tensions in the regional dynamics, Allawi drifted away from Turkey and Qatar's axis and consolidated his relationship with the KSA, Egypt and Jordan. Allawi's domestic and external politics hardly differ in his pursuit of broadening his support and alliances; for example, his common interests with Muqtada al-Sadr (Allawi supported al-Sadr's anti-corruption movement and protests in 2016) and other not staunchly pro-Iran Shia factions such as al-Hakim's *al-Hikma* movement as well as his ties with the Kurdistan Democratic Party (KDP). After the 2018 election Allawi backed the building of a Reform bloc *Islah* that included Sunni and Shia factions (Muqatada al-Sadr's, A'mmar al-Hakim's and Haider al-Abadi's parliamentary bloc) who were not in the pro-Iran camp. *Al-Wataniya* again earned twenty-one seats in the ICR. Allawi is leaning towards some major Shia factions who have no Iranian agenda. He is pro-Iraq's unity; nonetheless he did not support Baghdad's punitive measures in regard to Kurdistan's referendum and advocated for a diplomatic approach and the KRG to freeze the referendum's results (Irvine, 2017; Kassim, 2018a). Allawi continually projects to international and regional powers that pro-Iran Iraqi Shia factions and elites are sectarian and dysfunctional. He also stresses external interferences in Iraqi politics and decision-making with frequent reference to Iran. These have contributed to international and regional states losing trust and respect for the federal government in Baghdad, particularly al-Maliki's. Allawi as an opposing political force has added to the incoherence of Baghdad's foreign policy.

*The al-Nujaifi brothers*

The al-Nujaifi brothers have political forces, some local supporters (mainly Arab Sunnis) and regional allies. This makes them relevant actors among Sunni factions in Iraq and for regional states. Usama has been one of the top Sunni politicians in the post-2003 era; he has played a role in Iraqi foreign affairs by representing the Sunni constituency, particularly in Ninewa Governorate, alongside his brother Atheel al-Nujaifi. Usama was a prominent figure and member of Parliament in the Iraqi National List (INL) and served as minister of industry in 2005. Atheel leads Al-Hadba, which was founded in 2009 and became part of the *al-Iraqiya* coalition in 2010, endorsed by Usama. When *al-Iraqiya* fell apart he was in competition with Allawi. Atheel has close ties with Turkey, and Turkish support was vital for him to become the governor of Ninewa in 2009 (Martin, 2015).

Usama's emboldened external relations can be traced to when he became the Speaker of the ICR at the end of 2010. In 2012, he formed Uniters for Reform Coalition, a Sunni electoral bloc known as *Muttahidum*, which includes more than a dozen Sunni factions. Usama built bridges with the United States; he met with senior US officials in Baghdad. In 2011, he visited the United States and met Hillary Clinton, and in 2014, he met President Obama and gave a speech at the Brookings Institute (Abdelamir, 2014). In his US visits and meetings with the EU's former high representative of the union for foreign affairs and security policy in Brussels in 2013, Usama voiced his discontent with the Shia-led government – particularly al-Maliki's authoritarian behaviour, the marginalization of the

Sunnis and the crackdown on demonstrations in Sunni areas (Al-Mada Press, 2013b). Usama's foreign affairs messages and statements often contradicted those of the Shia-led government. He appealed for external forces to rescue Iraq from the alleged grip of tyranny (al-Maliki and Iran). He became vice president in 2014 and continued on the same trajectory. Following the parliamentary election of 2018, the influence of al-Nujaifi's political platform in policymaking and ability to cut favourable deals with other Iraqi factions has reduced as it lost seats in the ICR (from twenty-three to fourteen) and the Arab Sunnis have become more divided. *Muttahidum* in 2018 backed the formation of *Islah*, a coalition that includes non-pro-Iran Iraqi Shia factions led by Muqtada's Sairoon coalition (Mansour, 2019) as political and personal interests have led to more cross-ethnic sectarian alliances.

Usama and Atheel lobbied domestically and internationally for a Sunni federal region – or several regions in western and north-western Iraq, including Ninewa and maybe Anbar or another Sunni-majority governorate – that would have similar powers to the Kurdistan Regional Government of Iraq (KRG). Atheel lobbied in and received support from Ankara to build military forces to combat Daesh in Mosul, known as *Hashd al-Watani* or *Haras Nineveh*. Usama has also met with US officials to have concrete support on the ground and tried to establish a lobby for Sunni Arabs in Washington, DC (Mansour, 2016b). In 2016, Atheel said: 'We started to open a representation office for the Arab Sunnis in Washington DC that has begun its work. It includes myself, Rafi al-Issawi, Khamis Khanjar and some Sunni tribal figures' (Elaph, 2016). He hired the Chartwell lobbying and consultancy firm for lobbying in the US Congress, the Pentagon, the US Department of State and the National Security Council. The lobby aimed to support al-Nujaifi's efforts to reclaim the land from Daesh and backs *Haras Nineveh* (Sneed, 2014). This demonstrates the imperative external goal of al-Nujaifi and his allies to have a presence in the United States and to try and influence the United States' decision in their favour. Usama's then ally Khanjar, a multimillionaire and leader of the Arab Project Party, has also lobbied for the same purpose as well as to elevate his own profile and hired US firm Darren Morris of Morris Global Strategies (Parker, 2015; Piper, 2019).

According to leaked documents, Usama was accused of receiving more than US$500 million from the KSA's government in June 2014 (Fars News Agency, 2015; Saleh, 2015). He denies this, and on multiple occasions has called for the KSA to have a greater role in Iraq. His *Muttahidum* bloc called for Iraq to enter a military coalition with the KSA (CNN Arabic, 2015). Usama openly referred to his close relationship with the KSA and Turkey, where he announced he could assemble support in the fight against Daesh (Tohme, 2016).

Since the rift between the Arab Gulf States, there have been indications that leaders within *Muttahidum* have increasingly closer ties with Qatar (Wicken and Lewis, 2013). In a statement, Usama denied the interference of Arab countries in Iraq, including Qatar, and stated that it was unfair to accuse Qatar of terrorism and that Iraq has a good relationship with Qatar (Qanat al-Dijla al-Fathaia B, 2017; Alhurra Iraq, 2018). Although he publicly acknowledges the KSA's importance to

Iraq, it appears that al-Nujaifi was leaning towards alliances with Turkey and Qatar while being diplomatic with other Arab states, including the KSA (Kassim, 2018b).

Usama and Atheel's external efforts have had an outcome: their regional allies, led by Turkey, have provided their militia with material support, including military logistics, training and funding. However, since the liberation of Mosul in 2017, the relationship between al-Nujaifi and Ankara has been minimized, partly because of the rapprochement between Turkey and Iran and partly as a result of Turkey's new friends in Iraq, such as Khamis Khanjar, splitting from Usama's coalition and joining al-Bina, a pro-Iran Iraqi coalition in 2018. Al-Nujaifi has been critical of Iran's role in Iraq, and on many public occasions he referred to their interference (Kassim, 2018; Shafaaq, 2019). In 2017, he asked the United States 'to equip Arab Sunnis and to stop Iranian expansion in the Middle East *al-Tamadud al-Irani*' (Braun, 2017; Kurdistan 24, 2017). Usama's regional alliances have shifted from staunchly pro-Turkey to passive friend of Turkey.

Usama was against the punitive measures imposed upon the KRG for the Kurdish referendum, and in 2017 he and Allawi separately presented initiatives to resolve the crisis. However, in interviews, Usama applauded the collaboration between Turkey, Iran and Baghdad on their rejection of the referendum. The al-Nujaifi brothers have influence on the ground and are able to forge ties with regional states. Their external efforts in lobbying for an autonomous Sunni region within the framework of the Iraqi state and gaining support for their forces are strategic and consistent – this contradicts the Shia-led government's foreign policy. Another result of their lobbying is that they have managed to unofficially represent a segment of the Arab Sunni society, at least externally. Dhafer al-A'ni, a Sunni political leader and member of Parliament who joined the *al-Iraqiya* coalition in 2009 and the *Muttahidum* coalition in 2013 and became its spokesperson, said:

> 'The Shia politicians have special [close] relationships with Iran, Syria and Russia ... The Arab Sunnis – and I am one of them – have special relationships with Arab states, and the Kurds have special relationships with the international community ... Therefore the US call or discuss Iraqi issues with three separated delegations from the Iraqi government who represent the Shias, Arab Sunnis and the Kurds.' (Author's interview with al-A'ni, 2014)

Al-A'ni demonstrated the divergence of positions of all major Iraqi components and the stance of a (Sunni) coalition to which he belongs.

*Iraqi Islamic Party*

The Iraqi Islamic Party (IIP; *al-Hizb al-Islami al-Iraqi*) is a key Arab Islamic Sunni political party that shaped Iraqi domestic politics post 2003 by representing a significant segment of their constituency. It has gradually declined in popularity, lost its role in governance and moved to the periphery of Iraqi politics. The IIP was founded in the 1960s, and its ideas, objectives, agendas and actions reflect the ideology of the international Muslim Brotherhood (*al-Ikhwan al-Muslimin*)

(Sabir, 2012, 140). Nonetheless, Ayad al-Samarrai, the IIP's secretary general, stated that neither the IIP's policies nor the vast majority of its members are associated with the Muslim Brotherhood (Seloom, 2018). After the toppling of Saddam, its former secretary general Muhsin Abdul Hamid was given a seat in the IGC. The IIP boycotted the 2005 election and wanted to secure concessions from the IGC and CPA (Frankel, 2010). Despite this, the IIP led the *Jabahat al-Tawafuq* (Iraqi Accord Front or IAF), a coalition of Sunni political parties, and participated in the December 2005 election, in which it became the third largest bloc after the Kurdistan Alliance. The alliances between the Sunni political parties fractured, which has since become a frequent occurrence. Beyond their divergent views, they have had some common foreign policy perspectives; for example, until the end of al-Maliki's premiership they viewed Iran as a threat and a destabilizing force in Iraq. Meanwhile, they have sought close ties with the Arab world and Turkey. Despite the defection of key figures from the IAF, they continued to hold positions in al-Maliki's first government, such as in the Ministries of Higher Education and Planning. One of the two former vice presidents was Tariq al-Hashimi, a fugitive and former IIP leader. Iraqi IIP officials did not have significant influence on the government; nor did the IIP agree with the Shia-led government's domestic and foreign policies – yet they still conducted external relations.

Iyad al-Sammarai (IIP's secretary general and former Speaker) and Salim al-Jubouri (former deputy secretary general, former Speaker and a moderate politician who left the IIP in 2017) have more or less found a balance between domestic politics and foreign relations. During the US occupation, the IIP strongly denounced the United States but participated in the political process, in which – similarly to other engaged political factions – it became a target for jihadists (Dougherty and Ghareeb, 2013, 315). Post 2003, despite relying on Iraqi Sunni grassroots, the IIP's popularity declined.

Al-Maliki clashed with and persecuted IIP key figures in the Iraqi government and escalated his anti-Sunni strategy after the United States' withdrawal. This threw the political process in Iraq into peril. For instance, al-Maliki accused Vice President al-Hashimi, and former finance minister Rafi Issawi, IIP member, of treason, issued arrest warrants and sentenced them in absentia. Al-Maliki's attitude sparked regional resentment and internal instability, and damaged Iraq's image. Al-Hashimi fled to Turkey, which refused to hand him over to al-Maliki, and bilateral relations worsened. The IIP quarrelled with the Shia-led government on domestic and foreign affairs matters and withdrew from the government in protest.

High-profile conferences were held by regional powers such as Qatar, which resulted in angry responses from Baghdad and the I-MOFA as the conferences voiced anti-Shia-led government statements and included fugitives (senior official and former IIP members such as al-Hashimi and al-Issawi) (Middle East Monitor, 2015).

The IIP's vision of foreign affairs starkly contradicts that of other major Shia factions, especially in their views on regional powers. In its November 2005 manifesto, the IIP advocated for a relationship with the Arab world and voiced concerns about increasing Iranian influence and interference in Iraq. It blamed the United States entirely for Iraq's security deterioration and instability. Furthermore, allowing any foreign military bases to remain and normalizing a relationship with Israel is not acceptable to the party. The IIP seeks a foreign policy in harmony with the doctrines of Sunni Islam and considers its Arab and Islamic ties (Glenewinkel, 2005). After the United States' withdrawal from Iraq, the IIP and its key figures changed their view towards the United States, especially since al-Maliki's crackdown on Sunni officials. The same Iraqi officials who denounced the United States before the withdrawal now urged it to maintain its influence in Iraq, counter Shia Iran-backed militias and save Iraq from Daesh. The IIP wanted a close relationship with the United States; its leaders (such as al-Hashimi) visited Washington, DC, in December 2006 and met with George W. Bush (BBC News, 2006). Meanwhile, the United States was interested in the IIP becoming part of the political process as a leading and relatively moderate Sunni power. The IIP's Committee for Foreign Relations researched and prepared a plan to enhance its relationship with the United States in 2006. In the meantime, al-Hashimi and the IIP pursued lobbying in the United States. In September 2006, the IIP hired an Iraqi American expert in the United States to advise them on how to influence Washington, DC, policymakers (Radio Sawa, 2007; Wikileaks, 2007; Buratha News, 2009a).

The party's leaders have close relationships with Sunni-majority states, especially Turkey and Qatar, and have connections with Sudan (Luizard, 2007). Turkey has influenced the Iraqi political process through, for example, the Justice and Development Party's (AKP) close ties with and backing of the IIP. Davutoglu (former Turkish prime minister) played a role in mediating between Sunni parties to form the IAF (Stein, 2014, 23). Meanwhile, the AKP favoured the IIP's politics of advocating for a unified and centralized Iraq based on an Islamic identity; it was a major Sunni political bloc that engaged in electoral politics and a counterweight to the Kurds, and it balanced against the Shia political factions and Iran (23). The IAF political manifesto for the 2010 elections referred to Iraqi foreign affairs only briefly: 'We seek a balanced foreign policy and partnership regionally and internationally that serves international security' (Al-Tawafoq, 2010). The manifesto shows similarities between mainstream parties on theoretical principles, but differences regarding practicalities, regional alliances and lack of details remain.

The Shia-led government and ruling Shia parties are concerned about the close ties between Turkey and Sunni-majority parties, as Baghdad and Ankara's relationship is unstable and fragile. Turkey, Qatar and Morsi's Egypt were interested in strengthening Iraqi Sunnis through the IIP and other Arab Sunni parties and their leaders. The IIP and its leaders encouraged a close relationship between the Arab Gulf States and Iraq. Ayad al-Samarrai, the current IIP secretary general, said: 'They [the KSA] are strategically important for us. He [the King Salman] is leading the Arab and Islamic world ... We believe they are playing a vital role in Iraq to overcome its challenges' (Beth News, 2016). The Speaker of the ICR and the former deputy secretary of the IIP al-Jubouri has preserved a good rapport with the KSA and with other Arab Gulf States externally and also enjoyed good domestic relations with Prime Minister al-Abadi and al-Sistani. Since Qatar's boycott, and the removal of Egypt's Muslim Brotherhood President Mohamed Morsi, with whom the IIP had a close relationship, the IIP found itself in isolation and was unable to garner support (Seloom, 2018), thus further undercutting its regional status and ties. The IIP's relationship with Qatar has distanced the Saudis from them. In return this provided an opportunity for Iran to forge a relationship with the IIP, despite the IIP's long-standing criticism of Iran. Ayad al-Samarrai said, 'Today Saudi Arabia does not want to liaise or forge a relationship with us [IIP] whereas Iran, even with our disagreement, contacts us' (Qanat al-Furat, 2019). In 2018, the IIP supported pro-Iran *al-Bina* coalition led by al-Maliki and Hadi al-A'meri (Baghdad Post, 2018). This demonstrates the fluctuating dynamics of the IIP shaped by Iraqi and regional politics.

*Conclusion*

The influence of the Shia factions and figures on Iraq's foreign policy has been more tangible than that of the Arab Sunnis – and, to a certain extent, the Kurds. The opposing political factions are able to disrupt and fragment the process of exercising Iraq's foreign relations and foreign policy. The Iraqi state's weaknesses and the post-2003 political system, including the quota *al-Muhasasa* and the electoral system (proportional representation), have contributed to the rise of emerging political figures and parties. While *al-Muhasasa* has contributed to the divided foreign policies, the principle of inclusion of all three major ethno-sectarian political factions (Shia, Arab Sunni and Kurd) has prevented a complete fallout of the state's system and given every main political component a stake in Iraq. The interests and external ties of the political factions do not necessarily translate to benefit the public.

There are clear differences between the Shia elites and factions in terms of how to view regional and international powers. Thus, not all the Shia elites and factions are pro-Iran, and both al-Sistani and Muqtada seek to limit Iranian leverage while maintaining a competitive relationship with Iran. Muqtada and al-Abadi's supporters, unlike the pro-Iran factions, are more willing to restore ties with, for instance, the KSA. Despite the significant divisions between the Iraqi Arab Sunnis, they have maintained affinities and/or alliances with the Arab world and Turkey. However, the rifts between Arab states, such as Qatar's isolation and the emergence of Qatar and Turkey's axis, have resulted in some major Iraqi Arab Sunni factions taking sides. A few of them, such as the IIP, in a rare and unexpected tactical move are getting closer to their former foe Iran. The manifestos of the political parties regarding foreign policy are extremely brief and primitive – some are almost non-existent. The lack of a clear plan from all parties is therefore reflected in poor policymaking performance when politicians assume office.

Weak state institutions have led to non-state actors (political factions) having their own external relationships, which has weakened Iraq's foreign policy. Many

Iraqi politicians do not adhere to the official Iraqi foreign policy. There is no consensus on Iraq's national interests, national security, sovereignty or political identity. There is no concrete agreement on a foreign policy between and within the coalitions and major parties and their leaders. This shows that the interests and partisan politics of the elites overshadow Iraq's foreign policy. Iraqi politics has witnessed a plethora of coalitions and political parties, which have splintered and merged, but this has not fundamentally altered the external ties, interests and relationships of the parties and their leaders. As such, each political force has pulled Iraq's foreign objectives in a different direction, while external forces have exploited these differences to advance their own interests.

There are contradictory visions of Iraq's foreign policy. The Arab Sunnis want a distant relationship with Iran (excluding a few such as the IIP), while the Shia (albeit not all of them) want close ties. Al-Sistani, who backed al-Abadi's government, and Muqtada are not in line with the powerful pro-Iran Iraqi Shia militias, who want a more strategic relationship with Iran and strongly project the latter's interests in Iraq's foreign policy. Al-Hakim is closer to al-Sistani and former prime minister al-Abadi, has a relatively cordial relationship with current prime minister al-Mahdi and acknowledges the benefit of the relationship with the Arab world and Iran. Pro-Iran Iraqi figures and militias, as well as Muqtada and his factions, are anti-West (particularly United States), while al-Abadi, al-Mahdi and al-Hakim are not anti-United States. This shows the division in the Shia camp.

The leading Sunni actors – INA, IIP and their leaders, as well as the al-Nujaifi family – play a role in portraying a different picture and representation to other Shia leaders in the federal government. Post 2003, the contrast was strongest between the major Sunni and Shia elites and factions, in which some Sunni factions periodically lobbied regionally and internationally against the Shia-led government. However, gradually some leaders of Shia factions reduced their sectarian rhetoric, and this subsequently led to leaders such as al-Hakim and Muqtada reaching out to Arab Sunni states.

## Chapter 2

## THE FEDERAL GOVERNMENT'S CORE EXECUTIVE BODIES IN FOREIGN POLICY MAKING

The core executive bodies make the official bulk of Iraq's formal foreign policy. The post-2003 incoherence, poor governance, the overshadowing of competing elites and political factions in the federal government's executive bodies contributed to Baghdad's foreign policy dilemma. The core executives, the elites (particularly the officials) that dominate them, their roles in foreign policy making since June 2004 when the sovereign Iraqi Interim Government (IIG) was established, of which Ayad Allawi was prime minister, are identified and examined. While some characteristics of Iraqi foreign policy began to appear during this time, Baghdad's foreign policy has been more or less on the same trajectory since the elected Interim Transitional Government (ITG) of Prime Minister al-Jaafari, who was from the Shia Islamic Da'wa Party.

The prime minister; Iraqi Ministry of Foreign Affairs (I-MOFA) and foreign minister; the Iraqi Presidency, the Foreign Relations Committee (FRC) in the Iraqi Council of Representatives (ICR) and the Speaker of the ICR are the major formal actors that interact in policymaking, yet the prime minister holds a constitutional authoritative edge in representing the official foreign policy. The posts of prime minister, foreign minister, president and Speaker, as well as those of their deputies, are 'sovereign posts' (*Al-Manasib al-Siyadiyyah*); in terms of parliamentary seats, these are worth considerably more than cabinet seats, as it is a coalition government (Osman, 2015, 151).[1]

The elites who control key government positions, their political parties and the post-2003 quota system (*al-Muhasasa*, or *al-Muhasasa al-Hizbiya wa al-taifiyya*) have contributed to fracturing Baghdad's foreign policy. The quota system has resulted in Shias, Arab Sunnis and the Kurdish leaders and political parties in the ICR dominating particular posts. Post-Saddam communal sharing of sovereign positions has become a common norm or principle; the prime minister is a Shia, the president a Kurd and the Speaker of the ICR an Arab Sunni. In other key posts, there is more possibility of rotation between ethno-sectarian groups. Increasingly, and since al-Abadi's government, *al-Muhasasa* has been challenged by some major political factions and their leaders, mainly Muqtada, who calls for technocrats to assume office.

Post 2003, Iraq opted for a parliamentary system (Ishiyama, 2012, 183; Danilovich, 2014, 60). The Iraqi system provides limited power to the presidential council, in which the president is usually symbolic and is elected by a two-thirds majority of the parliament. The powerful prime minister heads the Council of Ministers. The president selects the prime minister and then requires parliament's approval. The prime minister's authority to dismiss ministers also requires parliament's approval. This shows the importance of the parliament. Iraq is a multiparty, representative system. The proportional representative (PR) of the electoral system and the parties that form a majority coalition in the parliament – with the principles of the quota system and political consensus or accord (*al-Tawafuq al-Siyasi*) – shape the core executive bodies. Iraq is a shared rule that has a consociational flavour.[2] However, there are arguments by McGarry and O'Leary (2007, 692) and Ahmad and Sabi' (2010, 41) that the federal executive is a hybrid or mixed presidential-parliamentary executive, in which the Council of Ministers (led by the prime minister) holds most of the executive powers. Although the structure appears to be closer to mixed system because there is a president and prime minister where the former has some limited jurisdiction. Besides the president being part of the executive authority with limited powers, it is largely ceremonial and is elected by the parliament. Therefore, Iraq is a parliamentary and a federal system.

At the time of interview, Iraq's former deputy prime minister Dr Barham Salih said: 'In Iraq we have three main foreign policies. We have a Shia policy or policies, a Sunni policy or policies, and a Kurdish policy or policies and this is one level' (author's interview with Salih, 2014). Within each ethnic-religious political group there is more than one foreign policy vision, often representing personal or political differences. The rivalries within communal groups have led to cross-communal alliances serving political and personal interests, which is more evident post-al-Maliki's tenure. Baghdad's incoherent foreign policy is the result of a temporary and fragile compromise between its core executive bodies and the political elite that controls them. Despite the incoherence in the federal government, the prime minister has the ultimate power to direct the official federal government's foreign policy. I will address what the role, performance and contribution of the various core executive bodies in making foreign policy are; where there are multiple executives, which, if any, enjoy superiority; and if they are coordinating.

## *Mapping the core executives in foreign policy*

Hammoud, the former undersecretary of the I-MOFA, identifies some Iraqi foreign policy sources: first, the Iraqi constitution; second, Council of Ministers' orders relating to foreign relations, including the I-MOFA's proposals and laws proposed by executives and voted on by the ICR; and third, Iraq's international agreements that apply to the international community (Hammoud, 2015). Some of these sources are legislative, some are obligatory and some are guidelines for actors conducting foreign policy. However, not all Iraqi officials completely adhere to them.

Salih stated: 'Since the elected government of PM al-Jaafari, the Prime Minister has been a very important player in deciding foreign policy but also the Foreign Ministry, and the President because he came from a different political background [Jalal Talabani, the Kurdish leader of the Patriotic Union of Kurdistan (PUK)], and the Speaker of Parliament' (author's interview with Salih, 2014). He further elaborated: 'As the government was not strong and was composed of different political rival entities we had a very confusing and unclear arrangement.' Salih indicated to the United States' previous significance in the state-building project, in which it engaged in reconstructing state institutions (including the I-MOFA) and assisting the prime minister. He also illustrated that 'the real foreign policy was a reflection of the political arrangement between mainly the Shia, Kurdish and Sunni political parties who are involved in the political process [al-A'malia al-Syasiya]' (author's interview with Salih, 2014).

Mohammad Sabir Ismail – former Iraqi ambassador to the United Nations Office at Geneva, who was interviewed by the author in 2015 – agreed that after initially toppling Saddam, the United States assisted in drawing up Iraqi foreign policy. After the first elected ITG in 2005, the United States' influence on Iraqi politics and foreign affairs slowly began to decline and for the most part remained dormant. Some of my interviewees argue that there are three levels on which foreign relations and policy in Iraq are shaped: an ethnic and sectarian level, a governmental level and a rival political parties level. These levels overlap and include the involvement of regional states. Post 2003, key actors in the federal governments witnessed a plethora of discrepancies, and since al-Abadi's government, the sectarian level has gradually paled, but it persists in some form even now. Subsequently, in late 2018, a cautious shift in foreign policy making appeared when Salih assumed office as president of Iraq and Adil Abd al-Mahdi became prime minister (independent Shia politician), Mohammad al-Halbousi (Arab Sunni) the Speaker of the ICR and Mohamad Ali al-Hakim (a Shia) the foreign minister, and at the time of writing there is a somewhat synchronized and coordinated position in foreign affairs. Their foreign policy perspective is more pragmatic, not ideological and less partisan; for example, they do not hold a firm position towards Iran or the United States and encourage working with both countries.

Abbas al-Bayati (Shia and pro-Maliki) – a member of Parliament from the State of Law Coalition (SLC), who was a member of the Committee of Defence as well as the FRC – shed an important light on policy in 2014:

> The making of Iraqi foreign policy is from the Council of Ministers. According to the Iraqi constitution, the Council of Ministers draws the general policy that includes internal and foreign ... and the FM is representing, executing, implementing and portraying the foreign policy ... The Foreign Minister comes to the Council of Ministers to announce and discuss his results and vision ... The decision will be taken by the Council of Ministers ... Therefore, the FM and Ministry of Foreign Affairs mirrors the Iraqi Council of Minister's foreign policy ... The President is conducting foreign relations ... the parliament [ICR] and

the FRC have legislative work and they monitor the performance [of executive bodies]. (Author's interview with al-Bayati, 2014)

In interviews, Baker Fatah (2015; Iraqi Ambassador to Sweden) and Ismail (2014) identified several bodies that contribute to and make foreign relations and foreign policy: the Council of Ministers led by the prime minister, the foreign minister and the Iraqi president, particularly former president Jalal Talabani, the ICR and the FRC. Fatah (2015), Ismail (2014) and al-Bayati (2014) argue that the foreign minister provides a proposal and discusses the policy with the Council of Ministers. The role of the National Security Advisory and Agency is complementary to the discussion as it influences the federal government's foreign policy imperatives – particularly security, where the advisory advises and assists the prime minister.

## The prime minister's role in foreign policy

In the post-2003 political system, the prime minister (*Rais Majlis al-Wazara*) has the highest executive power in the federal government. According to Article 78 of the Iraqi constitution, the prime minister is responsible for general state policy and directs the Council of Ministers. A significant part of the foreign policy making process goes through the Council of Ministers. The prime minister is the commander-in-chief of Iraq's Armed Forces, which also provides the prime minister with authority on domestic and foreign policy in security and defence. The international community looks to the prime minister to understand the federal government's official position and image.

There are a number of organizations available to help and support the prime minister. For example, al-Abadi's office has ten offices (*Makatab*) within the committee, each of which deals with different issues (Knights et al., 2011; PMO, 2015a,b). Another is the General Secretariat for the Council of Ministers, the main administrative duties of which are to assist the prime minister (including in foreign affairs) and act as the link between the prime minister and the Council of Ministers and the ministers' policies (General Secretariat for the Council of Ministers, 2014). The prime minister has a cluster of advisors, who are specialists on various issues related to governance, including foreign policy. Since 2003, the prime minister has had deputies appointed from different political parties as part of the quota system and consociationalism. Prime Minister Al-Abadi stripped these deputies and other positions for his government as part of the reform plan.

### Ayad Allawi (June 2004–April 2005)

Ayad Allawi is a secular Iraqi nationalist of Shia origin and the co-founder of the Iraqi National Accord (INA). He was a member of the Iraqi Governing Council (IGC), and was chosen by the United States and voted for by the IGC to become the first prime minister of the IIG (CPA Regulation 10, 2004). Occupying powers, in consultation with the IGC, appointed the IIG (Otterman, 2004).[3] Some of

Allawi's policies were reflected in the INA's political programme. He aimed to build the security and defence apparatus by reintegrating – with limited success – some of the Iraqis dismissed by the US-led coalition. Allawi enjoyed close ties and was friendly with many of the Sunni community leaders, neighbouring countries (excluding Iran), the Arab states and the West. His policies were modest and reflected his political background and external ties.

The IIG maintained some of the IGC's political configuration, which first introduced the ethno-sectarian distribution of portfolios and powers (Raphaeli, 2004). The cross-sectarian prime minister had relatively good relations with various Iraqi elites and factions and especially close ties with the Arab Sunnis. In spite of Bremer's formal blessing of Allawi's appointment, Symonds (2004) noted that UN secretary general Kofi Annan was more reluctant because the UN was sidelined from his appointment. US leverage was dominant at this time. Allawi (2013) had, at least theoretically, both legislative and executive powers.

Allawi is a liberal figure and was active in presenting and giving interviews and speeches in good English on international platforms and media. Notably, on 23 September 2004, Allawi said to the US Congress: 'A message from my people to you: Thank-you, America.' As prime minister, he was warmly welcomed by the Kingdom of Saudi Arabia (KSA) and other Arab states (Al-Mada Paper, 2004). Allawi lacked Iran's support, which he consistently accused of interference. His previous career with the Ba'ath Party and close ties with the US security circles made him an unpopular figure in a segment of the increasingly religiously conservative Iraqi Shia community.

The Transitional Administrative Law (TAL), announced in March 2004 and brought into effect in June 2004, had a temporary influence on the transitional period for approximately one year. Its laws were in effect for the IIG until a permanent constitution was confirmed (CPA, 2014). Article 25 of TAL granted the ITG the power over the country's foreign affairs but lacked clarity on the distribution of responsibility. Allawi granted himself credit for supervising the revitalization of Iraq's diplomatic and foreign relations; Allawi led the Sharm el-Sheikh international leaders' conference (November 2004) on Iraq's future, which included leaders of the UN, Arab League and regional and international foreign ministers. Within a month, Allawi gave a speech in the European Union headquarters regarding the stabilization of Iraq (Allawi, 2013). This showed the first Iraqi prime minister's proactive behaviour, post Saddam, on the international scene. He stated his intentions to integrate Iraq with the international community and the family of nations and to build state institutions (Council on Foreign Relations, 2004), including the security apparatus, and revive the economy.

Compared to Iraqi Shia Islamists, Allawi took a divergent stance on regional issues. While he was very cautious about improving Iraq and Syria's bilateral relations, he bluntly stated the tensions between Iran and Iraq, which are between him and Tehran. In September 2004, Allawi claimed that foreign fighters were coming from Iran and Syria. He said, 'There are tensions and problems between us [Iraqi government] and you [Iran]' (Council on Foreign Relations, 2004). Allawi stated 'When I was PM I did not allow for Iranian interference, but I respect

Iran' (Al-Sumaria, 2019). He became known for his critical anti-Iranian rhetoric, which escalated after he left office and when Iran favoured al-Maliki in 2010. He turned down numerous invitations from Iran and in August 2004, rejected Iran's call for a regional summit for the stabilization of southern Iraq (Berenson and Filkins, 2004). In the meantime, the Iraqi vice president Ibrahim al-Jaafari, a Shiite leader, visited Iran to mend bilateral relationships (Iran Focus, 2004). This was the beginning of Baghdad's foreign policy incoherence between one of the vice presidents and the prime minister. Post Saddam, the only period of time in which the Iraqi and Iranian governmental relationship were not at their best was during Allawi's government.

Allawi's government focused on emerging from isolation by building diplomatic relationships; setting up foreign affairs bodies, with the US-led coalition's assistance; opening up Iraq for foreign investment, approaching international and regional organizations and states and promoting security and military cooperation. The IIG was figuring out how to reach out to the world. These three areas (diplomacy, security and economy) are still present in Baghdad's foreign policy priorities.

*Ibrahim al-Jaafari (May 2005–May 2006)*

In January 2005, the first election resulted in the first post-2003 elected transitional government. Ibrahim al-Jaafari, the former Islamic Da'wa Party spokesperson, served as Iraq's first democratically elected prime minister for the ITG. Previously, in 2003, al-Jaafari had been the first president of the IGC; he then became the vice president from 2004 to 2005, and was a leading member of the United Iraqi Alliance (UIA).

Sectarian violence increased during al-Jaafari's time as prime minister. He had close ties with Tehran and welcomed their advice. He turned a blind eye towards Iran's increasing financial, military and training assistance for the Shia militias (Lukitz, 2011, 60; Yaphe, 2011b, 45). Al-Jaafari tolerated Jaish al-Mahdi (JAM), the anti-US-led coalition Muqtada al-Sadr's militia. Washington and the Arab Gulf States, particularly the KSA, were dissatisfied with al-Jaafari's appointment, as he had close ties with Iranian decision-makers. His deputies – Rosh Shawis, from the Kurdistan Democratic Party (KDP), and Ahmad Chalabi, a secular Shia favoured by the United States – have significantly different, moderate views.

There were contradictory visions for Iraq's future between Iraq's interim president Jalal Talabani and al-Jaafari. The latter gave lip service to federalism and autonomy, but advocated for a strong centralized regime (Eppel, 2011, 121). In al-Jaafari's article 'My Vision for Iraq' for the *Washington Post* in March 2006, he focused on security, backing Muqtada al-Sadr's integration into the political system and economic rehabilitation (al-Jaafari, 2006). The United States, some Shia factions and the Kurds were disgruntled by al-Jaafari's approach. Al-Jaafari was overwhelmed with instability and passing the new constitution, which was voted for by referendum in October 2005. This period marked the emergence of a disagreement between Iraqi elites and factions regarding the Iraqi constitution, which reflected the divergent views projected to the outside world.[4]

The new Iraqi constitution granted the prime minister domestic and foreign policy powers, such as in Article 78. While al-Jaafari was drawn into domestic challenges, he pushed for a strategic relationship with Iran in the areas of security, economy and natural energy; in July 2005, he was the first Iraqi prime minister to visit since the fall of Saddam (Obaid, 2006) and the era of close ties between Iraq and Iran began. Al-Jaafari had a tense relationship with the KSA, which he accused of not coordinating with Iraqi pilgrims for *Hajj* in the KSA. The Saudi government rebuffed al-Jaafari's accusations, which it described as 'a political ploy to improve his flagging political image in Iraq' (Saudi Embassy, 2006). This demonstrates the schism between Prime Minister al-Jaafari and Riyadh.

The Islamic Da'wa Party nominated al-Jaafari but discussed neither the governance and administration programme nor how their relationship would evolve after he presumed the premiership. The Da'wa Party viewed al-Jaafari to be taking a different direction from the party, and the link between them became very feeble. His efforts in foreign relations and diplomacy were compatible with the party's but were translated by his personal expertise rather than the party's agenda. He was sidelined in the party because of his poor relationship with the rest of the party's leadership, he and formed his own party in 2008 (Husseini, 2014).

Although the UIA won the December 2005 election, the Kurdish and Sunni political blocs lobbied for al-Jaafari's removal and the United States no longer backed him (Lukitz, 2011, 60; Yaphe, 2011a, 45).[5] He stepped down in May 2006 in favour of Nouri al-Maliki. Although the United States still played a role, this period witnessed the further gradual decline of US influence on Iraqi political configuration and policymaking. Iranian influence continued to increase in Iraq's politics.

*Nouri al-Maliki (May 2006–10 and December 2010–September 2014)*

Al-Maliki became prime minister in 2006 and was depicted as a compromise to al-Jaafari. Ali Khedery, a senior advisor to the US ambassadors, argued that he introduced al-Maliki to the Americans, who were looking for a leader to crush the Shia militias (viz. JAM) and al-Qaeda and unify Iraq. The US ambassador Zalmay Khalilzad contributed significantly to the negotiations leading to al-Maliki's appointment (Khedery, 2014). Initially, US officials did not disapprove of al-Maliki, and the new prime minister was warmly received when he addressed the US Congress in 2006 (C-Span, 2006).

On 22 April 2006, President Jalal Talabani designated al-Maliki to form the government. Al-Maliki was elected the leader (secretary general) of the Islamic Da'wa Party. He won three successive party elections as secretary general: in 2007, 2009 and 2013. Al-Maliki sought to appease the Da'wa Party more than al-Jaafari had. From 2006 onward, al-Maliki's goal was to dominate vital governmental bodies by appointing Da'wa members, cronies and loyalists.

In 2006, al-Maliki made his first visit as prime minister to the KSA where he met King Abdullah and top officials. They discussed border security, trade and investment. The KSA leaders were cautiously optimistic and waited for the Iraqi government to engage (KUNA, 2006; Wikileaks, 2006). However, al-Maliki's visit was fruitless; the relationship did not develop. Sdqian (2014) argues that the deterioration of Iraq's regional relationships with the Arab world was due to the turbulent regional dynamics and US occupation.[6] Without dismissing the latter two aspects, mutual suspicions and al-Maliki's rigid and sectarian policies also contributed, as well as his reactionary and undiplomatic statements – especially towards the Arab Gulf States and Turkey. The now deceased King Abdullah of the KSA told Obama's top advisor John Brennan, 'I don't trust this man ... he is an Iranian agent' (Gordon, 2010).

Al-Maliki clearly favoured a strong, centralized state in Baghdad. He carefully balanced the need to preserve US support with concessions to national sentiments (Henry and Springborg, 2014, 152). Al-Maliki asserted the independence of the federal government's authority in formulating and conducting foreign relations and policy. He articulated this in 2007: 'Iraqi foreign policy is designed and executed by the Iraqi federal government.' He further said: 'Our official foreign policy stance is having good relations with the neighbours and not intervening in their domestic affairs, and not allowing them [e.g. Turkey] to interfere in Iraq's internal affairs.' This comment was a response to statements from President Masoud Barzani and Turkish authorities from which he was excluded (al-Mustaqbal, 2007; Now, 2007). Furthermore, in the same statement al-Maliki grudgingly underlined foreign policies that emanated from the Kurdistan Regional Government of Iraq (KRG).

During al-Maliki's term, the Status of Force Agreement (SOFA) between Iraq and the United States faced opposition from many Iraqi Shia and Sunni elites and factions. Despite his inclinations, al-Maliki was unable to secure a small remnant of the US forces in Iraq. At the end of 2007, al-Maliki asked the UN Security Council to extend the mandate for the last time. On 26 November 2007, al-Maliki and Bush signed a Declaration of Principles for a Long-Term Relationship of Cooperation and Friendship between the Republic of Iraq and the United States of America (US Department of State Archive, 2007; Mason, 2012). Neither al-Maliki nor Allawi were ready to provide definite support (Jeffrey, 2014). Kurdish leaders and their members of Parliament in Baghdad supported providing immunity for residual US troops. Although the Bush administration agreed to the total withdrawal of US troops from Iraq by the end of 2011, negotiations for a number of US troops to remain in Iraq failed in 2011. Al-Maliki played a part in obtaining the support of some Shia elites for an agreement with the United States – the Strategic Framework Agreement (SFA) – which was signed in November 2008 and covered political, diplomatic, security, economic and cultural spheres (Bruno, 2008; Mason, 2008, 17; White House, 2014). As immunity was not granted for the residual forces and the entire force had to withdraw, in November 2008, the ICR voted in favour of the SFA pact 149-35, despite opposition from Muqtada al-Sadr's bloc.

In this period, al-Maliki – who appeared to be becoming a strong politician – preserved a balanced relationship with the United States and Iran, despite the rise of critics (Alsis et al., 2011, 22). A few days before al-Maliki's visit to Iran, the Iraqi defence minister and his Iranian counterpart signed a memorandum of understanding to develop defence cooperation (Global Policy Forum, 2008; Relief

Web, 2008). Al-Maliki met President Ahmadinejad and the Supreme Leader, who he reassured that the US agreement would not harm (Iran Focus, 2008). Al-Maliki played an intermediary role in bringing the Americans and Iranians into direct talks in his office in Baghdad in 2007. These meetings focused on the security situation in Iraq, and aimed to create a common interest in supporting the new Iraq (Soffar, 2010, 226) as al-Maliki stated it was breaking the ice between the two countries (Euronews, 2009). Therefore, al-Maliki achieved the support of the United States and Iran to cement his position, despite his differing agenda (Dodge, 2012, 183).

Al-Maliki's military campaign countered the growth of the Sunni jihadists and Al-Qaeda in Iraq in 2007 with the US-backed Awakening movement (*Sahwat*) of local Sunni Arab tribesmen. In addition to his military campaign against JAM, al-Maliki's position was strengthened domestically and abroad; his key support came from the United States and Iran. He started to rely on Iranian support to counter JAM when Iran began to splinter Muqtada's militia (JAM) into many militias, such as Asa'ib Ahl al-Haq (AAH) and Kataib Hezbollah (KH) (Mansour and Jabar, 2017). In his first term as prime minister, al-Maliki favoured Tehran's interests, as they were convergent to his. From the end of al-Maliki's first term, authoritarian tendencies began to appear; he and his loyalists sought to control the key pillars of the Iraqi state security and oil revenues (Rayburn, 2014, 55). Al-Maliki interfered on a granular level to cement his grip over the Iraqi Security Forces (ISF) and intelligence services. He established two extra-constitutional organizations, which spanned Iraq's military and security forces (Dodge, 2012, 127, 128). His approach to foreign policy was similar to his approach to other areas in governance – concentration of power and the micromanagement from the prime minister's office of all internal and foreign policy making (Sirri et al., 2013, 12). Al-Maliki drew up a subjective foreign policy and had the support of the Da'wa Party.

Al-Maliki's accumulation of power and sidelining of adversaries was a gradual strategy. He sought to project himself as a strong leader, able to formulate foreign policy. His first term witnessed a deliberate diversifying of Iraqi foreign relations to include France, Eastern Europe and Russia for security and investment. Al-Maliki preferred to have allies who would not place restrictions or conditions on buying weapons. Additionally, having more allies provided him with the space to outmanoeuvre the United States if necessary.

Al-Maliki's SLC was second to Allawi's (*al-Iraqiya*) in the 2010 election. Al-Maliki's controversial second term in 2010 was secured after eight months of bargaining between the major elites and factions. Iran engineered al-Maliki's reinstatement to power by persuading other elites and factions – particularly his rival, al-Sadr (Younis, 2014). Al-Maliki became more indebted and akin to Iran, which also coincided with the US-led forces' withdrawal from Iraq. Al-Maliki is an Iraqi nationalist, not an Iranian puppet. His interests converge with Tehran's; both have a proximate worldview of Western conspiracy against the Muslim world.

The government meeting al-Maliki headed on 22 December 2010 discussed the priorities of his new government: developing foreign relations and the security file

(Al-Arab, 2010). Al-Maliki wanted to show his ability to draw up an independent and centralized foreign policy and foreign relations. However, fragmentation in the federal government's foreign relations and foreign policy persisted, including between him and his deputies. His agenda originated from drivers such as strengthening his constituency's impact on domestic politics and creating a new foreign policy that would help him in his political struggle internally (Bacik, 2012, 1). Al-Maliki's foreign policy tendencies and statements reflected his political campaign to attract wider segments of the Shia community. His close inner circle included Falah al-Fayad, who he appointed as acting national security minister in June 2011. Al-Fayad played the major role in assisting al-Maliki on Syrian issues. Al-Maliki had more than a dozen advisors in different fields, many of whom were from the Da'wa Party. Foreign Minister Zebari, from the KDP, had less say in shaping al-Maliki's perspectives on foreign relations than his advisors or inner circle.

In the new Iraqi constitution, Article 78 confers on the prime minister the legitimacy to draw and steer the policies of the state. The constitution has been subject to various interpretations, although it lies under the power of the Federal Supreme Court, which is a victim of political manipulation. Al-Maliki was accused of subjecting many institutions to his domination, including the Iraqi Judiciary (Yaphe, 2012).

A key feature of al-Maliki's second term was internal conflict. In December 2011, Obama praised al-Maliki for leading the most inclusive government yet (White House, 2011). On 13 December 2011, Iraq's deputy prime minister Saleh al-Mutlaq (a Sunni politician) told CNN he was 'shocked' by Presidents Obama's remarks. He said: 'Washington is leaving Iraq with a dictator who [al-Maliki] has ignored a power-sharing agreement' (Damon and Tawfeeq, 2011; Beinart, 2014). The Iranians supported al-Maliki, and President Talabani rejected demands for a vote of no confidence (Ali, 2014, 6; Pollack, 2014). Al-Maliki's foreign policy perspective was increasingly coloured by the conservative Shia Islamic and sectarian vision. He displayed increasingly authoritarian tendencies and favoured Iran's interests regionally, such as removing Sinan al-Shabibi, governor of Iraq's Central Bank, as Iran desired. Al-Shabibi and his deputy blocked the smuggling of hundreds of millions of dollars from Iraq into Iran. Al-Maliki's loyalist replaced al-Shabibi, to financially support Assad's regime (Latif, 2012). Al-Maliki expanded hegemony in all vital sectors, including finance.

Al-Maliki prosecuted his opponents, such as the Iraqi vice president Tariq al-Hashimi (now based in Turkey), on terrorism charges. This case had regional and international repercussions, and Iraq's relationship with Turkey, Qatar and the KSA deteriorated as they received al-Hashimi as vice president and refused to hand him over (*Alwasat News*, 2012; Reuters, 2012a). This harmed Iraq's already damaged image and further distanced al-Maliki from the aforementioned states. It illustrates al-Maliki's disenfranchised approach to the Sunnis in the government and in Iraq, which had regional ramifications. While Iraq and the KSA had a poor relationship, al-Maliki's attitude worsened it (Stansfield, 2010a).

Al-Maliki's deputies had different visions and statements relating to foreign policy. His deputy Salih al-Mutlaq presented a picture of Iraq's politics, security and economy to the outside world that completely differed from that of al-Maliki. Al-Maliki's government faced challenges in formulating a united foreign policy and all participating (in the government) political parties agreed (Al-Knani, 2012). His offensive on Sunni politicians escalated; former deputy prime minister and finance minister Rafie al-Issawi's house was raided. This can also be portrayed as al-Maliki's politicization of security. The minister of communications Mohamad Allawi (from the *Iraqiya* alliance) published a letter detailing al-Maliki's interference in the ministry and eventually resigned (Al-Ali, 2014, 152).

Al-Maliki appointed himself acting interior minister and defence minister and acting minister of state for national security in 2010, with the premise of retaining the posts until he found suitable candidates. He had a different vision of foreign policy than Ayad Allawi, Masoud Barzani, Ahmad Chalabi and other leaders. Al-Maliki usually accused the politicians who disagreed with him, including the aforementioned, of conspiring against Iraq and having special links and interests with external states.

Likewise, the chasm between al-Maliki and Foreign Minister Zebari widened. Adel Murad, Iraq's former ambassador to Romania and a Kurd, said: 'I have suffered from the hatred of the Shia-led government to the Ministry of Foreign Affairs where the structure of the ministry was not dominated by Shia party affiliated members' (author's interview with Murad, 2014). The prime minister's national security advisor al-Fayad confirmed the gap between the Shia-led government and the foreign minister:

> Political and social strife, a weak national identity and disunity still influence Iraq's representatives abroad ... With respect to the Foreign Minister, we have yet to craft a political policy that reflects the identity of the new Iraq ... Another factor is that the administration is preoccupied with domestic issues and internal security, which in itself is a serious structural flaw. (al-Kadhimi, 2013)

Al-Fayad described Iraq's foreign relations dilemma by showing the I-MOFA's shortcomings. The collision of interests within governmental bodies has been noticeable. During the upsurge of the Islamic State of Iraq and al-Sham (ISIS/Daesh), al-Maliki's deputy prime minister al-Mutlaq said: 'During my work in the office we [Arab Sunnis] were almost isolated from decision making especially in all security issues, military, interior, and intelligence ... They were run by al-Maliki or his party ... we call on the US to change the political process in Iraq' (CNN, 2015). Al-Mutlaq's statement shows the marginalization of Sunni elites from decision-making in the Iraqi government and was critical of al-Maliki's government even on official visits to foreign states. Al-Maliki's supporters have accused al-Mutlaq of receiving funding from Turkey, KSA and Jordan (Daudey, 2006).

Despite these allegations, al-Mutlaq fiercely rejected Iran's role in Iraq and welcomed proactive engagement from Arab Gulf States led by the KSA in Iraq (al-Fayad, 2014). He denied KSA interference in Iraq and accusations of receiving money from the KSA. Al-Mutlaq argues that Iran's decision-makers created the Shia-led government in Baghdad and interfere in policymaking (al-Kadhimi,

2014). This is one of many significant contradictory foreign policy messages from a senior Iraqi official. Al-Mutlaq lobbied in Washington, DC, to try to influence US decision-makers. He met senior US officials, including the president and House Foreign Affairs Committee, and addressed academic circles in the United States (Lake, 2014). One of his efforts was an attempt to influence the United States not to sell fighter jets to the Shia-led government; this involved hiring independent consultant Sam Patten in January 2014 for US$20,000 per month and a US$100,000 'win' bonus (Johnson, 2017, 401). Meanwhile, al-Maliki was lobbying to receive these weapons; he hired the Podesta Group lobbying firm, which has close relationships with the Democrats, to repair Iraq's damaged image in Washington, DC, and relationship with the Obama administration (Palmer, 2013; Ditz, 2014). This is a clear clash of foreign relations within the key circle of senior officials.

One of al-Maliki's alleged foreign policy trends – observed by Tareq Najem, a political advisor to al-Maliki, and Thamir Ghahban, chairman of the Advisory Commission to the prime minister – is not interfering in the domestic affairs of other countries. Al-Maliki has adhered to the principle of non-alignment of state policy in regional and international politics. Najem and Ghahban stated that al-Maliki was not involved in any regional axis (Sirri et al., 2013, 13). Al-Maliki also stated he was against any political axes or geopolitical camps in formulating Iraq's foreign policy (Al-Bawaba, 2010). During his tenure, there was a two-faced foreign policy – an official and an unofficial policy – with the latter constituting the real foreign policy. Al-Maliki's regional policies are biased, for example, superficially, he showed a relatively unbiased stance by announcing he was not taking sides regarding the Syrian Civil War. However, Iraq abstained on voting to suspend Syria's membership from the Arab League. In December 2011, al-Maliki sent his trusted ally al-Fayad to Syria to meet President Assad (Al-Jazeera, 2011; Sirri et al., 2013, 14). Furthermore, al-Maliki turned a blind eye towards Iran sending logistic support to Syria via Iraqi air space, and the Iraqi Shia militias that went to Syria to fight alongside Assad's army. While al-Maliki's government played a role in making a historic leap in Iraq's relationship with Iran, a further policy repercussion was the undermining of the Arab Gulf States' interests.

Al-Maliki has, in multiple speeches, accused the KSA and Qatar of interfering in and destabilizing Iraq. At the beginning of 2014, he said the aforementioned were waging war on Iraq. Al-Maliki's foreign policy caused a backlash from regional powers; the Saudi and Qatari media fiercely attacked his position towards Syria. The fragile and low level of rapport between Iraq and the Arab states was demonstrated in 2012 in the first Arab League summit in Iraq since 1990. Although the summit showed progress in Iraq's foreign relations, many Arab states (excluding Kuwait – the Emir Sheikh Sabah al-Sabah attended) deliberately sent low-level representatives to convey to al-Maliki's government their frustration with his policies. Qatar's former prime minister Sheikh Hamad bin Jassem al-Thani said: 'By sending only an ambassador (KSA also sent an ambassador) to the summit, Qatar was sending a message to Iraq' (Al-Jazeera, 2012; Wicken, 2012b). Al-Maliki accused the KSA of destabilizing Iraq: 'Saudi Arabia supports terrorism in the region including in Iraq … We are at war with Saudi Arabia but not with armies' (Al-Manar, 2014). Furthermore, he said: 'Qatar and Saudi Arabia are agitating and supporting the sectarian violence in Iraq … They declared war against Iraq similarly to their war in Syria … Both countries are primarily responsible for Iraq's insecurity' (France 24 Arabic, 2014). These accusations notably increased the strain and isolated al-Maliki's foreign relations regionally. Tension was also evident in the relationship between Iraq and Turkey. This was partly caused by the KRG's and Turkey's rapprochement and Turkey's stand on the Syrian Civil War, and certainly by the sectarian depiction. The strained relationship moved to a personal level between Recep Tayyip Erdogan and al-Maliki.

One of his foreign policy objectives was to revive a relationship with Iraq's old ally, Russia. When he visited Moscow in October 2012, their relationship focused on, but was not limited to, defence and security cooperation and buying heavy weaponry. Only a few months earlier, the Iraqi defence minister had visited Moscow and signed a military deal valued at US$1 billion. The revival was partly due to the United States' delay in the delivery of F16 jets to Iraq, Iranian encouragement and the Iraqi and Russian governments' similar stances on the Syrian conflict. Sunni politicians and religious figures raised concerns about the weaponry deals with Russia and Eastern Europe (al-Hashimi, 2012; Al-Arabiya, 2015; Usama, 2015).

In 2013, al-Maliki argued that Iraq's independent foreign policy would not repeat Saddam's policy with its neighbours. He stated that Iraq was a sovereign partner of the United States, but that they did not see eye to eye on the Middle East's challenging issues such as supporting the Syrian rebels and opposing Assad (al-Maliki, 2013). Although the language might appear diplomatic (because it was published in the *Washington Post*), the article shows that al-Maliki was gradually drifting away from the United States.

Any other prime minister would face similar challenges to finding consensus among elites and political factions and to unify Iraqis in foreign policy. However, al-Maliki's policies further divided the Iraqi state. He projected a narrow and rigid perspective in foreign relations and policy, relying on conspiracy theories to explain his views. He securitized Iraqi politics and foreign relations by portraying any adversaries as conspirators aiming to destroy Iraq and making them an agent of external actors. He depicted the Sunni Arab world and Western states as seeking to weaken Iraq. Al-Maliki's policies contributed to Iraq's failure in approaching regional powers such as Turkey, Jordan and the Arab Gulf States. Although al-Maliki curbed insurgents and Shia militias (JAM), he presented himself as the leader of the Iraqi nationalist campaign, SLC, and slowly reversed his stance to support pro-Iran militias to serve his and Iran's interests. This was particularly the case at the end of his second term, when he moved away from the Da'wa Party's tradition of not having or not sponsoring opposing armed militias. Moreover, in 2014, al-Maliki became the godfather of the Popular Mobilization Forces (PMF).

Finally, the continuous increase of Iraqi Sunnis' grievances against the Shia-led government, and al-Maliki's harsh responses to Sunni demonstrations across Iraq at the end of 2012, widened the gap between them. Consequently, the Sunni areas became a fertile ground for Daesh to grow and seize a third of Iraq's territory. This had global consequences and caused a failure in al-Maliki's domestic and foreign policy outcomes. The United States signalled they would not provide support unless a new government was formed without al-Maliki as prime minister. Thus, the United States played a role in forcing al-Maliki out of office, despite his first election victory in 2014 (al-Qarawee, 2016, 1). Regional powers, namely, Iran, approved of the changes in Baghdad. Despite this, post 2014, al-Maliki had limited alternatives; this led to him further consolidating his ties with Iran and its allied proxies, such as AAH and KH.

*Haider al-Abadi (September 2014–18)*

Al-Abadi's tenure appeared, to the outside world, to revitalize Iraq's weak foreign policy. Prime Minister al-Abadi was from the Islamic Da'wa Party. He is a moderate politician among the Shia elite with a Western educational background. In August 2014, the new president, Fuad Ma'sum, named al-Abadi prime minister and requested that he form a new government. After ICR approval in September 2014, al-Abadi was voted into power as head of the fifth cabinet.

Following internal, regional and international pressure, al-Maliki was sidelined. In a continuation of external involvement, rival powers (the United States and Iran) backed al-Abadi's appointment. He received al-Sistani's blessing; Muqtada al-Sadr, most Kurdish and Sunni political elites and parties, and regional and international powers welcomed him. The scale of internal and external support of this Iraqi prime minister was unprecedented in Iraq's history.

Al-Abadi inherited Iraq's political, security, economic and foreign relations challenges, which al-Maliki had exacerbated. The previous government (by al-Maliki) did not project the real picture of Iraq to neighbouring states, especially Arab states (Sdqian, 2014). Another internal obstacle was the division within the Da'wa Party, in which two camps were formed: al-Abadi's (moderate wing) and al-Maliki's (pro-Iranian and conservative wing). This rift has had internal and external ramifications; the fragmentation within the party, rise of the pro-Iran Shia militias and division within the Shia house (al-Bayt al-Shi'i) weakened al-Abadi's position on internal and foreign affairs. Nonetheless, compared to al-Maliki, al-Abadi represented a new page in Iraq's foreign relations and foreign policy, one composed of progressive and friendly engagement.

Al-Abadi's cabinet received global attention, as the Iraqi state was on the verge of complete collapse and Daesh threatened Baghdad. In al-Abadi's first speech as prime minister in September 2014, he said: 'The Iraqi government will focus more on Iraq's foreign policy, particularly security' (Sky News Arabia, 2014). Given that Iraq lost a third of the country to Daesh, the security context of foreign policy was a logical priority. Al-Abadi showed a cordial face, at least diplomatically, in his foreign relations. He is open to the Arab states and has been viewed as friendly to Western countries, while also preserving close ties with Iran and Russia. Ford stated: 'Abadi does not want to be in the middle of the United States and Iran's disputes … Iraqis need good relations with Iran and with the United States … the best outcome for them is to benefit from both' (Middle East Institute, 2015). He claimed that when al-Abadi was in Washington, DC, al-Abadi said: 'We [Iraqis] are the ultimate arbiters of our fate, and we [Iraqi government] have told the Iranians to back off a little bit' (Middle East Institute, 2015). Al-Abadi benefited from Iran and the United States but tacitly pushed back against Iranian domination. This was despite the fact that al-Abadi's first visit abroad after assuming office was to Tehran, as Iran assisted Iraq in defending against Daesh.

Al-Abadi's foreign policy strategy was to assemble support from a broad range of states to defeat Daesh, and to try and project this in coherent messages from Iraqi officials. As a consequence of long demonstrations and resentment, al-Abadi cancelled the posts of deputies of the prime minister and president and other ministerial posts in August 2015. This was part of a reform plan to reduce the government expenses, nepotism, which indirectly reduced the number of contradictory voices in the government. However, the Iraqi Supreme Court revoked his abolition of the president's deputies in October 2016, because it was unconstitutional. Since Saddam's fall, deputy prime ministers have usually contradicted the statements of the prime ministers or presidents in all cabinets. The pro-Iran and al-Maliki's allied Shia militias continued to contradict al-Abadi on foreign policy, despite not being foreign policy bodies.

The Iraqi government hosted the fourth conference of the Arab ambassadors in April 2015, which the three key officials – the prime minister (al-Abadi), president (Ma'sum) and Speaker (al-Jabouri) – attended. In the conference, al-Abadi stated: 'Foreign policy is the second stage on the war on terror' (Nasiria, 2015). Here, al-Abadi articulated the importance of facing security challenges alongside the Arab states. Prime Minister al-Abadi and Foreign Minister al-Jaafari participated in the six partners' summit in Brussels on 3 December 2014 at the invitation of former US secretary of state John Kerry; this reiterated support for Iraq in combating Daesh (US Department of State: Diplomacy in Action, 2014). Additionally, al-Abadi and NATO secretary general Jens Stoltenberg reaffirmed their partnership, discussed security cooperation and requested defence capacity-building support from NATO (Wales Summit Declaration, 2014). A ministerial-level conference in London in January 2015 included al-Abadi, Kerry, Hammond (UK secretary of state for foreign affairs) and other international leaders to provide more military support to Baghdad. These events aided the evolution of the international coalition's strategy to focus on their fight against Daesh and to back Iraq. Al-Abadi's first year witnessed the invigoration of al-Maliki's period of dormant foreign policy, which focused on reaching out to states and security.

Al-Abadi was better received by the Arab states than al-Maliki and al-Jaafari during their premierships. The Arab world, particularly the Gulf States, welcomed al-Abadi's appointment. The Saudi foreign minister Prince Saud al-Faisal and King Salman invited the new prime minister to visit. In 2015, the Saudi ambassador began to work in the embassy in Baghdad. However, the Syrian Civil War and Iraq's political and security instability made it difficult but not impossible for al-Abadi to balance the region's rapprochement with Iraq.

Al-Abadi's participation in international conferences and diplomatic speeches in English provided a positive image. On 30 September 2015, he addressed the

UN regarding Iraq's security threats and the war on Daesh. He also addressed its economic condition in the 2015 and 2016 World Economic Forums in Davos, and in 2015 and 2016 at the Munich Security Conferences. Al-Abadi's foreign policy reflected the dire necessity to broaden Iraq's military, intelligence and security allies and restore its economy. Al-Abadi was more open to potential partners; Iraq increased cooperation with the United States, Iran and Russia. Therefore, Baghdad built closer ties with contentious bedfellows. Iraq is partnered in the war against Daesh with the Russian- and Iranian-led alliance, as well as the US-led global coalition.

Iraq has increasingly been plunged into economic and financial meltdown. This is due to reliance on oil revenues, which have fallen; chronicled and systematic corruption; the expensive war on Daesh; internal displacement; and an unproductive economic structure (which burdens the state with a massive number of public employees). Consequently, al-Abadi lobbied internationally for financial aid. In April 2015, he visited Washington, DC, to lobby for further US support; his top priority was obtaining military equipment and financial aid. Iraq received US$200 million in humanitarian aid, and the first batch of US fighter jets were delivered in July 2015. After a few months, a visit to Moscow concentrated on military and security cooperation to revitalize and create new military contracts.

Like previous governments, al-Abadi faced difficulty in producing a unified foreign policy. Divisions remerged between senior officials and actors associated with the government. Iraqi vice president Usama al-Nujaifi disagreed with al-Abadi's rapprochement with Russia: 'Our political bloc is against any new coalition with Russia … as this worsens the situation in Iraq and Syria' (Al-Khaleej Online, 2016a). Al-Nujaifi's statement reflected his position against the establishment of the sharing intelligence cooperation centre in Baghdad, which includes Damascus, Moscow and Tehran. Indeed, many Arab Sunnis rejected Russian involvement; this may have been influenced by Moscow backing Assad's regime and bombing the Syrian rebels. Comparatively, Vice President al-Maliki and pro-Iran Iraqi Shia militias backed and encouraged Russian, Iranian and even Lebanon's Hezbollah's engagement in Iraq. Meanwhile, al-Abadi tried to downplay the importance of the intelligence centre in Baghdad: 'The centre is very low level, it is not high level … there is no military cooperation whatsoever' (PBS News Hour, 2015). Al-Maliki and pro-Iran Shia militias depicted al-Abadi's general policies as a failure because they did not serve their interests.

Although al-Abadi's government was less shambolic in Iraqi foreign policy messaging than al-Maliki, it experienced differences even between al-Abadi and Foreign Minister al-Jaafari. For instance, al-Jaafari was more sympathetic to Syria's government and their allies than al-Abadi (Abdullah, 2018; Ali, 2018). Al-Abadi wanted to maintain support from the US-led coalition without losing the Iranian and Russian-led coalition's support. His foreign policy approach appeared to convey a non-sectarian policy that managed the rapprochement between Baghdad and Arab Gulf States.

Al-Abadi devised punitive policies towards the KR-I after its referendum in September 2017. These included: a ban on international flights to and from the

KR-I that lasted for around six months and coordination with Tehran and Ankara to put pressure on the KRG economically and politically. His rigid stance was because he sought to appease the Iraqis who are against the KR-I's independence, the international community's lack of support for the referendum and the regional powers' – particularly Iran and Turkey's – fierce rejection. The aftermath of the Kurdish referendum caused al-Abadi to formulate a joint policy with Iran and Turkey to counter the referendum and the KRG's ambitions.

*Adil Abd al-Mahdi (2018–19 and continued as a caretaker)*

Al-Abadi's successor prime minister Adil Abd al-Mahdi as a moderate independent Shia politician has continued on al-Abadi's path, particularly in engagement with the Arab world and the West but not at the expense of Iran. The prime minister's first official foreign visit was to Egypt where he met President al-Sisi and King Abdullah II of Jordan; following this he visited Iran and the KSA in the same month. This indicated a balanced foreign policy behaviour among rising tensions in the Middle East. Al-Mahdi was sworn in in October 2018. He has formerly been a vice president and finance minister, and a member of the Islamic Supreme Council of Iraq (ISCI). Prime Minister al-Mahdi represents a departure from Da'wa Party domination on the premiership between 2005 and 2018. Nonetheless, Prime Minister al-Mahdi does not have firm political sponsorship and his appointment was the outcome of negotiation between major Shia elites and factions that are more fragmented than before. This will have at least two potential consequences: First, other actors within and outside the government will step up their activities and this might weaken the prime minister's role in formulating policies; second, the Presidency and the Speaker might have stronger leverage in foreign policy making, but this has constitutional limitations. Domestically and externally Prime Minister al-Mahdi has been viewed as a beacon of hope because of his attempt to push to strengthen the state's institutions, but the rise of conservative pro-Iran Shia militias, their political wings and leaders as part of the Iraqi state's security apparatus means the government might remain vulnerable in formulating tangible and independent policies.

The prime ministers in the six cabinets demonstrate that the prime minister has the leading role in making foreign policy. Ambassador Faily, who worked directly with all the aforementioned prime ministers excluding Prime Minister al-Mahdi at the time, articulated how they viewed Iraq and the world:

> Al-Maliki wanted to focus on projecting power in his foreign relations for instance 'we are strong' … Al-Maliki did not have clarity regarding his views about the West and maybe he didn't trust the West and he saw they are not reliable … al-Abadi wants to present to the outside that we need you [outside world] more than anything else and he sees the need for the West … Ibrahim al-Jaafari sees the world from civilisation and ethical perspectives rather than real politics; I can't say that he is a pragmatist … Ayad Allawi wants to have a liberal country and to westernise Iraq. (Author's interview with Faily, 2016)

These interpretations of the four prime ministers are realistic spotlights on their personalities. All five prime ministers' continuous foreign policy priority is maintaining a stable relationship with the United States (with varying degrees of enthusiasm between successive prime ministers) and Iran (excluding Allawi). Al-Jaafari, al-Maliki, al-Abadi and al-Mahdi had an interest in strengthening the relationship with Iran (al-Abadi and al-Mahdi being moderate in this). All prime ministers had a continuous period of instability and – excluding Allawi – distance from the Arab states and Turkey. This is despite their differing approaches to foreign policy, in which al-Abadi and al-Mahdi appeared to be diplomatic and receptive to external counterparts. The last four prime ministers had an uneasy relationship with regional powers, excluding Iran, albeit al-Abadi's and al-Mahdi's regional policy being somewhat reconciliatory. A pattern of continuous disagreements on foreign policy between the aforementioned prime ministers and their government officials has resulted in an incoherent foreign policy.

### *The foreign minister and the Iraqi Ministry of Foreign Affairs*

The Coalition Provisional Authority (CPA) built the I-MOFA (*al-Wazara al-Kharijiyah al-Iraqiya*) from scratch between April 2003 and June 2004, and the IGC between July 2003 and June 2004 as part of the process of building the new Iraqi state. The reconstruction took place in three stages. The first was to rebuild the bureaucratic institutions; in 2005, the Foreign Service Institute, which is part of the I-MOFA, sent 385 Iraqis on thirty-six training courses around the world. The second stage was the foreign minister meeting with diplomats based in Baghdad and abroad, as well as media outlets, to give reassurances that they were on the right track. Third, Iraq sought to regain its presence in international organizations and to represent itself in international fora (Soffar, 2010, 240). The I-MOFA's structure includes: the foreign minister; three to four undersecretaries (*Wakala al-Wuzara*), each focusing on a particular issue or issues in foreign affairs and aiding the foreign minister; ambassadors; and I-MOFA's official spokesperson. The I-MOFA has around a dozen departments and each one has specialized sections. It is structured according to function and on a geographical basis into departments, which are supposed to function as two-way channels, passing information to higher echelons and directives to lower ones (Soffar, 2010, 222). The I-MOFA's main priorities are to emerge from isolation and revive Iraq's diplomatic ties with the international community; protect Iraq's security, promote stability and preserve unity; contribute to building the economy; continue upgrading its work and performance level, guided by the constitutional basis and legal controls; support international multilateral bodies; and free the country from the sanctions and reparation obligations to which it was subjected under chapter seven of the United Nations Charter (Maggiolini, 2013; Republic of Iraq, Ministry of Foreign Affairs, 2015; author interview with Faily, 2016).

Demonstrating the achievements of the I-MOFA post Saddam, Ismail said:

Despite the domestic political instability and lack of genuine institutionalisation in Iraq post-2003, in a decade Iraq was successfully able to repair a great number of diplomatic relations. Iraq has 89 missions abroad whereas before 2003 Iraq did not have professional diplomatic relations. It was more intelligence relations conducted by intelligence officers. (Author's interview with Ismail, 2014)

The I-MOFA restored diplomatic representations and normalized Iraq's relationship with other states and international organizations, and the federal government was able to free itself from the UN sanctions and chapter seven in 2013. However, the I-MOFA partially failed in other areas: unifying foreign policy messages; corruption and *al-Muhasasa* throughout the I-MOFA, which even reached the embassies and their staff; lack of sufficient professional cadres, diplomats and coordination; and failure of the I-MOFA members to adhere to, understand and have a common interpretation of the Iraqi constitution. In 2015 Sinjari, Iraq's ambassador to Romania, stated:

> When Iraq has a strong government then you will have strong embassies and diplomacy but Iraq is very weak ... There is no teamwork in the Iraqi Foreign Ministry ... Many times we [ambassadors] write to the centre [ministry] and don't get an answer ... we don't get anything [informing about the formal policies] from the centre ... there is very little correspondence ... In 2015 in the Baghdad conference for all the Iraqi Ambassadors, everyone was complaining about the ministry in some way. (Author's interview with Sinjari, 2015)

Ambassador Murad revealed similar sentiments. Murad also mentioned ambassadors' contradictory statements regarding a political position in foreign affairs. For example, a number of diplomats in Arab Sunni states disagreed with Iraq's official foreign policy positions (author's interview with Murad, 2014).
Ambassador Faily said:

> There are major administrative and management problems in how you manage embassies, how you define priorities for them and how you facilitate relevant things for them ... For example, they send staff to embassies abroad to English speaking countries or when English is required and a number of them do not speak English. (Author's interview with Faily, 2016)

Faily said: 'These shortcomings negatively affected the influence of foreign relations where we don't have tools [effective embassies] that provide effective messaging' (author's interview with Faily, 2016). Ghanim Alwan al-Jumaily, Iraq's ambassador to the KSA, stated in 2013: 'The majority of our diplomatic cadres are new and have little experience' (al-Jumaily, 2013, 127). The diplomat's perspectives underline the political, administrative and tactical shortcomings of the I-MOFA. Therefore, rebuilding the institution post 2003 faced significant challenges in bringing coherence to the ministry and has contributed to incoherent and weak foreign policy messages. However, in 2018, Dr Fareed Yasseen, Iraq's ambassador to the United States, said: 'Early on at the I-MOFA everyone used to pass the promotion exam but now standards have been applied it is not like this' (Hudson Institute, 2018). Although, after more than a decade of rebuilding the I-MOFA, there are fewer contradictory messages from diplomatic circles, the extent of these shifts on the bureaucratic levels and diplomatic performance are unclear and lack concrete evidence. The majority of the diplomat interviewees accepted that ambassadors have different opinions and positions about how Iraq should conduct its foreign policy towards a particular state. There is a lack of a unified vision for foreign policy throughout the I-MOFA and across the ambassadors. A partial response to this, in mid-2017 when Ibrahim al-Jaafari (a Shia Islamist politician) was foreign minister, was when the I-MOFA formed a committee that had various governmental bodies, including clandestine security organizations, and sidelined and revoked the diplomatic status for around forty diplomats, mostly Arab Sunnis, who were accused of incompetence and exploiting their positions for personal gain. Arab Sunni politicians condemned the I-MOFA's order because it targeted experienced Arab Sunni diplomats (Abdulrazak, 2017). While this policy seems to appear to reduce the incompetency, it minimizes the role of Arab Sunnis who have or could have contradictory or undesirable perspectives within the I-MOFA that do not align with those of the Shia ruling elites, including Foreign Minister a-Jaafari.

Officially, the conventions Iraq has signed govern its diplomatic interaction with the international community. The Iraqi constitution provides broad principles, which suffer from a lack of detail and guidelines over the purview of actors in foreign policy. Article 110 states that the federal government has the authority to draw up foreign policy, Article 78 gives responsibility to the prime minister to direct the general policies as well as some legislative powers to the ICR and Article 61/4 and 61/2 monitor the executive performance and ratification of international treaties and agreements. However, the vagueness is in the lack of details and the degree of adherence by the key actors, which are critical in a fragmented and a complex executive state structure like Iraq. Former foreign minister Zebari (2014) called for a review of the articles that have caused tension in the Iraqi constitution (Kurdsat, 2014). There appears to be a consensus between decision-makers and academics regarding the deficiencies of the Iraqi constitution in relation to many issues, including foreign policy.

*Hoshyar Zebari (2003–14)*

Zebari was the first Iraqi foreign minister post 2003 who led in the construction of the I-MOFA. He is a Kurd and a senior member of the KDP and as the head of the KDP's International Relations Bureau from 1992 to 2003, he gained experience in public diplomacy. Under Zebari's supervision during the CPA and IGC, the I-MOFA achieved a number of goals, including restoration of diplomatic relations. Zebari stated: 'The Ministry of Foreign Affairs' most difficult task has been to develop an independent Iraqi foreign policy at a time when our country is under legal occupation' (qtd in Soffar, 2010, 195). Since the occupation ended, challenges in foreign policy development have been ongoing.

Zebari emphasized the need to direct Iraq's foreign policy to promote its stability and integrity and rehabilitate its economy (Salem, 2013, 5). When reviewing Zebari's speeches and interviews between 2003 and 2014, it can be seen that his approach focuses on Iraq's sovereignty, foreign relations, security, domestic integrity and economy. One of Zebari's policies was to try to convey the domestic political process and state building to the outside world.

In the I-MOFA's Law 2013/36, Article 1 states: 'The Foreign Ministry implements the foreign policy of the Republic of Iraq and is represented by its Foreign Minister or whoever represents him' (I-MOFA's Law, 2013). Therefore, legally, officially and theoretically the I-MOFA and the foreign minister do not create foreign policy; rather, they execute it. However, the foreign minister contributes to shaping foreign policy because of the lack of any agreed – or even existing – detailed foreign policy plan. Simply put, the foreign minister fills the political void with perspectives based on personal efforts, expertise and/or worldview shaped by their political background. Therefore, Zebari had a degree of freedom in conducting foreign relations and projecting the foreign policy. He tried to avoid significant clashes with the prime minister, president and the Speaker of the ICR in foreign policy statements. A number of diplomats and ambassadors did not adhere to official foreign policy endorsed by the Foreign Minister Zebari.

Zebari, who was the longest-serving minister in Iraq post Saddam, pointed out several achievements. First, he emphasized the ending of the US occupation: 'The key issue for us after 2003 was to regain our sovereignty, to become a normal country and to reach an amicable agreement with the Americans for the troops' withdrawal, I think our interests coincided to reach that and that was a major achievement' (qtd in Sirri et al., 2013, 10). Zebari signed the SOFA agreement between Iraq and the United States, and under the US-Iraq SFA Zebari attended meetings with many US officials and discussed issues related to mutual cooperation regarding Iraq's domestic and regional challenges. In 2013 the United States expressed concerns about weapons flowing from Iraq to Syria and Foreign Minister Zebari denied the Iraqi government's role in these activities (United States of America Department of State, 2013). Second, Iraq's foreign relations with the international community were revived. Normalizing broken diplomatic relations with many countries on a bilateral basis is a process that is still ongoing. Third, pulling Iraq from the UN's Charter Chapter VII was considered a victory for Iraq's foreign policy actors and freed Iraq from restrictions. However, Ismail said:

> The Foreign Minister reflected Iraq's foreign policy and is the official who is responsible for the country. In that regard we see another minister or member of parliament seeking to articulate and drive Iraq's foreign policy ... this shows the disunity, the vulnerability of the process of democratisation of the new political system in Iraq, and mirrors the internal tensions. (Author's interview with Ismail, 2014)

In al-Maliki's second government, disagreements between Zebari and al-Maliki and his supporters escalated because Zebari did not entirely represent Prime Minister al-Maliki's vision. A meeting between Zebari and the FRC in April 2011 resulted in clashing statements over the foreign minister's approaches and policies. Sami al-A'skari, a member of the FRC and ruling Da'wa Party, argued that the foreign minister is not properly coordinating with the FRC and tries to impose the I-MOFA's will (Al-Sumaria, 2011). Al-A'skari further stated: 'The performance of the I-MOFA is bad and we have problems with the individuals who are running it' (Al-Sumaria, 2012). Disagreements between lawmakers and executive bodies are common in democracies. The disputes were also an extension of internal political disputes between the then KRG's president (Masoud Barzani), Prime Minister al-Maliki and their elites.

Prime Minister Al-Maliki consolidated and centralized power in the government, which resulted in overshadowing Zebari. The prime minister's office made all of the vital decisions on Iraq's foreign policy. For example, in 2012, al-Maliki's office imposed restrictions on US visas (Dodge, 2012, 186; Schmidt and Schmitt, 2012). In the same vein, in 2014, Ismail said:

> There are different visions between Zebari and al-Maliki, mainly internally which occur in respect to administrating the Ministry of Foreign Affairs and the mechanisms of running it. For example, when the former Foreign Minister Zebari with the former President Jalal Talabani were in the United Nations General Assembly, al-Maliki issued an order to retire a number of ambassadors without consultation from FM Zebari. This should not have happened in this way. (Author's interview with Ismail, 2014)

The lack of coordination between, and ignorance of, the government bodies was mainly (but not only) a feature of the prime minister's office. Al-Maliki abused his position and the distribution of powers. He expanded his authority, imposed his will on the ministries and interfered in other ministries and officials – including the I-MOFA and Foreign Minister Zebari – without considering the implications.

Ismail stated there were differences between al-Maliki and Zebari regarding regional foreign policy perspectives, but no differences when dealing with the United States or the UN (author's interview with Ismail, 2014). For instance, as al-Maliki's relationship with Riyadh deteriorated, Zebari tried to amend what was left (Fordham, 2012). These differences are expected; the elites adhere to different perspectives emanating from their personal and their parties' interests. This naturally leads to different outcomes. Hassan al-Hamdani, the former head of the FRC and from Ayad Allawi's al-Wataniya bloc, said: 'Hoshyar Zebari acted as an Iraqi not as a Kurd, this counted [credit] for him. For example, he led the successful Arab League summit [in Baghdad in 2012] while Erbil and Baghdad's relationship had deteriorated' (author's interview with al-Hamdani, 2015). To an extent, al-Hamdani's statement is accurate. His perception is also influenced by the friendly relationship between Ayad Allawi's bloc and the KDP, in which Zebari is a key figure. Therefore, the government functions when the political factions and elite have amicable relationships and common interests.

Aggravation between the Iraqi officials, including Erbil and Baghdad, reflected tensions over Iraq's territories (disputed areas), politics, natural energy and security, as well as the KRG welcoming prominent Sunni tribal leaders and working with them. Prime Minister al-Maliki accused the Kurdish leaders of harbouring terrorists: 'We will not be silent that Erbil has become a base of operation for Daesh, Baathist, Al-Qaeda, and terrorists ... I call those [Kurdish Leaders] who want partnership to stop this ... They [Kurdish leaders] who harboured them [terrorists] will lose' (Afaq TV, 2014). Within hours, the KRG strongly condemned these baseless accusations, and the political parties reached a consensus that Kurdish ministers – including the foreign minister – would boycott the Iraqi cabinet. Moreover, in July 2014, Zebari asked al-Maliki to apologize to the KRG (Al-Sumaria, 2014).

The domestic turmoil between the KRG and Baghdad reflected on the performance of the foreign minister and I-MOFA and the fragile unity of the government. In July 2014, al-Maliki temporarily replaced Kurdistan Alliance members Foreign Minister Zebari and Trade Minister Khairalla Hassan Babiker, as the Kurdish ministers had boycotted the government. Hussain Shahristani – an independent Arab Shiite who joined the SLC and became deputy prime minister responsible for energy from 2010 to 2014 – replaced Zebari as acting foreign minister. Immediately, the Kurdistan Alliance in the Iraqi government declared it would not take part in the cabinet meeting of al-Maliki's government, as they were protesting the accusations and reshuffle. Zebari publicly denounced the general failure of al-Maliki's policies that led to the rise of Daesh and stated that this was evident during his work in the cabinet (Al-Bawaba, 2014; qtd by Zand, 2014). This demonstrates how fragile the federal government is in the face of any political, security or economic difficulties, in which the foreign minister has not been safe. Finally, the disputes between Zebari and al-Maliki have weakened the image of Iraqi foreign relations actors and brought internal disputes into Iraqi foreign policy representations. Faily said:

> I used to work directly with the PM and FM because of the country [the United States] I worked in ... A lot of ambassadors think they are only related to the Foreign Ministry. We [ambassadors] in reality represent the state not the government if the government changes we do not change ... the Foreign Affairs Ministry primarily is the direct boss and facilitator for you [ambassadors] to interpret the foreign policy. (Author's interview with Faily, 2016)

Although Faily's assertion shows that the ambassador's priority is representing the state, they represent the government too. He recognizes the lack of collaboration and coordination between the prime minister, the foreign minister and the president regarding foreign affairs at least until al-Abadi's government.

*Ibrahim al-Jaafari (2014–18)*

Al-Jaafari executed a foreign policy that aimed to assemble support in the war against Daesh, and he projected an Islamic Shia rhetoric. Foreign Minister al-Jaafari, who was a former prime minister and vice president, took part in al-Abadi's cabinet in September 2014. Similarly to other cabinets, al-Jaafari's appointment was the result of compromise, bargaining and accord (*al-Tawafuq*). Al-Jaafari defected from Da'wa in 2008, founded the National Reform Trend (Shia-based) and led the INA (a broad alliance of Shia political parties). He has a reputation of being a traditional Islamic Shia intellectual and politician with little pragmatism in foreign policy. As prime minister, he was accused of sectarian policies and having close ties with Iran and the Sadrist militias. However, there have been indicators of a slight shift in his approach and policies, which Prime Minister al-Abadi's practicality may have influenced. Ismail said:

> Al-Jaafari could have changed, people change … The new foreign policy of Iraq involves al-Jaafari and al-Abadi. Both officials coordinate and do not want to repeat the lack of cooperation in al-Maliki's government … al-Jaafari and al-Abadi are focusing on regional matters and pursuing a peaceful and reconcilable approach. (Author's interview with Ismail, 2014)

As both al-Abadi and al-Jaafari come from a Shia Islamic political background, they were expected to be more likely to agree than their predecessors (al-Maliki and Zebari), and to slightly reduce the incoherence in foreign policy. Nonetheless, al-Abadi's pragmatism and al-Jaafari's Shia conservatism were often prone to different viewpoints, particularly towards regional affairs. Al-Jaafari allegedly conducted a reform campaign to fight corruption and remove unqualified diplomats and employees from the I-MOFA and, as the Iraqi budget was under strain, reduce and review the number of diplomats and officers in missions abroad, many of whom were appointed according to *al-Muhasasa*. However, his campaign's achievements were limited. Abdul Bari Zebari, the new head of the FRC, said: 'We [FRC] have our observations during both Hoshyar Zebari and al-Jaafari's ministries … However, the conduct of the previous ministry is slightly better than al-Jaafari's I-MOFA' (author's interview with Zebari, 2016). The I-MOFA's problems lie in the Iraqi political system, in which al-Jaafari has been a key figure since the beginning, and corrupt elite.

Al-Jaafari was appointed at a time when Iraq was the centre of global attention because of Daesh. Therefore, al-Jaafari and President Ma'sum formally visited the KSA to repair the strained relations from al-Maliki's tenure. Al-Jaafari met the Saudi foreign minister, who stated the KSA was ready to amend and improve the relationship. Al-Jaafari visited regional states to show Iraq's desire for rapprochement. He also paid many official visits to European countries, Asia and the United States, where he expressed Iraq's enthusiasm to enhance diplomatic ties.

Several interconnected summits have highlighted Iraq's efforts in diplomacy and security relationships with other states, particularly in combating terrorism and seeking humanitarian and financial aid. The Iraqi government, via the I-MOFA, proposed a draft resolution for the Arab League Foreign Minister's summit on 7 September 2014, which resulted in Resolution 7804 urging collaborative efforts against Daesh and support of Iraq (Al-Arabiya, 2014). On 11 September 2014, ministers from the Gulf Cooperation Council (GCC), Iraq; Jordan, Lebanon and the United States attended the Jeddah Communiqué and emphasized the Arab League's resolutions (US State Department: Diplomacy In Action, 2014). This represented a new (but fragile) reconnection between Iraq and the Arab Gulf States. On 15 September 2014, the Iraqi president and Foreign Minister al-Jaafari attended the International Conference in Paris on Peace and Security in Iraq, which emphasized the role of the Arab League and European Union as long-term strategic partners with Iraq (France Diplomatie, 2014). Al-Jaafari participated in the UN Security Council's session for combating Daesh and gave a speech to the UN Security Council, which stressed the international community's role in supporting Iraq in its humanitarian catastrophe and fighting terrorism (UN Meetings Coverage and Press Releases, 2014).

The last three summits provided Iraq with international recognition in its struggle against Daesh and laid the foundation for channels of support. Al-Jaafari asserted that Iraq was receiving unprecedented international endorsement and support: 'The Head of the Security Council session told me that he has never witnessed in his life such kind of consensuses and unification in the United Nations for a cause' (al-Jaafari, 2014). Nevertheless, the Syrian Civil War, the war in Yemen against Houthis, the rise of the Shia militias and clashes in foreign policy visions regionally between the Arab Gulf States and the Iraqi federal government made it temporarily difficult for real Iraqi-Arab/Turkish rapprochement.

Al-Jaafari agreed with the theme of the 'Iraq's foreign policy in the turbulent region' forum at the Brookings Institute in Doha (Brookings Institute, 2015). He claimed that Iraqi foreign policy is built on several constants. First, good bilateral relationships with neighbouring and regional states. Furthermore, al-Jaafari recognized the differences between the Arab states and Iraq, but argues that progress has recently been made and there are more shared than divergent values. Second, Iraq does not want permanent foreign military bases. Third, not allowing external powers to interfere in Iraqi domestic affairs, and vice versa. Fourth, Iraq is avoiding the regional axes; al-Jaafari argues that Iraq is siding with neither the Iranian nor the Saudi-led axes. He argues that Iraq's foreign policy cannot separate itself from internal matters, such as the fight against terrorism, and Iraq's foreign policy and diplomacy cannot distance itself from regional turbulence, such as in Yemen and Syria (Brookings Institute, 2015).

Reality contrasts with al-Jaafari's aforementioned constants. He has criticized the Arab states' policies. In the opening of the Arab Ambassadors Conference in 2015, the I-MOFA criticized the Arab states for not consulting Iraq earlier regarding building an Arab military force (Nasiria, 2015). Al-Jaafari asserted Iraq's reservations on a joint Arab force or army (*al-Quwa al-A'rabia al-Mushtaraka*). Al-Jaafari, and to an extent al-Abadi, have moderately reinforced the Shia Islamic endorsement. In 2015, the Iraqi government and foreign minister asked to remove some Iraqi Shia militias, such as Badr Organization and AAH, from the UAE's list of terrorist organizations. At other events, the I-MOFA has protested against and summoned the UAE ambassador for calling for the dismantling of the PMF (*Asharq Al-Awsat*, 2015; Mamoun, 2016).

While many of the Arab states deplore al-Assad, Foreign Minister al-Jaafari met al-Assad and the Syrian foreign minister Muallem, in Damascus, about a week before the Arab League session regarding Yemen. In 2015, the Iraqi government strongly rejected the Arab League's Operation Decisive Storm (*A'sifat al-Hazm*) against the Houthis in Yemen. Additionally, in the Arab League foreign ministers' session in 2016, Iraq abstained from voting to label Lebanon's Hezbollah, which the majority of its members agree is a terrorist organization. Al-Jaafari called the leader of Hezbollah Hassan Nasrallah, 'the savior of Arab dignity', which caused the Saudi envoy to leave the session until al-Jaafari finished his speech (Alsharif, 2016). Al-Jaafari played a coordinating role between the US-led coalition and the Syrian regime regarding the US airstrikes in Syria. He said: 'When the US decided to bomb Syria the US State Secretary Kerry called me to inform us and send a message to the Syrian regime ... I informed the Americans that Assad's regime should not be targeted in the airstrikes' (al-Jaafari, 2014). This shows the wide gulf between the Arab states and Iraq. Al-Jaafari's attitude towards regional issues has agitated some of the Arab states and caused deterioration of political ties, despite limited diplomatic revival. Regarding al-Jaafari's third and fourth points, there are regional powers interfering in Iraq.

The PMF's relationship with the I-MOFA might shape the latter's performance towards pro-Iran Shia militias' interests. Al-Jaafari invited the spokesperson of the PMF, al-Asadi, to the I-MOFA's conference in 2016 to provide support for the Shia majority umbrella (I-MOFA, 2016a). Additionally, the I-MOFA's senior delegation has included PMF members. Labeed Abbawi, Iraq's former undersecretary at I-MOFA, said: 'I think the ruling, especially the Islamic parties have a big influence on the running of the foreign ministry, especially in the present administration' (Rudaw, 2017a).

Al-Abadi and al-Jaafari applauded Iran for being the first country to provide Iraq with logistic support – including weapons, ammunitions, funding and military and security advisors – in the fight against Daesh. Al-Jaafari's views on political and foreign affairs do not significantly differ from al-Maliki's but are different from those of Hoshyar Zebari. His views show less flexibility (but they are not hostile) towards the Sunni Arab world/Turkey. The slight differences between al-Abadi and al-Jaafari became more obvious towards the end of Al-Abadi's government. For example, in April 2018 al-Jaafari condemned the United States, French and British airstrikes against Syria, whereas official sources from the prime minister's office announced that Foreign Minister al-Jaafari's position did not reflect that of Prime Minister al-Abadi, who preferred not to take sides in this particular case (Abdullah, 2018; Ali, 2018).

However, al-Jaafari took a similar stance to al-Abadi's against Kurdistan's referendum. He attended the Arab League summit in Cairo on 13 September and the closing statement called the referendum unconstitutional, thereby supporting the position of the federal government in Baghdad (Aboulenein, 2017). On 21 September 2017, Foreign Minister al-Jaafari, Turkish foreign minister Mevlut Cavusoglu and Iranian foreign minister Javad Zarif had a meeting in New York. They presented a joint statement in which they voiced concern about the Kurdish referendum and expressed their strong commitment to maintaining Iraq's territorial and political integrity (Reuters, 2017). The referendum motivated the governments of Ankara, Baghdad and Tehran to increase their coordination to streamline countermeasures, including punitive actions towards the KR-I.

*Mohammed Ali al-Hakim (since October 2018)*

The current foreign minister al-Hakim is a Shia politician who makes fewer ideological statements compared to al-Jaafari. Nonetheless, he presents the continuation of the Shia leaning positions that have dominated the process of decision-making in previous governments. Foreign Minister al-Hakim has adopted similar foreign policy orientations to those of al-Jaafari and al-Abadi and defends Iraq's previous foreign policy positions, such as calling for supporting Assad's regime and its return to the Arab League (NBC News, 2019). Al-Hakim is an experienced diplomat who has a British and American educational background. He stated that the source of his diplomatic work is the prime minister, the Council of Ministers and the Iraqi constitution, and he recognizes the importance of liaising with the FRC in the ICR (Al-Sumaria, 2019). As of the time of writing, al-Hakim's work has witnessed coordination with the prime minister and Iraqi president Barham Salih in conducting foreign relations. He stated that internally executing foreign policy is a struggle as Iraqi members of Parliament disagree on certain bilateral relations with a country or policies (Al-Sumaria, 2019). Post 2003, diplomats in Iraq and their missions' representatives showed divided visions and statements. Iraqi officials, including diplomats, define Iraq according to their political and communal identity as well as their own interests.

*Iraqi president's role in foreign policy*

According to Article 67 of the Iraqi constitution: 'The President is the head of the state, the symbol of unity of the country and represents the sovereignty of Iraq ... The President shall guarantee the commitment of the constitution.' The president is not only symbolic, he is part of the executive authority according to Article 66. The president has the constitutional power to reject laws or refuse to approve a bill that influences the country's economy, domestic politics and foreign relations. Kamaran Karadaghi, Iraq's former spokesperson and chief of staff of President Jalal Talabani (2005–7), said:

> According to the Iraqi constitution, the Iraqi President does not have a direct oversight on Iraq's foreign policy ... but because he is the head of the state he represents Iraq in international conferences and summits and he can directly request that the Foreign Minister explains to him his activities and work ... When the President goes abroad for formal visits he usually takes with him the Foreign Minister ... according to the Iraqi constitution the highest executive powers are granted to the Head of the Council of Ministers [the prime minister]

... However, it is also stated in the constitution that the executive powers consist of the President too. (Author's interview with Karadaghi, 2015)

Khalid Shwani, Iraq's former president's spokesperson and legal advisor, stated:

The President's external activities try, through his constitutional and political position, to consolidate Iraq's foreign relations internationally and particularly to normalise relationships with the states that Iraq has problems or tensions with. (Author's interview with Shwani, 2016)

Presidents (Talabani, Ma'sum and Salih) have adopted a conciliatory approach to regional powers. Therefore, the president has an input in Iraq's foreign policy despite it being a largely ceremonial post with limited powers. After the first president, who was an Arab Sunni, the post was allocated to the Kurds due to the ethnic-religious quota system and power-sharing agreement. The federal executive powers consist of two pillars – the president and the Council of Ministers – with most powers held by the prime minister. Both are subject to the influential role of the ICR. A majority of the ICR elects the president and vice presidents. They form the Presidency Council, 'which shall be elected by one list and a two-thirds majority' of the ICR elects, according to Article 138/2/A. Prior to the 2010 legislative elections, all members of the Presidency Council had veto power on laws or issues that were sent to them. The members of the Presidency Council are appointed by unwritten norms as part of the ethnic-religious quota system and the power-sharing agreement and arrangement of three main components of Iraq: Kurds, Shias and Sunnis. The Presidency Council must unanimously approve any piece of legislation the ICR passes. After Jalal Talabani's 2010 re-election, the president was able to sign bills passed by the ICR without concurrent unanimity of his two vice presidents (Danilovich, 2014, 52 and 53). Occasionally, a meeting is held between the federal government's top three constitutional authorities, who are known as the three presidencies *al-Riasat al-Thalatha* (Iraqi president, prime minister and the Speaker) to discuss policymaking and streamline their vision. Although this occurred during al-Abadi's government, it has been more systematic in al-Mahdi's government.

### *Ghazi Mashal al-Yawer (June 2004–April 2005)*

As the transition of authority from the CPA to the IIG began, al-Yawer was appointed the first president of Iraq. Previously, he had been a member of the IGC. Al-Yawer is a prominent figure in the Shammar tribe, one of the largest Arab tribes in Iraq. He is a moderate Sunni, educated in the United States, who led the newly founded Iraqis Party (*Hezb I'raqyoon*) – a secular party with Arab nationalist sentiments. Paul Bremer, members of the IGC and UN Special Envoy Lakhdar Al-Ibrahimi were involved in the process of al-Yawer's selection (Raphaeli, 2004). However, the United States had preferred the candidate Adnan Pachachi, while in a rare display of defiance the IGC selected al-Yawer (Stansfield and Anderson, 2009,

118). The Arab League, Egypt and Arab Gulf States' foreign ministers welcomed the appointment of al-Yawar and the new government, which Allawi headed.

Al-Yawer was a relatively unknown figure, but he had worked and spent years in the KSA and had close ties with the monarchy. Additionally, he, like many Arab Sunni figures, had pan-Arabism orientations and sought to develop Iraqi-Arab relationships and assert Iraq's place in the Arab world. Al-Yawer was critical of the US occupation and its security policies. He asked the US coalition forces to stay for a short time and then leave Iraq (Fairweather, 2004). He demanded a larger role for the Iraqis in running the state alongside the US-led coalition and multinational forces. In December 2004, he said some Iraqi candidates and parties allied with Iran received funding (*Ashraq Al-Awsat*, 2004; Cordesman and Khazai, 2014, 158). In the same month, the Iranian Foreign Ministry's spokesperson formally expressed its frustration with al-Yawar's statements (Addustour, 2004; Elaph, 2004).

In his short tenure, he discussed the transitional period of Iraq when visiting countries, including the United States, Europe, Arab states and Turkey. He also engaged in several meetings at which he addressed key figures, including world leaders at the G8 summit on Sea Island, the EU foreign policy chief in Brussels and the NATO's chief of Iraq's security file. In June 2004, he said: 'Although we have a premiership system in Iraq where the PM has the most responsibilities on most entities, but on issues concerning foreign policy we [al-Yawer and interim prime minister Allawi] have more team work and partnership' (al-Yawer, 2004). Al-Yawer and Allawi expressed very similar views on foreign affairs, particularly regional affairs.

In March 2004, the CPA imposed TAL. The Presidency Council is part of the executive authority, alongside the Council of Ministers. In TAL, foreign affairs powers were not clearly identified between the National Assembly, the Presidency Council and the Council of Ministers. While TAL gave the ITG the right to formulate foreign policy, sign treaties and negotiate, according to al-Yawer, the IIG had limited lasting powers; he said the Iraqi government could conduct and exercise foreign relations, but could not make agreements or commitments lasting more than one or two years (al-Yawer, 2004).

Al-Yawer, his first interim vice president al-Jaafari and second vice president Rosh Shaways, all had differing views on foreign policy. Al-Yawer welcomed the proposal for Arab states' engagement in Iraq as part of the multinational forces (Cole, 2004b). Although his views were compatible with Prime Minister Allawi's, they were not with the majority of Shia officials, including al-Jaafari. Al-Yawer was part of the process of rebuilding the new political system, in which the focus was to diplomatically liaise with the international community and build new institutions.

*Jalal Talabani (April 2005–12, but held the position officially till July 2014)*

Jalal Talabani was one of the co-founders of the PUK and the first Kurd that the Transitional National Assembly democratically elected in 2005 as president in Iraq's history. Al-Yawer, the former president, became a vice president; the other vice president, Adil Abd al-Mahid, was from ISCI. Despite the difference of views between Talabani and al-Yawar, such as Iran and the timetable to withdraw US troops, Talabani maintained stable relationships in the Presidency Council due to his political weight, acumen and diplomatic skillset. However, there were rifts between President Talabani and Prime Minister al-Jaafari regarding internal and foreign policy. Although President Talabani discussed his external relations activities with former prime minister al-Jaafari, the latter took unilateral decisions and actions in foreign affairs (Author's interview with Karadaghi, 2015).

The ICR elected Talabani as president in 2006 and 2010 after talks. In the 2006 al-Maliki-led government, sectarian animosities and clashes on domestic and foreign affairs appeared between Prime Minister al-Maliki and Talabani's new vice president Tareq al-Hashimi. Vice President al-Hashimi lobbied in the United States and regionally, without Talabani's agreement, against al-Maliki's policies. This demonstrates the divisions within the Presidency Council and the al-Maliki-led Council of Ministers, which sent different messages internationally and regionally. Talabani tried unsuccessfully to alleviate and resolve these hurdles. Confrontations escalated until al-Maliki accused al-Hashimi of running death squads and persecuted him. However, Talabani maintained a relatively good relationship with al-Maliki, while many Sunnis and Masoud Barzani pushed twice for votes of no confidence against al-Maliki in 2012. President Talabani refused; while he disagreed with al-Maliki's policies (Wicken, 2012a), Talabani's principle was to keep the house integrated.

Talabani's charismatic leadership of the PUK (major power house in the KR-I) provided him with advantages in foreign policy making, as he and the party enjoyed good relationships with Iran and Western countries. Talabani was known in the international media as Iraq's safety valve, like a non-religious Kurdish version of al-Sistani. Karadaghi said:

> There were additional factors regarding constitutional powers for the President in foreign policy. Namely the personality of Jalal Talabani as he is charismatic and has political weight incomparable to other politicians and his good interrelationships with other Iraqi politicians … This gave him influence on foreign policy more than the constitutional powers. (Author's interview with Karadaghi, 2015)

All interviewees agreed that Talabani brought additional importance to the post of the Presidency, which was projected onto Iraqi foreign relations and policy. He emphasized the Kurdish commitment to the integrity of Iraq (Eppel, 2011, 113). He was known as *Mam* 'uncle' to Kurdish people, underlining his wise and subtle manner and political prudence that enabled him to navigate Iraq post Saddam and qualified him to resolve a number of internal and international issues related to Iraq. Between 2006 and 2008, he paved the way for peace-making negotiations between the United States, some Arab Sunni insurgents and the Shia-led government (Al-Fayhaa TV, 2014a). He prevented the escalation of the situation between al-Maliki's government and the KRG, especially with Masoud Barzani. Talabani also had historical cordial relationships with Iranian leaders in

Tehran. Meanwhile, Talabani was a close ally of the United States and had a close relationship with the George W. Bush administration. He also played a role in mediation between Iran and the United States to mitigate their animosities. Ryan Crocker, former US ambassador to Iraq, said, 'He [President Talabani] would host meetings at his residency and everybody would come, there was not another figure who could do that including the prime minister' (Calamur, 2017). Furthermore, his role extended beyond Iraq's borders; for example, he was the vice president of Socialist International.

Talabani recognized the importance of the role of the prime minister in consolidating Iraq's relationship with neighbouring countries. For instance, he said:

> Our relationship with Jordan has improved very much ... As you know we [Jalal Talabani] visited Jordan a lot of times but the last visit of al-Maliki [prime minister] has supported the visits that I have conducted with my governmental delegations including ministers, and approved the success of our discussions with Jordan. (Fatha al-Hurriya, 2012)

This statement underlined his ability to have a working relationship with al-Maliki. During the strained Turkey-Iraq relations in 2008, Turkey bombarded Iraq's borders in the north and targeted the Kurdish Workers Party (PKK), which the Iraqi government called 'unacceptable violations of its sovereignty' (*Today's Zaman*, 2008). The airstrikes stopped and Talabani visited Ankara by invitation of the Turkish president Abdullah Gul and bilateral relations temporarily improved. Mr Sabah Omran, Iraqi ambassador to Turkey, said: 'The visit was successful ... the President is a practical man ... he is never affected by criticism. If he had listened to criticism this visit might not have happened ... the President Talabani is the central figure in the Iraqi government apparatus and he made it clear against terrorism' (*Today's Zaman*, 2008). Talabani's peaceful relationships with regional leaders and most Iraqi elites and factions facilitated the government's foreign relations. Despite the constitutional limitations of the president's powers, Talabani's personality played a significant role.

His absence due to a stroke at the end of 2012 created a vacuum of a consolidatory elite in Baghdad and of power in the PUK-controlled areas. Al-Hashimi remained fugitive and the remaining vice president, Khodair al-Khozaei, was a Shia Islamist from the Islamic Da'wa Party-Iraq Organization. This party is different from al-Maliki's ruling party, but shares relatively similar Shia political objectives. Al-Khozaei has a good relationship with al-Maliki and has defended the Shia-led government's policy. After Talabani, political exclusion worsened and resentment rose among the Kurds and the Arab Sunnis, further fragmenting the state and contributing to the rise of Daesh and Kurdish nationalist sentiment.

*Fuad Ma'sum (July 2014–18)*

In July 2014, the ICR elected the veteran Kurdish politician Ma'sum, from the PUK, to be the new president. Ma'sum said: 'I became President after all the Kurdish political parties selected me and there is a decision to stay in Iraq' (Council on Foreign Relations, 2014). Ma'sum as a politician has no influence on the PUK, in which he is a member of the political bureau; nor does he have any significant influence on other Iraqi political leaders. He also lacks Talabani's charisma and is thus less effective in policymaking.

However, Ma'sum was involved in international platforms relating to Iraq's security and its place in the international community. Ma'sum and Foreign Minister al-Jaafari attended an international meeting in Paris, along with the leaders of more than thirty countries, which aimed to aid the Iraqi government against Daesh. In October 2014, Ma'sum said: 'The Paris meeting convened according to coordination between President François Hollande, and me. We agreed to convene this meeting and send invitations to forty-one countries' (Alhurra Iraq, 2014). The president and his advisors participated in preparing the programme for that summit (author's interview with Shwani, 2016). This shows the president's efforts and contribution to conducting Iraq's foreign relations.

There were divisions in the Presidency Council. Ma'sum had three vice presidents: al-Maliki, Usama al-Nujaifi and Allawi. All three had different approaches to foreign policy. Shwani, President Ma'sum's spokesperson, said:

> There was some understanding between the Presidential Council members in that the foreign policy address should be united; representing the Presidential Council, not representing individuals' views ... However, the President was sometimes embarrassed by the VPs relationships or because of their political stances and statements towards some regional states that were outside the Presidential programme. (Author's interview with Shwani, 2016)

Vice President al-Maliki's policy and position was against Prime Minister al-Abadi's in general, as he was sidelined from the prime minister position. Al-Maliki pursued a more rigid, aggressive and narrow approach to projecting foreign policy. He encouraged closer ties with Iran and Russia. Vice President Al-Nujaifi and Vice President Allawi persistently criticized the domination of the Shia-led government and Iran. These perspectives were different from those of Ma'sum, who is moderate in his views, and he encouraged the US-led global coalition against Daesh and acknowledged the importance of the relationship with Iran; Ma'sum visited Tehran and Riyadh to consolidate Iraqi bilateral relationships. Al-Abadi and Ma'sum tried to reactivate the stalemated Iraqi foreign relations during al-Maliki's tenure, especially after the absence of Talabani. However, Ma'sum's and al-Abadi's efforts yielded limited results. Ma'sum did not have Talabani's political base and binding relationships with internal, regional and international figures; his internal and external engagement therefore gave the impression of being rather weak. When al-Abadi stripped the vice presidents from their posts – although this was later revoked by the Supreme Court – as part of the reform plan, it was without consulting Ma'sum, whose later intervention failed.

In the run up to Kurdistan's referendum, Ma'sum's effort to reconcile the differences between Baghdad and Erbil was unfruitful. On 16 September Ma'sum's office called for the initiation of dialogue '*Mubadarat al-Hiwar*' between Erbil and Baghdad without indicating support for the referendum (Mustafa, 2017) and cancelled his trip to the United States and his speech at the UN General Assembly on 18 September due to the sensitivity of this issue. On 29 September 2017, Ma'sum mentioned that his initiative – to defuse the tension between Baghdad and Erbil – was not accepted by either government. However, he said that he was successful to a degree in mediating between Baghdad and Erbil because the latter did not declare independence (Alhurra Iraq, 2017).

*Barham Salih (since 2018)*

Ma'sum's successor President Salih, a Kurdish politician (from the PUK), is a promising reinvigoration of the Presidency's role in foreign policy making as he has long-standing relationships with regional and global powers' leaders and prominent scholars. His professional and Western educational background, fluency in multiple languages and diplomatic skills aid him in balancing the delicate relationship between Iran and the United States and the Arab world. President Salih began his tenure with official regional visits, namely, to the KSA, Turkey, Iran, the UAE, Jordan, Kuwait, Qatar, and global visits, including to France and the UK. At the time when Prime Minister al-Mahdi was facing political rivalry and vulnerability, Salih's visits were in the context of improving bilateral relations; this matches with al-Mahdi's approach for amending Iraq's ties with regional powers. It is unprecedented that the approaches of the president, the prime minister and the Speaker are relatively compatible; this was partly due to the goodwill and open lines of communication between them. Although Iraq's presidency does not have a significant influence on foreign policy making, the president's contribution can be weighed by the skillset of the personality, prudent use of constitutional powers, their network and their political party's support as well as their relationship with other key actors in the government. They usually have a mediating role in order to produce a less contentious policy.

## *The Speaker, the Iraqi Council of Representatives and its Foreign Relations Committee*

The Speaker of the ICR does not have executive powers. However, in Iraq's parliamentary system he is a prominent figure domestically and internationally, as the position unofficially represents the Arab Sunnis in Iraq's power-sharing agreement and quota system. From 2005 to 2016, the successive speakers were Arab Sunni politicians from Sunni political parties – apart from Fuad Ma'sum, who was Acting Speaker for five months.

According to Article 33 of the ICR's Rules of Procedures, 'The Speaker is the person who represents the ICR, and speaks in its name.' He plays a role in foreign relations and bilateral relationships, the effectiveness of which depends on his efforts and political base. For example, in 2008, Mahmoud al-Mashadani

(Speaker from 2006 to 2008) argued that the US-Iraq SOFA agreement should be discussed with neighbouring countries. As Speaker, he was involved in bilateral talks about the security pact with a number of regional powers, including Iran (Al-Jazeera Arabic, 2008). Usama al-Nujaifi (Speaker from 2010 to 2014) aired Sunni grievances, lobbied regionally and internationally for an Arab Sunni region in Iraq and strongly disagreed with al-Maliki's domestic and foreign policy. All Iraqi speakers have played a role in contributing to or contradicting the Shia-led government's foreign policy statements.

The Speaker not only meets foreign delegations but also visits foreign states and meets foreign officials. Shia-led government officials have critically noted that the Speakers represent their political and sectarian backgrounds, rather than the ICR. The US head of Congress and the US president invited al-Nujaifi to the United States as Speaker to discuss bilateral relationships. Al-Nufaifi used these visits to demonstrate al-Maliki's government's marginalization of the Sunnis. On many occasions, Speakers – including the former Speaker Salim al-Jubouri, previously from the Iraqi Islamic Party (IIP) – have clashed with the Shia-dominated executive authorities regarding foreign policy.

The current Speaker Muhammad al-Halbusi's foreign affairs statements are fairly compatible with that of the prime minister and Iraqi president. However, there is divergence emerging around each role's jurisdiction. Al-Halbusi is a young Arab Sunni politician from the Arab Sunni political faction 'Solution' (*al-Hal*). In a turning point in the 2018 elections he received the backing of the pro-Iran Shia factions' coalition '*al-Bina*' led by al-A'meri. Al-Halbusi has been active in foreign affairs and visited Riyadh, Tehran and the United States. In April 2019 he headed the Iraqi parliamentary summit for neighbouring countries hosted in Baghdad which brought two rivals, the KSA and Iran. This Speaker is carving a less contradictory course than his predecessors.

According to Article 112 of the Rules of Procedures, Speakers coordinate with the FRC regarding their foreign affairs–related legislative activities. However, they lack coherent coordination. In October 2015, Speaker al-Jubouri met with FRC members to enhance relationships with foreign parliaments to improve Iraq's image internationally (Parliament Iraq, 2015b). In November 2015, the FRC and Speaker al-Jubouri organized a forum that included Iraqi academics, all of whom recognized that Iraqi diplomacy and foreign policy faced obstructions in designing diplomacy. Former Speaker al-Jubouri emphasized that

> their [Iraqi officials] loyalty should be to Iraq; it is dangerous that Iraqi internal political parties are conducting external diplomacy where each political party or component build ties with the international community and beyond the border where Iraq loses its compass [directions]. (Parliament Iraq, 2015a)

Al-Jubouri's statements highlight the splintered foreign policies, to which he and his former party (IIP) contributed by portraying different pictures of it.

The ICR has a role in foreign relations enacting federal laws, and it monitors the performance of the executive bodies, including that of the I-MOFA and the foreign minister. Therefore, the ICR has legislative oversight of the executive and the power to consent/declare/approve the declaration of war and state of emergency based on a joint request from the president and the prime minister. It ratifies Iraqi international agreements with states, which executive bodies have signed, and has the power to approve or reject them. More than one committee is involved in studying the agreement (law project; *Mashroo' al-Qanoon*) to ratify it. In foreign affairs these usually include the FRC and a specific committee related to the area of the agreement. Abdul Bari Zebari was head of the FRC and represented the ICR's Kurdistan Coalition for three terms. In 2016, he said:

> The Iraqi constitution compelled the Iraqi government to obtain the approval of the ICR when they make agreements whether its trade, security or military ... The government should present the agreement to the ICR to ratify it. Without it, it is not a legitimate law ... Moreover, the significant agreements with huge military or economic impact needs the approval of two-thirds of the ICR, while other agreements require a simple majority 50 plus 1 ... Nevertheless, the memorandum of understating between Iraqi executive bodies and foreign states do not need the approval of the ICR. (Author's interview with Zebari, 2016)

This demonstrates that the ICR can influence Iraq's bilateral or multilateral relationships and commitments with foreign entity or entities. It monitors the performance of all Iraq's international agreements. Therefore, it is a legislative authority (*Sulta al-Tashria'ya*) that contributes to Iraq's foreign relations. In particular, the ICR provides legitimacy to the core executive bodies. It is a theatre of political debate, lobby and bargain, which also reflects on foreign policy performance by sometimes questioning executive figures. The ICR's support strengthens or weakens the foreign relations and policy of the prime minister and foreign minister. It has constitutional powers to remove the core executive bodies, including the cabinet members, by withdrawing confidence from one of the ministers, such as Defence Minister al-Obeidi and Finance Minister Zebari.

The FRC is an important body, but less critical than the aforementioned foreign policy making apparatus. It has two major functions: to facilitate legislation inside the ICR with respect to foreign affairs issues necessary for all governmental bodies; and to monitor the performance of the I-MOFA and foreign minister. Essentially, in relation to legislation, the FRC studies and presents a report regarding the agreements and treaties Iraq has signed, which is then sent to the ICR and voted on. Abdul Bari Zebari, the chair of the FRC, said: 'The I-MOFA send the agreement to the Council of Ministers then the latter send it to the ICR where all the FRC and other related committees depending on their specialization and the agreement specification are involved' (author's interview with Zebari, 2016). This shows some degree of functionality between the executive bodies and the ICR. Occasionally, some FRC members participate in formal Iraqi government delegations with the prime minister and other officials (author's interview with al-Bayati, 2014; and al-A'ni, 2014). The FRC does not formulate foreign policy but tries to monitor foreign relations and related agencies.

Different perceptions regarding foreign policy were expressed in the author's interviews with ICR members and FRC members from various parliamentary blocs (conducted in 2014, 2015 and 2016). Members of Parliament from Sunni and Kurdish political factions are dubious of the effectiveness, representation and formulation of the government's foreign policy, while members, for example, of the SLC (Shia) advocated for al-Maliki's government's foreign policy. This is not representative of all the Shia members of Parliament or blocs. These views became more fractured and divided even within each ethnic-sectarian political faction. For example, in al-Abadi's government some Shia members of Parliament from the SLC allied with al-Maliki showed great distrust of the government. Regarding the power-sharing agreement, interviewees reported that the Arab Sunnis claim they are marginalized in decision-making and the Kurds criticized the Shia-led government for dominating it. For example, al-A'ni, a prominent Sunni leader and member of the FRC, said:

> The role of the committee is weak, and the decision-making process was opaque in al-Maliki's government. Al-Maliki had overridden all other governmental institutions. When he was shaping cooperative or animosity relations with countries he was conducting relations in isolation from the parliament, the political forces and even the Ministry of Foreign Affairs which resulted in clashes between the Prime Minister's office, Parliament and the Ministry of Foreign Affairs. (Author's interview with al-A'ni, 2014)

Al-A'ni's argument underlines that foreign affairs bodies are at loggerheads. It also asserts Prime Minister al-Maliki's undermining of institutional and key figures. In 2014, Abdul Bari Zebari said: 'Iraq's foreign policy is a controversial topic that is a prisoner of the Iraqi people and the Iraqi people are manipulated by the slogans of some Iraqi politicians.' His argument illustrates that the fragmentation of Iraq's foreign policy reflects the influence of the political parties and leaders, who follow their party's and/or personal agendas, including but not limited to ethno-sectarian tendencies for political and/or personal gain. The chasm in comprehension and interpretation of formulating Iraq's foreign policy between various ICR members was clear in the interviews. It can be concluded that the ICR and FRC are notably contributing to the legal framework and legitimize the foreign relations of both the executive bodies and those allocated to create and implement foreign policy.

## Conclusion

The incoherence of Iraq's foreign relations and foreign policy emerges between and within core governmental bodies and agencies. The divergence goes even further: into the Presidency Council, Council of Ministers and ministries, including the I-MOFA and its departments, embassies and consulates. To various degrees, the core executive authorities and the ICR contribute to shaping foreign policy. Nevertheless, as head of the Council of Ministers, the prime minister has superiority in drawing up foreign policy and directing Iraq's diplomacy. The foreign minister implements the foreign policy; he has some input that is based on personal and partisan interests due to the lack of coordination or a detailed, concrete and comprehensive agenda, particularly until al-Mahdi's government. The president conducts some foreign relations activities, but he has limited authority in foreign policy; his role is symbolic, shaped by his personality, political base and domestic and external interrelationships. Although the ICR does not execute policy, occasionally their role could be significant as they are able to remove the officials if there is an adequate majority.

The lack of detail in the new Iraqi constitution and different interpretations of it, as well as the dearth of understanding among officials of the magnitude and responsibility, has contributed to incoherent foreign policy. Although from 2005 to 2018 there were successive governments with prime ministers drawn from Shia-based parties (excluding Allawi) competition and clashes between officials persisted, which resulted in tenuous processes and weak foreign policy outcomes. The Iraqi constitution provides the federal government with some general principles for formulating foreign policy. Article 3 identifies Iraq as part of the Islamic world and an active member in the Arab League. Article 8 stipulates Iraq shall adhere to principles of good neighbourliness and non-interference in the internal affairs of other states. Article 9/E states the Iraqi government shall respect and implement Iraq's international obligations (Iraqi Constitution, 2005). Iraq's foreign policy is supposed to reflect the Iraqi constitution's values. Iraq has successfully implemented its international obligations. However, as Faily (2016) emphasized not all Iraqi officials and diplomats have adhered to all principles nor the official federal government's political stance. This was particularly evident when examining Iraq's aloof relationship with most members of the Arab League. Besides these few generic principles, the constitution is ambiguous about the requirements of foreign policy making on a granular level.

Following the tenure of Prime Minister Allawi and President al-Yawar in the IIG, no other Iraqi president or prime minister has issued hostile statements towards Iran. More frequently until al-Mahdi's government the Arab Sunni deputy prime ministers and vice presidents, the Arab Sunni Speaker and some Kurdish and Arab Sunni diplomats contradicted the Shia prime minister or Kurdish Iraqi presidents on many foreign policy issues, including statements against Iran.

In 2016, Faily said: 'The core executive bodies, they may not be complementary to each other ... there is a lack of coordination between them, specifically what the PM and FM want from a country ... they may not be as cohesive or fully in agreement but there are negotiations going on' (author's interview with Faily, 2016). Since 2005, the Shia elites and parties (particularly the Islamic Da'wa Party until 2018) have dominated the major posts (primarily the prime minister) and bodies responsible for drawing Iraq's foreign policy. The institutionalization of the quota system and the crippled power-sharing agreement between Iraqi actors has contributed to Iraq's incoherent foreign policy; yet it provided every major ethnic and religious political faction with a platform and a say in the political process. Although the United States has had a substantial role in reconstructing the governmental institutions, including those involved in foreign affairs, it was unable to establish sophisticated independent bodies or maintain influence after its withdrawal. Nevertheless, Iraqi officials were compelled to have a relationship with the United States, as the regional powers (excluding Iran) did not have prosperous relationships (since al-Abadi's government, Iraq's relationship with the KSA has slowly improved) with the Shia-led government and the political elite maintained a rapport with the United States.

Until 2018 there was an obvious lack of coordination and cooperation between various governmental bodies and elites relating to foreign affairs and their duties; the Iraqi constitution and laws have not addressed these loopholes. Disparate statements and messages from Iraqi foreign relations representatives have confused Iraqi public opinion and regional and international powers. The Iraqi people despise the rotation of the political elite in every government's posts. For example, Ibrahim al-Jaafari has been the president of the IGC as well as the vice president, prime minister and foreign minister of Iraq. The endemic bureaucratic corruption, nepotism, cronyism, favouritism, clientelism and patronage network in the weak institutions are contributing factors to incoherent foreign policy. The majority of officials blame others for the failure to adopt a coherent foreign relations and policy. In fact, they should all accept a degree of responsibility. However, the government has had some success in foreign policy; it has built foreign affairs and governmental organizations (albeit fragile ones), regained Iraq's seats in transnational organizations and started to improve Iraq's global image compared to Saddam's era.

Regardless of position or constitutional limitations, politicians and officials with a significant number of political party supporters and relationships have more power and influence over foreign affairs than officials without a support base. However, the prime minister is the primary actor and leads the Council of Ministers in formulating the bulk of foreign policy and conducting foreign relations. The foreign minister has secondary importance conducting foreign relations, and fills the vacuum in Iraqi foreign policy. The president of Iraq has limited executive power; only Talabani and Barham have had an exceptional role in shaping Iraq's foreign policy. The Speaker of the ICR has relationships with foreign officials and – with the FRC – monitors executive authorities in foreign affairs. He has an informal but exceptional role in foreign affairs as Iraq is a parliamentary system and he represent the Arab Sunnis. The National Security Advisor and Agency play a supplementary role to the prime minister in pinpointing Iraqi foreign policy security imperatives. There are no clear-cut provisions and laws that grant powers to the vice presidents and prime minister's deputies in foreign policy, and they do not have a great input in the official foreign policy making. Rather they appear as political and partisan actors who are able to make the policy incoherent and weak. Due to Iraq's fragmentation and the communal quota system the posts – including that of the Speaker of the ICR and the deputy prime minister and vice president positions – are viewed as important governmental voices by external powers such as the United States, Turkey and Arab states as they represent their constituencies, particularly the Arab Sunnis. However, external states do not make official agreements with them without the consent of the executives that hold constitutional powers such as the prime minister. Since 2003, the prime minister has not had control of the members of the Council of Ministers – including ministers and his deputies – as they are appointed according to the *al-Muhasasa* and *al-Tawafuq al-Siyasi*. This lack of commitment to the prime minister's policy vision has also made Iraq's foreign policy incoherent.

## Chapter 3

### THE KURDISTAN REGIONAL GOVERNMENT'S FOREIGN RELATIONS AND FOREIGN POLICY

*Introduction*

The Kurdistan Regional Government's (KRG) need for a foreign policy is a central part of the state-building project of the Kurdistan Region of Iraq (KR-I) and reflects its sociopolitical and economic evolution. The KRG's foreign policy often differs from and contradicts that of the central government in Baghdad, which further fragments Iraq's foreign policies. I explain why the KRG needs a foreign policy, how it is made and who is making it. The KRG's foreign relations and policy diverge from those of Baghdad. From the KRG leadership's perspective, drawing up a foreign policy is urgent. This is because foreign policy lays out the external agenda, priorities (imperatives that have international dimensions) and alliances, most of which are different from those of Baghdad. The KRG's decision-makers agree that having a foreign policy is imperative to achieve the interests of the KR-I. KRG officials said that its foreign policy will not contradict or clash with Baghdad unless the latter seeks to curb the interests of the KR-I. The KRG seeks to have a role and a distinctive voice in the international arena as the need for recognition for its rights, including self-determination and, ultimately, independence. It has temporarily ceased its pursuit of independence after the regional backlash and the international community's unwillingness to recognize and accept the KRG's non-binding independence referendum and its outcomes.

The former president of the KR-I held the major authority in formulating the KRG's foreign policy until he resigned in 2017; yet he maintains leverage. The prime minister was the second most influential figure until 2017 when the president resigned, and he became the highest executive authority. Bureaucratic bodies such as the KRG's Department of Foreign Relations (DFR) implement the president and prime minister's unwritten foreign policy agenda.[1] An important consequence is that the KRG's foreign policy is independent and often contradicts Baghdad's official foreign policy. Analysing the structure of the KRG's core executive bodies, it appears that the region has a mixed or hybrid presidential-parliamentary system where political factions and key figures are most powerful.

The KR-I is an unrecognized state and a relative success in state building; since 1991, the region has shown sociopolitical development in a post-conflict setting (Stansfield and Caspersen, 2011, 3). The KR-I has developed from a quasi-state into one that conducts the activities of a federal state in foreign relations (Mohammed and Owtram, 2014, 65). Post 2003, the KRG was a leading force in the establishment of the federal constitution to secure its status and powers. Despite the differences between the two main parties, the Kurdistan Democratic Party (KDP) and the Patriotic Union of Kurdistan (PUK), they have, since 2003, been working on two tracks: first, the KR-I state-building project, which includes foreign relations; and second, securing recognition from Baghdad and external powers of the rights and powers of the KR-I as well as pursuing their partisan interests. The Kurdish senior positions in the federal government have protected the KR-I from potentially unfriendly interventions by neighbouring states, such as Iran and Turkey (Romano, 2010a, 1350). Since the first government in Baghdad, the Kurdish positions in Baghdad gave them a stage where they were able to seek their interests. Meanwhile, the elites in Erbil have adopted active foreign relations and a foreign policy, which serves the priorities of their region and their partisan interests. Post referendum, the KRG's foreign relations entered a dormant phase due to the absence of international support, yet the external ties have gradually revived.

## The evolution of the KRG's foreign policy

There are three main stages of the KR-I's progress in foreign relations and policy and the key Kurdish political parties' engagement with Baghdad's foreign relations and policy. Historically, it is essential to recognize the Kurdish leaders' (such as Sharif Pasha and Sheikh Muhammad Barzanji) engagement in foreign affairs at the beginning of the twentieth century particularly interacting with superpowers for the Kurdistan region's self-rule.[2] Although their efforts failed to carve out a region for the Kurds, it was the beginning of Kurdish international interactions with nationalist purpose. There are three interconnected phases: from the 1940s to 1991; post 1991, which saw the development of basic foreign relations; and post 2003, which saw the development of the KRG's foreign relations and foreign policy. The Kurdish political parties in the KR-I began their limited relations with regional and global powers after the formation of the major Iraqi Kurdish political parties: the KDP in 1946 and the PUK in 1976. Along with other, smaller parties they built bridges with Iraqi political parties, regional powers and then beyond the Middle East. They focused on promoting the Kurdish cause with and via the Kurdish diaspora. Dr Fuad Hussein, the KRG's former president's chief of staff, said:

> The Kurdish movement began as a revolutionary movement in the 1960s, trying to make relations to spread awareness about the Kurdish cause and mobilise the Kurds. For example, to tell the European people and countries beyond that the Kurds are here and do exist and they are victims ... this can be called public relations. (Author's interview with Hussein, 2014)

The first phase, the Iraqi Kurds' external relationships, can be classified as public relations. The Kurdish political parties still have clandestine or covert relationships with various intelligence agencies in the region and beyond. The second stage of Kurdish external relations began in 1992 and can be identified as foreign relations. Since 1992, the powers of the KDP and PUK have gradually expanded. This is the result of the rebellion against Saddam's regime, known as *Rapareen*; the Iraqi Kurds and Kurdish political parties were able to control a considerable swathe of Kurdish territory during the first Gulf War in 1991. Operation Provide Comfort in 1991 secured a safe haven for the Kurds in the KR-I, which had a historic opportunity to hold democratic multiparty elections in 1992 and to build a parliament and governmental bodies despite their chronic shortcomings and rivalries. Hussein said: 'When the Kurds controlled the land and the establishment of the KRG and Kurdistan Region's parliament, the KRG started its foreign relations to facilitate its activities, such as economic and cultural relations' (author's interview with Hussein, 2014).[3] Before 2003, the international and regional powers were cautious about interacting formally with the KRG, as it was a nascent, unpredictable and unrecognized entity. Internally, the KRG was not at a sufficient level to formulate a strategy and so did not have a foreign policy as conventionally understood.

As a result of the Iraqi-Kurdish Civil War (1994–8), known as *BraKuji* (the killing of brothers between the two major parties), two administrations with binary cabinets were established: the KDP's government in Erbil and the PUK's in Sulaymaniyah. Both parties have had external relationships with international aid organizations and non-governmental organizations (NGOs), as well as some regional and international powers. Their ties with states were often unofficial and fragile and restricted to security and economy. The political parties' bureaus of foreign relations, intelligence services, party leaders and other nascent governmental bodies (e.g. Ministry of Humanitarian Aid and Cooperation) conducted external relations (author's interview with Sayfour, 2014). These efforts were incoherent and without a professional approach or foreign relations objectives. The external activities of the two local governments represented the two divided parties' control of political affairs.

Then prime minister and current president of the KR-I Nechervan Barzani divides the KRG's foreign relations into two phases: from 1991 until 2003, and post 2003:

> The KRG's foreign relations in the first stage was limited and restricted, which was not based on recognition of the KRG ... We had relationships with the US, Turkey and Iran ... We can define these relationships as not having a high level of rapport ... we did not even have diplomatic relationships ... Our relationships were more with intelligence agencies and with some foreign affairs ministries, such as the Turkish Ministry of Foreign Affairs. (Author's interview with Barzani, 2014)

As Iraq's future was ambiguous, Prime Minister Barzani believes that pre-2003 states were dealing with the KRG as a temporary entity, that relations would diminish over time and that Iraq would become as it was before (author's interview with Barzani, 2014). The prime minister's views reflect the conditions that the KRG experienced before 2003. This was a preparatory phase for the period post 2003 and can be seen as the second stage of developing foreign relations.

Nechervan Barzani stated that the second stage began after 2003 and the KRG's foreign affairs are reflected in the Iraqi constitution, which states that the KRG can conduct foreign relations but Baghdad will draw up foreign policy. Nevertheless, in reality, the KRG's independent status in foreign policy is de facto. Barzani called this period the stage of developing institutions (author's interview with Barzani, 2014). In 2006, in the KR-I, the Kurdish parties (KDP and PUK) formed a unified government in the fifth cabinet. This period witnessed a slow integration of governmental bodies and the start of institutionalization of robust foreign relations. This institution building can be understood as the third phase of developing foreign policy and its organizations.

Post 2003, the KDP and PUK led the Kurds in Baghdad. They participated in defeating Saddam alongside the US-led coalition, particularly in the periphery of the KR-I. The two leaders of the parties were in the Iraqi Governing Council (IGC), and the KDP and PUK formed a coalition in December 2004 to participate in Iraq's elections in 2005. Despite their differences in foreign relations (such as disparities between their top-down sets of priorities and varying degrees of ties with regional allies), they joined with other smaller parties to form the Democratic Patriotic Alliance of Kurdistan (DPAK), also known as the Kurdistan Alliance (KA) or *Al-Tahalf al-Kurdistani* and renamed the Kurdistan List (*Listi Kurdistani*) in 2009. The KRG and the two major Kurdish factions recognized the limitations of their aspirations as a sub-sovereign entity in achieving their objectives. The Kurds sought to make changes in Baghdad by engaging there to consolidate the KR-I and make it a recognized entity. They had a major role in the new political process and system in Baghdad to secure their rights and enable the KRG to exercise external relations.

In Baghdad, the Kurdish elite have had an input in Iraq's foreign relations since the re-establishment of the Iraqi Ministry of Foreign Affairs (I-MOFA). The former foreign minister Hoshyar Zebari held a vital role from 2003 to 2014. Although he is from the KDP, the PUK (which was closer to the major Shia parties) has held the Presidency. The KDP and PUK remained in coalition in Baghdad for the parliamentary elections in January and December of 2005 and 2010. The Kurdish coalition's political manifesto in the elections emphasized Kurdish rights; in foreign relations, they sought to develop relationships with Iraq's neighbours and not interfere in the domestic affairs of other countries, so as to develop cooperative and peaceful relationships and combat terrorism (Munther, 2005). Adding to the 2005 programme, the 2010 manifesto also included promotion of economy and access to foreign direct investment (FDI) in Iraqi infrastructure (al-Jumaili, 2010). However, in 2014, the unity of the two major Kurdish parties weakened in the Iraqi elections as they ran separately in several provinces. The schism widened, and in the following Iraqi election in 2018 they ran as separate lists, this is in parallel to the deepened division between the Shia and Arab Sunnis.

Their political parties' ideologies promote Kurdish nationalism and further devolution of powers for the KR-I. However, Kurdish elites in Baghdad maintain a balance between their Iraqi counterparts and regional powers. Since 2003, Kurdish elites have adopted two approaches: one tries to adhere to the official Iraqi foreign policy, particularly by those who are based in Baghdad; the other formulates de facto foreign relations and policy in Erbil. These two approaches were not synchronized among the Kurdish leadership but materialized as an imperative for the time and circumstances.

The KRG's foreign policy has contracted and endured setbacks since its referendum on 25 September 2017 mainly because of the lack of support from the international community. Subsequently, the KRG faced regional isolation which has had harmful economic and political ramifications on its foreign policy objectives. In the run up to the referendum, coordinated regional threats emerged particularly from Iran and Turkey. For example, on 21 September 2017 the foreign ministers of Iraq, Iran and Turkey, in a joint statement at the UN in New York, announced countermeasures against the KRG's referendum. The KRG's Western allies either rejected or asked to postpone its referendum; In August 2017 the US secretary of state Tillerson asked the KRG to postpone the referendum; an official EU statements on 19 September emphasized support for Iraq's unity, sovereignty and territorial integrity and advocated for the KRG to avoid the referendum. Nonetheless, the referendum was conducted, and 93 per cent voted in favour of independence. In response, Baghdad shut down the KRI's airspace, cut off the banking system, delayed the salaries of KRG's employees and retook Kirkuk with a military assault. As a consequence, the president of the KRG resigned. The KRG's referendum coincided with world silence regarding Spanish suppression of Catalonia's independence referendum on 1 October. This underlines the fact that the international community is neither ready nor accepting of emerging new sovereign states.

To ease the political and economic pressure exerted on the KRG, Prime Minister Nechervan Barzani received supportive phone calls from Rex Tillerson, the US state secretary, and Theresa May, the UK prime minister. President Emmanuel Macron invited Prime Minister Barzani and his deputy Qubad Talabani to the Elysee Palace in Paris in the first week of December 2017. This event reinvigorated the KRG's foreign relations and provided it with a platform at a meeting with top-level leaders and a prospect to resolve the predicament between Erbil and Baghdad and support the KRG's rights within the Iraqi constitution. After the Kurdish referendum the Kurdish elites slowly restored their rapport with their counterparts in Baghdad and gradually recovered their relationships with regional great powers (Iran and Turkey). The latter have become more cautious, distanced and apprehensive of the KRG's political ambitions

*The debate around the KRG's foreign policy*

The KRG's international activities went through two phases of development: from 1991/1992 to 2003, and post 2003. In the first phase, the KRG had limited foreign relations with the outside world. Post 2003, the KR-I became more secure than the rest of Iraq, the KRG set up specialized foreign affairs bodies and flourished economically and gradually international actors (states and transnational corporations) began to be interested in the KR-I. Consequently, it broadened its foreign relations and the KRG began to draw up foreign policy. The KRG has an interventionist foreign policy, which opposes Iraqi foreign policy. This means, for example, that there are different policies towards the Syrian Civil War, where Iraqi Kurds have interests and are engaged in Rojava (Stansfield, 2013, 279). The KRG has a proactive foreign policy that is mainly drawn up by the KDP. The PUK has a secondary role and its own foreign policy approach. In some cases, different interests have emerged between the KDP, the PUK and Baghdad, such as in Rojava.[4] The KRG is another centre of a foreign policy that emanates from Iraq (279). The emergence of the KRG's foreign policy is a reflection of its evolution in policymaking and international actors' interactions. Officially, there are two governments' foreign policies: that of the Baghdad-based federal government, and that of the Erbil-based regional government. Both possess incoherent actors in their foreign policies. Nevertheless, the KRG's formulation of foreign policy is more coherent than that of the federal government – mainly until al-Abadi's government in 2018 – and this is despite the stark division in domestic politics and policies between the major Kurdish parties. The president, the prime minister and the Council of Ministers (including the DFR and most of their representatives) are unified in foreign policy statements; the majority of the KRG's representatives adhere to its policies. For example, Tahir, the KRG's highest representative to the UK, from the PUK, would not criticize the KDP or their officials and said in 2015 that he is implementing the KRG's official foreign policy (author's interview with Tahir, 2015).

There is debate among scholars and policymakers regarding whether or not the KRG has a foreign policy or foreign relations or both. It is critical to point out the distinction between both terms because identifying a foreign policy would underline the KRG's international objectives, while the day-to-day practise of the officials with foreign entities is foreign relations. All agree the KRG has foreign relations. The different perspectives of the KRG officials emanate from distinctive interpretations of the KRG (based on personal experience), ideologies, beliefs (whether based on academic theory or practicality), partisan loyalties, interpretations and, to a degree, interest in legitimizing the KRG's foreign policy. Hussein argued: 'When the KRG was established [1991/1992] it started foreign relations. I do not believe currently that we [KRG] have a foreign policy' (author's interview with Hussein, 2014). Hussein argues that when Kurdistan becomes an independent state it will be able to have a foreign policy.

Barham Salih argues that the KRG has something in between a foreign policy and foreign relations. He leans towards the argument that the KRG has a unique, messy and independent foreign policy, which reflects the political reality on the ground in the KR-I. In many cases, he emphasizes the distinctiveness of the KRG's foreign policy in comparison with Baghdad, such as the policy towards Turkey, the United States and even Syria: 'The KRG is reflecting the continuation before

2003 when it had its relations ... by and large the KRG has a unified foreign policy but the KDP and PUK have their own foreign policy priorities' (author's interview with Salih, 2014). Salih underlines the differences between the KDP's and PUK's distinctive regional outlooks; they have relatively similar foreign policy priorities, but differ in how much value they place on them. For example, while both parties aspired for independence, this was more of a time-sensitive imperative for the KDP. The prime minister believes the KRG has a foreign policy but not a written strategy. Nechervan Barzani said:

> We don't have a written strategic plan in foreign relations but we know the KRG's strategy ... The world political leaders know that the KRG became a factor of stability in the region ... balancing and strengthening the relations with neighbouring countries based on mutual respect ... The KRG has solid relations with the US, UK and other Western and European countries ... Our new plan will focus on developing our relationships with the European countries. (Author's interview with Barzani, 2014)

The KRG's foreign policy has generic principles, which are known, but their approach and lobbying methods have not so far been written about in detail. Falah Mustafa has a similar vision to Nechervan Barzani: 'We [KRG] have got a parameter of foreign policy which is in line with Iraqi foreign policy, but at the same time we are conducting and implementing that policy through the KRG's DFR' (author's interview with Mustafa, 2014). Mustafa said the KRG leadership knows what the KRG stands for, what they want to achieve and how they want to go about it. He argues the KRG has a foreign policy and foreign relations to communicate with the outside world (author's interview with Mustafa, 2014). His argument is compatible with Nechervan Barzani's; both agree they have the tools to draw a foreign policy and pinpoint its priorities. Nechervan Barzani said:

> We view foreign policy from the interests of the Kurdistan Region, this is a reality ... Therefore, the first priority is the Kurdistan Region's interests and it is above everything as our work and responsibility is for the Kurdistan Region of Iraq ... therefore our conduct of foreign relations is a reflection of the Kurdistan Region's interests. (Author's interview with Barzani, 2014)

Barzani reiterates that the KRG's purpose is to conduct foreign relations and policy to serve the KR-I. The KRG's foreign policy objectives have not been clearly announced or formally agreed upon by the PUK or other political factions. The PUK's officials in the government have not formally rejected them, and representatives, including Deputy Prime Ministe Qubad Talabani, are contributing to them.

There are obvious clashes between the KRG's and the federal government's foreign policy priorities and objectives on almost all issues, including security, economic and energy policy and recently full sovereignty. There are differences in foreign relations between Erbil and Baghdad in approaching regional powers.

Baghdad, during al-Maliki's governments, had a strained relationship with Turkey and the Arab Gulf States, particularly the Kingdom of Saudi Arabia (KSA). Meanwhile, Erbil has enjoyed excellent relationships with these states.

The KRG's policy of expanding its relationships and foreign states' increasing acceptance of its foreign relations efforts were evident till the referendum and since then have slowly been restored. Its interactions with external powers could be understood in the context of states viewing the KRG as a friendly and useful entity and a political non-state actor rather than an equal. In interviews with the author, Prime Minister Barzani and the president's chief of staff underlined the differences between Baghdad and Erbil in foreign relations. All the decision-makers in the KR-I agree that the KRG has foreign relations and the majority agree that the KRG has a foreign policy that pursues distinctive interests.

## The Kurdistan Region's Presidency

The Kurdistan Region Presidency (KRP; *Sarokayati Haremi Kurdistan*) is a political, administrative and legal body that the Kurdistan National Assembly (KNA) promulgated in 2005 (Kurdistan Region Presidency, 2014). The president formulated and had the major role in foreign policy until he resigned on 1 November 2017; the position was vacant until Prime Minister Nechervan Barzani was elected on 28 May 2019 by the Kurdistan Parliament (KP). Since Masoud Barzani stepped down, he does not hold executive authority, but he still has an influence on all the KDP's officials as he is the president of the KDP. The president holds the highest executive authority in the KRG, according to Article 1 of the Presidency Law (PL) of the KR-I in 2005, and in the draft constitution Article 60/1 (Kurdistan Regional Government, 2005, 2015; author's interview with Zebari, 2014; Kurdistan Region Presidency, 2015). Masoud Barzani was the first president of the KR-I. The KNA elected him, and he was sworn into office on 12 June 2005; he was re-elected by popular vote (roughly 70 per cent) in 2009. The KDP predominates politically by controlling Erbil and its institutions, and economically by controlling the KRG's oil revenues.

According to PL Article 12 and draft constitution Article 60/2, the president also serves as the commander-in-chief of Peshmerga Armed Forces. Moreover, PL Article 10/10 and draft constitution Article 65/13.2 state the president has powers over security forces; for example, mobilizing forces against Daesh to retake territories and sending Peshmerga forces to Kobani in Syria.[5] Although the draft constitution is not yet operative, Masoud Barzani has exercised these powers. Practically, in the PL and draft constitution, the president is responsible for domestic security and defence policy. This and the aforementioned executive articles of the KR-I granted Masoud Barzani a stronger position to draw foreign policy. Reflecting on draft constitution Article 60, Mustafa Said Qadir, the former minister of Peshmerga affairs, said:

> The Article is operative although the constitution is not there yet as we have a constitutional project which has to be amended and there is a committee working

on it ... However, we have laws for the President of the Kurdistan Region and give powers to the President which is similar [to the draft constitutional Article] ... and we have laws for the Council of Ministers and Ministry of Peshmerga and Interior Ministry and Kurdistan Region Security Council, they operate according to the laws. (Author's interview with Qadir, 2015)[6]

Qadir tries to underline that, at the time of interview, the president was the major actor in defence and security policy. According to draft constitution Article 65/21, the president can issue a resolution establishing special offices for the KR-I in foreign countries, based on a proposal from the prime minister and in coordination with the federal government. Former president Masoud Barzani already exercised these as-yet unsanctioned powers, which provided him with a base to lay out the KR-I's foreign relations. The president has power over most of the KRG's representatives, as he gives his permission for their appointment. Hussein said:

Legally the President is the face of the KRG to the outside world ... The President and the Kurdistan Region's Presidency conduct the genuine and fundamental articulations of foreign relations, as they are responsible for this task. Thereafter, there are other governmental bodies which have foreign affairs activities. (Author's interview with Hussein, 2014)

Hussein's statement was accurate until Masoud Barzani resigned from his post, yet he still holds leverage and has a say on the KDP's governmental officials and has zealous loyalists within the party. Dindar Zebari underscored the president's role in foreign policy and his connections with other agencies:

Formulating foreign policy is the combined effort of several bodies headed by the President in collaboration with the Council of Ministers, the PM and his Deputy and cabinet, in partnership with the political stand of the KRG supported by political parties, elites, and parliament ... The President is formulating policy in line with the Iraqi constitution so far and in line with the draft constitution of the Iraqi Kurdistan Region. (Author's interview with Zebari, 2014)

While the president plays the central role in foreign relations, other governmental bodies, political parties and elites are also influential. Masoud Barzani represented the KRG in the international theatre and international summits such as the World Economic Forum in Davos in 2013 and 2014. This is a new horizon for the Kurds' interactions in international relations that have developed post Saddam.

The former president directed relations between the KRG and the Iraqi federal authorities and overseas (Kurdistan Region Presidency, 2015). There is consensus among officials and politicians that the former president played the major role in directing foreign relations. Dr Barham Salih, the KRG's former prime minister, emphasized the president's role in making the KRG's foreign policy. He also underlined the role of the PUK, which holds unique external orientations; he described the PUK as a parallel to the KDP:

According to the law the President is in charge of the KRG's foreign policy and national security policy. Fundamentally it is the President who is formulating the foreign relations or foreign policy. But the reality in Kurdistan shows that the PUK has its own direction of priorities in formulating foreign policy. This demonstrates that the KRG has foreign policies. (Author's interview with Salih, 2014)

The KDP is the leading driver in the KRG as it holds the major positions of president, prime minister and head of the DFR that are engaged in foreign relations. This aided Masoud and it will aid Nechervan in external activities and in having a relatively coherent foreign policy, which the government designs and he leads.

## The KRG's prime minister

The KRG's prime minister (*Serok Wazirani Hukumati Haremi Kurdistan*) is – depending on who assumes the post – the second most powerful actor in conducting its foreign relations and drawing up foreign policy. The breakdown of the fragile government in the KR-I, which was established in 1992, divided it into two administrative governments led by two prime ministers from 1994 to 2006. The KDP's base of authority is in Erbil and the PUK's in Sulaymaniyah. According to Adnan Mufti, the KRG had unofficial and unannounced representatives from Erbil's and Sulaymaniyah's governments in a few countries (author's interview with Mufti, 2014).

During 2003, rapprochement between the main political parties was consequential with the evolution of the political process. Since 2006, this has produced a unified government in the fifth cabinet, which Nechervan Barzani, the deputy president of the KDP, headed. The unified government was according to a strategic agreement between the PUK and KDP. The KDP has more influence on the accord that extended the term of premiership in their favour (James, 2013, 21). The prime minister is the head of the KRG's cabinet; he has executive powers according to the KRG's laws, which the KP and the Council of Ministers enacted.[7] He can exert authority on foreign relations, such as proposing to the KRG's president to establish offices in foreign countries. The prime minister and his deputy are elected by a parliament majority, and therefore the political parties with the most seats bargain over who takes the positions (usually it is a coalition government). The president's approval is required for the prime minister to go ahead and form the government (Kurdistan Regional Government, 2015). Certainly, the members of Parliament adhere to the political parties' leadership instructions to form the government, and this is dependent on compromises between the parties.

Prime minister Nechervan Barzani and his deputy Qubad Talabani were in close coordination with the head of the DFR in the Council of Ministers. The prime minister plays a pivotal role in conducting foreign relations, such as formal meetings with officials from various countries (e.g. ministers and ambassadors).

The former prime minister Nechervan Barzani, who is also the deputy president of the KDP, had a personal input that shaped the KRG's foreign policy, which is to a considerable degree in line with Masoud Barzani's vision. Nechervan Barzani said:

> We [the KRG] draw a policy and I had role in drawing it ... The policy is on the basis to have normal relationships with all our neighbours and we managed to have balanced relationships with the neighbouring countries for instance with Iran and Turkey without being biased to one side ... I had a progressive role in designing the KRG regional policy with Iran, Turkey, Syria and even with Baghdad. However, other political forces had a role, adopted and contributed to the policy. (Author's interview with Barzani, 2014)

The prime minister plays a crucial role in building the KRG's capacity to develop its foreign relations, particularly regional relations. He is a key negotiator in the KRG's security and economic affairs with Turkey, Iran and Baghdad. Nechervan Barzani said:

> The KRG's foreign policy is mainly drawn by the KRG's Presidency and government [Cabinet] ... The implementation and execution of the policy is by the DFR ... For example, some of the files [particular relationships] which are related to some states are conducted by the DFR, while the KRG's Presidency deals with regional states because it is a sensitive issue for us. (Author's interview with Barzani, 2014)

Former prime minister Nechervan Barzani has encouraged foreign investments, businesses and trade to engage in both the public and private sectors in the KR-I. This was asserted in his inauguration speech for the eighth cabinet in June 2014 (Kurdistan Regional Government, 2014). Therefore, he is shaping the KRG's economic diplomacy. Dr Najmaldin Karim stated: 'PM Barzani has strengthened relationships with Turkey and frequently visits Istanbul for mutual economic and security purposes' (author's interview with Karim, 2014). For example, although the relationship between Ankara and Erbil deteriorated after the KR-I referendum, the prime minister had a key role in the economic integration between the KR-I and Turkey and in mediating previous peace process negotiations between the Kurdish Workers Party (PKK) and Turkey.

Karim argues: 'The Presidency and the Council of Ministers in particular, the President [Masoud] and the Prime Minister [Nechervan] of the KRG, are the primary actors in formulating the KRG's foreign policy, not the DFR which advocates that policy' (author's interview with Karim, 2014). The president and the prime minister provide cohesiveness in the KRG's foreign policy. They recognize the effect of their involvement in the development of exploration and production of oil and gas. Moreover, the prime minister underscores the engagement of his deputy and the president in the DFR and subsequently in the KRG's foreign relations.

Nechervan Barzani said in 2014:

The DFR's Minister has a formal relationship with me [prime minister] and my Deputy [Qubad Talabani] who supervises and provides instructions to some foreign affairs files while I supervise the other files. We do the work together ... in respect to Dr Fuad Hussein, as he is in the Diwan and close to the President, he has awareness about all the work of the DFR. (Author's interview with Barzani, 2014)

There has been progressive coordination in foreign affairs between Prime Minister Nechervan Barzani and his deputy Qubad Talabani from the PUK. Article 18 of the KRG's Council of Ministers' law gives the deputy prime minister an oversight role (after the prime minister) over the DFR (KRG's Council of Ministers' Law, 2006). They all share responsibilities in foreign affairs, for example, Qubad and Hussein supervised and developed the US-KRG and Europe-KRG relationships. There have been far fewer differences in foreign affairs between the KRG's prime ministers and their deputies, who are from a rival party, than between Baghdad's prime ministers and their deputies. The KRG's foreign relations, duties and responsibilities are distributed and organized between the officials – especially the president, the prime minister and his deputy, as well as the head of the DFR – but they all adhere to former president and the KDP's leader Masoud Barzani. Salih's and Nechervan's fifth, sixth, seventh and eighth cabinets have had functioning governments and made progress in foreign relations excluding the fact that after the referendum the KRG faced hurdles in foreign affairs. Finally, mapping the core executive actors, the prime minister is the second most powerful actor in decision-making and laying out international objectives. After the president, the prime minister has a notable role in designing diplomacy, mainly with regional states, but also with European states and Russia. On 10 July 2019 Masrour Barzani was elected by 88 of 111 members of Parliament in the KP as the successor of Prime Minister Nechervan Barzani, and his deputy Qubad Talabani remained in the same position with the support of a majority of members of Parliament (73) for the ninth cabinet. The forthcoming years will expose how Masrour and Qubad work together. Speculations about their collaborations have to be framed cautiously as both parties have been engaged in a bitter rivalry since the non-binding independence referendum.

## *The KRG's Department of Foreign Relations*

The KR-I's elites, particularly of the KDP, realized the need for the DFR amid the gradual rise of the KRG on the international scene politically and economically. Although the DFR is not a ministry, its head holds ministerial rank and is part of the KRG's cabinet, with a variety of responsibilities regarding foreign relations. Previously, the conduct of the KRG's foreign relations was disorganized and carried out mainly by political parties with less specialized governmental bodies. Post 2003, the process of institutionalizing foreign relations began. The Iraqi constitution paved the way for the establishment of the DFR, which was set up in September 2006 by the KRG's Council of Ministers, according to Article 22 of the

KRG's Council of Ministers' Law no. 1, under the supervision of Prime Minister Nechervan Barzani (author's interviews with Mustafa (2014) and Zebari (2014)). Prime Minister Nechervan Barzani appointed Falah Mustafa Baker as head of the DFR; he is close to former president Masoud Barzani, for whom Mustafa acts as occasional translator during important events. Mustafa participates in all Council of Ministers meetings in which foreign relations and policy are discussed. The DFR is officially under the premiership of the KRG's Council of Ministers. The KRP also supervised it – particularly the president's chief of staff Hussein – which resulted in the KRP directing the DFR according to the president's vision. In July 2019, British-educated Safeen Dizayee from the KDP, a former spokesperson for the KRG, became the DFR's new head for the newly formed cabinet.

The DFR is an administrative body; or, as Salih put it, 'a technical service body of the KRG, which has yet to be finalized by the Kurdistan Parliament' (author's interview with Salih, 2014). Mustafa said: 'The KRG has parameters of foreign policy which go along the lines of Iraqi foreign policy. But, at the same time, the DFR is on the ground implementing and conducting the KRG's foreign policy' (author's interview with Mustafa, 2014). It can be argued that the DFR is an executive body that conducts the KRG's foreign relations and implements the foreign policy that the KRG's former president and prime minister create.

After the DFR's inception, Prime Minister Barzani wrote a letter to the federal government asking for cooperation, particularly from the I-MOFA (author's interview with Mustafa, 2014). Meetings were convened to study sufficient areas of cooperation between the DFR and the I-MOFA. The results of the collaboration between the DFR and I-MOFA are evident in the representation of more than thirty countries in the KR-I and visiting delegations, many of which come via Baghdad. However, the relationship lacks genuine and comprehensive cooperation between both institutions (I-MOFA and DFR), including the Iraqi embassies and the KRG's representations abroad (author's interview with Mustafa, 2014). There have been complaints by KRG officials about the lack of coordination between both representatives, such as the Iraqi embassy providing some diplomatic leverage to the KRG representative's officers that the I-MOFA was reluctant to provide. Tahir argued that Iraq's Council of Ministers issued an order to form the committee, which should have been composed of representatives from both sides. The DFR drafted a paper on how the KRG would be represented abroad and how to work with Iraqi embassies. The meetings were unfruitful during al-Maliki's rule. Tahir suggested that Baghdad's committee members might not have a political order on how to act (author's interview with Tahir, 2015). Although in some areas there has been some progress in terms of coordination, in general the level of suspicion on each side has depended on the political instability between Erbil and Baghdad. Mustafa indicated the cooperation between the I-MOFA and the DFR, especially during Hoshyar Zebari's tenure. He mentioned the limited support of the ministry that facilitated the DFR to be part of the I-MOFA's delegation in the General Assembly in the United Nations for the first time in 2013 (al-Fayad, 2013). The existence of a Kurdish political elite, members of which belong to the same political party in both Baghdad's and Erbil's governmental bodies, relatively eased some coordination and collaboration between these institutions. At the end of 2014, Mustafa said:

> The cooperation between the DFR and I-MOFA could be better and we hope for more. In general, regarding coordination between Erbil and Baghdad, we had difficult relationships with the federal government especially the two terms of the former PM al-Maliki, it was not a healthy relationship because we did not find al-Maliki as a partner. (Author's interview with Mustafa, 2014)

The insufficient coordination reflects on all ministries' coordination between Baghdad and Erbil to various degrees. Discussions are continuing with respect to the DFR being part of the Iraqi Diplomatic Mission (Review Kurdistan Region of Iraq, 2013, 11). Karim argues:

> Despite the fact that the two officials are Kurdish, there has never been good coordination between the Iraqi Ministry of Foreign Affairs and the KRG's DFR. They were on a collision course; the DFR would be more effective if there was better coordination. Nevertheless, they have begun to establish a relationship. (Author's interview with Karim, 2014)

In addition to the fragile relationship between the I-MOFA and DFR, the political instability in Iraq and tensions between Baghdad and Erbil have slowed the progress between the two. When Ibrahim al-Jaafari became foreign minister, the two institutions became further polarized. Therefore, on an administrative level there is feeble coordination, and politically there are increasing differences that have curbed the collaboration.

According to Article 121/4 of the Iraqi constitution, 'Offices for the regions and governorates shall be established in Iraqi embassies and diplomatic missions, in order to follow cultural, social, and development affairs.' Controversially, the DFR's representatives are supposed to be within Iraqi embassies, but they have separate offices outside the buildings of Iraqi embassies abroad. Therefore, they conduct the work without the interference and observation of the Iraqi embassies (Mansour, 2014, 1187). Their relationship also depends on the personalities of those representing both governments between the Iraqi embassy and the KRG's representatives. Neither the KRG nor Baghdad has disabled their representatives' relationships with each other. However, there is ambiguity and suspicion from each side about the other's performance. The poor coordination at the bureaucratic level (between the I-MOFA and DFR, as well as between the embassies and representatives) reflects the dilemma of the political process between Erbil and Baghdad, which further divides Iraq's foreign policies.

*The purpose and activities of the DFR*

The KRG's primary body for international ties is the DFR. It is actively involved in building and broadening foreign relations with states and multinational organizations (Invest in Group, 2014). Dindar Zebari argues,

The DFR is a key partner in the implementation of Iraqi foreign policy when it comes to expansion of international presence and enhancing foreign relations. The de facto status of the DFR has led it to be involved in pressurising Baghdad for certain policy orientations – for instance, in terms of an 'open door' policy with neighbouring countries. (Author's interview with Zebari, 2014)

However, the Shia-led government perceives the DFR with scepticism, viewing it as part of the KRG's effort to further devolve powers and ultimately achieve independence. The DFR is preparing Kurdistan for the next step with more economic, administrative and devolved political power, including implementing independent foreign policy.

The DFR's activities also include organizing conferences and exhibitions in the KR-I and abroad. It regulates the KRG's interaction with the outside world and helps to provide a positive impression to the international community regarding the evolution of the KR-I (author's interview with Mustafa, 2014). The relevant responsibilities of the DFR are: strengthening bilateral relations with the regional and international community; promoting trade, investment, tourism and institutional ties; organizing the visits of political and economic delegations to the KRG; conducting and supporting activities that enhance the image of the KR-I; and coordination with the I-MOFA, and consular and some legal services (Department of Foreign Relations, 2014). Mustafa said:

> We laid out the DFR's strategy since day one of its establishment. It is working on two levels: first, with the I-MOFA to encourage the Iraqi embassies in Baghdad to have representations in Erbil; second, going abroad and reaching out to the international community through representations, initiating visits, accepting invitations to encourage businesses, parliamentarian, cultural, and educational delegations to come to the KR-I, and to have a strong presence in media, think tanks and universities. (Author's interview with Mustafa, 2014)

This strategy reflects the KRG's policy of adopting two tracks: one in Baghdad, trying to contribute to Iraqi foreign policy making, and a second for the making of foreign policy for the KRG. The first track aims to serve the KRG's interests, including securing and defending its rights in Baghdad, and the second promotes the KRG's interests and political identity internationally. Regarding the latter track, for example, the KRG's representatives abroad are engaged in public diplomacy. According to officials in the DFR and the department's website, the DFR performs its duties based on the KRG's legislation and the Iraqi constitution (Department of Foreign Relations, 2014). However, the Shia-led government claims the DFR violates the Iraqi constitution in some of its exercises of foreign relations.

The KRG's representatives have several purposes: they assert the economic ties, governmental collaboration and coordination with foreign entities; and enhance diplomatic relations. These representatives abroad (pseudo-diplomats akin to Quebecois, Scottish or Basque foreign representatives) have become familiar faces regionally and internationally (Romano, 2010a, 1358). The numbers of DFR representatives and offices abroad have gradually increased – there are now fourteen representatives. Western countries such as the United States, UK, Australia, Italy, Spain and Germany have hosted the KRG's representatives and its mission to the European Union in Brussels. There are representatives in Russia and Iran (Department of Foreign Relations, 2014), and forty foreign countries' representations and intergovernmental entities are based in the KR-I. The DFR's policy is to broaden its relations from West to East. The presence of multiple intergovernmental bodies, including the United Nations Assistance Mission in Iraq (UNAMI) and the EU delegation in the KR-I, disclose the political and economic atmosphere in the KR-I to the outside world while contributing to the region's development. The DFR organizes and supervises the relations between the KRG and the aforementioned international organizations in three main areas. First, it makes sure the KRG is in full cooperation when there are areas of engagement for Iraq with international organizations. Second, the KRG participates in full discussions with the UN and multinational organizations as a federal entity that has the right to exercise self-representation within Iraqi delegations. Third, the DFR oversees international presence in Erbil to ensure they are supported to help the KR-I in terms of democracy, development, peaceful transition of power, human rights, construction, humanitarian support and transparency. Since the 1990s, the KR-I has had extensive relations with international organizations and NGOs that have been vital humanitarian corridors for the Iraqi Kurds (author's interview with Zebari, 2014).

The DFR is a crucial instrument in conducting foreign relations and being a proponent of the Kurdish leadership's vision. One reason for the coherence of the KRG and the DFR in foreign relations is coordination between the critical bodies in the KRG's foreign affairs. For example, the DFR and its former head (Mustafa), in coordination with the former president's chief of staff (Hussein) and deputy prime minister (Qubad Talabani), have together engaged in systematic, organized and extensive lobbying in Europe and the United States to promote many of the KRG's interests, including financial, security and political support.

The DFR represents a nexus between the president, the prime minister and the Council of Ministers, each of which has an input in the DFR to direct foreign relations. It manages to balance, contain and synchronize these engagements to coherently execute foreign relations and foreign policy statements. As the head of the DFR, the president and the prime minister are from the KDP; this helps to ease coordination. The DFR conducts foreign relations (day-to-day practice) and implements the foreign policy that is designed by the president, and the prime minister has some input. Nonetheless, some PUK leaders and opposition parties are dissatisfied regarding the KDP's control of these bodies. A number of concerns remain regarding future political bargaining between Baghdad and Erbil, heralding a fragile future and further polarizing the foreign policies.

## *The Iraqi Kurdish political parties' foreign relations*

The parties' leaders, led by the KDP, determine the KRG's foreign policy positions. The PUK does not have the power to decide the direction of the KRG's foreign affairs, even though it controls areas and runs local administrations and has the deputy prime minister's post. The KDP has superiority in drawing up and executing the KRG's foreign policy. Before and after 2003, the KDP and PUK have conducted external relations and activities. The political parties' external ties have supported the KRG's foreign relations, particularly in bargaining with regional powers. Hussein elaborated: 'The Kurdish political parties were struggling for their rights in the mountains and for decades the party leaders have established relations with regional and international countries. Post 2003, these parties continued their relations with foreign countries' (author's interview with Hussein, 2014).

The KDP is nationalist and conservative and has considerable tribal loyalties; in the past decade it has incorporated educated party loyalists. It has a more cohesive structure than the PUK, which is made up of some leftist and progressive intellectuals, includes fewer hyper-nationalists and has been fragmented since its foundation. It can be argued that the PUK is centre-left and the KDP centre-right; both have nationalist sentiments for a greater Kurdistan. Their disparity includes a power struggle; competition for interests and revenue sharing; divergence in domestic policies and disagreements about the shape of the political system. These have led to different regional alliances that have mainly been shaped by geopolitics, and even divergent periodic changes on how to view Baghdad.

Territorial control, in which each party has a specific area to exercise authority, has confined each party's foreign relations because the PUK is bordered with Iran and the KDP with Turkey. Geopolitics has pressured both parties to give concessions to their neighbours for economic, political and security purposes. This paved the way for the regional powers to interfere in the KR-I's domestic politics and economics. It is crucial to note that enclave borders have curbed alternative regional relations options (Hira and Jabary, 2013, 103). Both parties utilize their political weight and capabilities in regional relationships, which helps the KRG and their parties. Regional powers have testified (excluding in the process of Kurdistan's referendum) to their shrewd and pragmatic approach, which has prevented confrontation.

Both political parties aim to compromise and prevent clashes with regional powers as their military and economy are vulnerable. Post 2003, the Turks have been heavily involved in the KR-I in many private and public sectors. The Iraqi Kurdish position with respect to Syrian Kurdish political parties varies between the KDP and PUK. The KDP has a tense relationship with the Democratic Union Party (PYD), the powerful Syrian Kurdish party, and the KRG's official stance reflects the KDP's, whereas the PUK and much of its leadership have close ties and coordinate with the PYD. The PUK has a friendly rapport with the Kurdish parties in Syria and Turkey that rival that of the KDP and their allies.[8] In Rojava, the PYD (PUK ally) and the Kurdistan National Council (KNC) (KDP ally) are competitors. This is to the extent that the PYD does not allow KNC fighters into Rojava. The gap between the parties' external relations widened for several reasons: Jalal Talabani's stroke and subsequent death; the internal political stalemate regarding the future of Kurdistan's political system, namely, power sharing; the halt of the progress of the KR-I due to the war on Daesh; significant numbers of internally displaced persons (IDPs); and the deficit in revenue. The KDP dominates the vital foreign affairs bodies, and the PUK does not actively seek to disrupt it. Both parties have their own separate external ties, which in some ways support the KRG's foreign affairs. The parties bargain with Baghdad on issues that benefit the elites, the parties and the KRG's interests.

Before and after 2003, the KDP and PUK have had representatives and offices abroad, including in the United States, the UK, Iran, Turkey and Egypt. Gradually, the number of the KRG's representatives increased while the parties maintained their own representatives overseas. As Salih said: 'Abroad in Europe and the United States, there is a KRG representative but also we see the KDP and PUK offices. This reflects the political reality on the ground' (author's interview with Salih, 2014). He underlines that the parties' representatives reflect the KR-I, which is divided between the two major powers. The political parties' offices abroad facilitate the parties' activities in host countries to augment their ability to reach out to the Kurdish diaspora.

Traditionally, the KDP has a friendly rapport with Iraqi-Arab Sunni political factions, while the PUK has friendly relationships with the Iraqi Shia political factions. However, these dynamics have shifted which has compelled both KDP and PUK to have cross-sectarian alliances in Iraq to secure a strong position in the government. Both parties seek a strong relationship with the United States, European countries and Russia. Falah Mustafa argued: 'The KRG's foreign policy principle is one that all the political parties agree on. For example, consistently good relations with neighbours and the outside world and good strategic relationships with countries such as the US, UK ... I don't believe any political party is against that principle' (author's interview with Mustafa, 2014).

Romano (2010a, 1359) stated that the Iraqi Kurds reached the outside world with a united voice, and neighbouring states grew more accustomed to that voice. However, their voice became more fractured when interests of some elites and their political factions clashed. This was clear when Shaswar Abdulwahid, a rich businessman and an opposition leader of 'The New Generation', opposed the Kurdish referendum and portrayed his views externally, for example, at US-based think tanks, and met with a number of US congressmen in Washington, DC (Kurdistan 24, 2017). In general, the oppositions' activities did not alter the KRG's trajectory in foreign affairs. The two major parties have the most influence due to their enriched roots in various sectors in the KR-I. Romano (2010a, 1352) argues that the major Kurdish opposition party, Gorran, criticized the KDP and PUK for failing to achieve Kurdish foreign policy goals in terms of oil. The now-deceased Nawshirwan Mustafa, leader of the Gorran movement, which was in the government until the KDP expelled them, often criticized systematic corruption, lack of transparency about the budget, oil contracts, relationships between Kurdish leaders and Baghdad and between Kurdish leaders and the US administration (Romano, 2010a, 1353). The main predicament from the oppositions' perspective is parties' and officials' lack of openness about foreign affairs, including bilateral relationships with states and energy contracts with transnational corporations.

There is a high degree of coordination between the KDP leadership and the KRG's foreign relations core executive bodies, because the KDP controls the heads of all the key posts. In the meantime, there is limited influence and coordination between the PUK and the KRG's foreign affairs bodies, as the PUK does not dominate the main positions. There are limited degrees of cooperation between the parties' representatives and the KRG's representatives abroad.

## *The Iraqi constitution and the KRG's foreign relations and foreign policy*

There are different constitutional interpretations by various political factions (particularly between Shia and Kurdish factions) regarding the extent and legality of the KRG's foreign relations and policy. Articles 117/1 and 141 of Section 5 of the Iraqi constitution acknowledged and accepted the KR-I's existing authorities' laws, organizations and activities before writing the constitution. Therefore, Kurdish politicians view the KRG's foreign relations as part of its previous activities, which have been exercised since 1992. The new Iraqi constitution recognizes the KP, KR-I and KRG and all of their laws and contracts since 1992 and grants power and autonomy to the KP in terms of legislation, with limited powers given to the federal government (O'Leary, 2008, 38). Kurdish politicians reiterate Articles 117/1 and 141 of the Iraqi constitution to legitimize their external activities and foreign policy. This contradicts Article 110/1, which stipulates: 'The federal government shall have exclusive authorities in … Formulating foreign policy and diplomatic representation; negotiation, signing, and ratify international treaties and agreements; negotiation, signing and ratifying debt policies and formulating foreign sovereign economic and trade policy.' The article states that the federal government has the sole power to design and manage the country's foreign relations and foreign policy. However, KRG officials argued that the KRG does not violate the Iraqi constitution because it is in line with Iraqi foreign policy. The KRG has developed its structure and the right to issue laws and orders in conducting foreign relations.

Article 121/1 emphasizes Baghdad's exclusive power over formulating foreign policy while granting the KR-I executive, legislative and judicial powers. Meanwhile, Article 121/4 granted some limited powers to regions to conduct foreign relations in narrow terms, as well as to have representations and diplomatic missions abroad. This article provides the KRG with a platform to develop its foreign affairs and facilitate the implementation of its policies.

While the article restricts the KRG's foreign relation powers to only cultural, social and developmental affairs, the KRG has a powerful lobbying machine, which in some countries is more salient than the Iraqi embassies. This is the case where the KRG's representatives have close ties with groups of lawmakers in the UK parliament and the US Congress. Arguably, this is due to the weakness of Iraqi diplomatic missions and the proactiveness of the KRG. Most of the KRG's representatives do not admit to exercising powers beyond the Iraqi constitution. In 2014, Shwani said:

> According to Iraqi constitution Article 121, the KRG is permitted to have offices in Iraqi embassies for economic and cultural purposes … The Iraqi constitution

does not prohibit the KRG from having independent [separate] offices abroad to conduct relationships with these states. Therefore, I don't see that the KRG is violating the Iraqi constitution, but the KRG should consider that these relationships should be in the framework of Iraq's political strategy. (Author's interview with Shwani, 2014)

Shwani, who was the chairman of the legal committee in the Iraqi Council of Representatives (ICR), provides a valid legal perspective with which a considerable Shia and Arab Sunni officials disagree; the latter interpret the articles differently and place more emphasis on Articles 110 and 121/4 which state that the KRG's representatives should be inside the embassies. Tahir said:

The KRG has the power to establish any department, and this is totally in line with the Iraqi constitution. This order [to establish the DFR] did not grant the DFR power to draw foreign policy. However, we have ambitions to increase our capabilities and become more than a department. (Author's interview with Tahir, 2015)

Although the DFR was established by order no. 143 of the KRG's Council of Ministers, in line with the Iraqi constitution, the KP should stipulate how far the DFR will be involved in the KRG's foreign affairs (author's interview with Zebari, 2014). The KP was inactive from October 2015 to September 2017 due to the political stalemate mainly between the KDP and Gorran about the president's powers and the end of his term, which resulted in the blocking of the KP's Speaker from the KR-I's capital and the expelling of Gorran's ministers from the cabinet. The KP does not have direct influence on foreign relations and policy. One of the aims of activating the KP in September was to approve the Kurdistan's referendum. This was to support the KRG's referendum appeal internally and more importantly externally (international community) to provide a legal framework from the KRG's parliament. For the time being, the KP's laws and Council of Ministers' orders fill the Iraqi constitutional vacuum and ambiguity. The KP's laws have the right to amend Iraqi legislation that falls outside the federal government's exclusive powers (Kurdistan Parliament, 2016; Kurdistan Regional Government, 2016).

In 2010, Talib Rasheed Yadgar, general director of the Presidential Diwan, argued that the KRG has the legality in the constitution to perform its foreign relations. His conclusion was redrawn and based on a number of articles in the Iraqi constitution that do not reject the KRG's right to have foreign relations (Mohammed and Owtram, 2014, 70). Meanwhile, discrepancies in reviewing the KRG's scope of foreign relations reflect domestic, political and economic friction between the KRG and the federal government, the differences in interpretation of the constitution and the different visions between and within the Iraqi Shias and Arab Sunnis and the Kurdish elites.

Post 2003, foreign relations actors became a legitimate tool for the KRG as Articles 117/1 and 141 legitimize the KRG's existing authorities; in July 2014, Mustafa said: 'We [KRG] had de facto independence from Iraq from 1991 to

2003 where we had our own foreign relations' (Washington Institute, 2014). Formulating foreign policy is not a right of the KRG, as the central government has the sole power to formulate foreign policy (as stated in Article 110/1); however, it identifies neither the practicality nor the process of implementing foreign policy and foreign relations. Furthermore, Article 115 mitigates Article 110, which grants residual authority; all of the powers not stipulated in the exclusive powers of the federal government automatically belong to the authorities of the regions or federal entities in Iraq. Hence, the constitution does not prohibit the KRG from performing foreign relations and providing legalities for its activities, but it is prohibited from forming foreign policy (Mohammed and Owtram, 2014, 71).

In 2011, Bayan Sami Abdul Rahman stated that the KRG has no representative in any country in which Iraq has no embassy (Mohammed and Owtram, 2014, 71). Although Abdul Rahman's statement is true, the KRG's agencies and officials might have clandestine ties with states that do not have a relationship with Baghdad but those relationship are not formal.

Between 2014 and September 2017, Erbil officially adopted a de facto foreign policy and publicly sought independence. The Iraqi constitution does not give any region the right to self-determination or to seek independence. However, the Kurdish leadership argues that the Iraqi constitution is not fully implemented and has been violated by Baghdad and there was a constitutional case for the KR-I's referendum. The preamble to the Iraqi constitution stipulates 'free union of people, land and of sovereignty', which can be interpreted as the KR-I's inclusion in Iraq not being mandatory. Some Kurdish elites mainly in Erbil argued that when this constitution was violated by Baghdad and the contract (constitution) broken, the voluntary union could be dissolved and the KRG and KR-I being part of Iraq was not compulsory. Another argument stated by the KR-I's referendum proponents was that it was constitutionally lawful; under Article 110, the federal government does not have exclusive jurisdiction over elections or matters related to a referendum, Articles 115 and 121/2 provide the KRG with authority to repeal or modify any law passed by Baghdad preventing it from having a referendum (O'Leary, 2018). Therefore, the KRG's argued that the referendum was lawful as it was a proposal to secede not the secession itself. This view is strongly rejected by Baghdad.

The KRG resorted to a referendum that Baghdad did not consent to and its pursuit of independence increasingly matched with the KRG's external activities and was also in line with the contentious dynamics that existed before 2014 between Baghdad and Erbil. Post 2003, Baghdad became suspicious about the KRG's activities to fulfil the growing Kurdish ambitions, and discrepancies have manifested over several matters; for example, oil control, including exports, and the KRG lobbying for their interests, including in Western capitals. The different interpretations, loopholes and ambiguity of the constitution have led to further disputes. These problems are interrelated and influence the foreign affairs of both Baghdad and Erbil. Iraq further fragmented after the rise of Daesh, and since then the KRG loudly asserted its intention to have a referendum for more decentralization – or even separation.

After the lack of support from the international community for the referendum, the KRG retracted its proactive foreign policy behaviour to pursue independence and began to invest in restoring ties with Baghdad and regional powers who were vehemently against the referendum.

*The Iraqi constitution in Erbil's and Baghdad's foreign policies on natural energy*

Post Saddam, controlling oil and gas became a major tension between the central government and the KRG. The vague Article 112 in the Iraqi constitution is heavily cited in a controversial debate on who has the sole power of formulating foreign policy in terms of oil and gas management and control. Article 112/2 states the regional and federal governments together draw a coherent energy policy. Article 112/1 and 2 underline the requirement for cooperation between Erbil and Baghdad in the energy sector. However, the KRG argues that this cooperation refers to current oilfields, not future oilfields, which were developed after writing the constitution and therefore not referred to in the article. It argues that it exclusively controls future oilfields in the KR-I (author's interview with Shwani, 2014), an interpretation with which Baghdad disagrees. Baghdad heavily cites Article 110 that grants the federal government the 'exclusive authority' to formulate economic and trade policies (including energy/trade in hydrocarbon). Baghdad often cites Article 111 that stipulates that 'oil and gas are owned by all the people of Iraq in all regions and governorates' which supports Baghdad's argument that wherever oil is in Iraq, including the KR-I, it belongs to all the people of Iraq and the federal government has control over it.

In 2007–8, the United States tried to solve the contentions between Erbil and Baghdad and pushed for a new hydrocarbon law but both sides were adamant in sticking to their positions and conflicting interpretations (Jeffery and Wahab, 2018). Internal issues, such as those in the oil and gas sector, can become internationalized; extraction and production will be performed with the assistance of transnational companies. Erbil argues it has the right to negotiate agreements with international actors and corporations regarding oil and gas; anything not prohibited by the Iraqi constitution is permissible for the KRG – its laws that have priority are based on Article 115 (author's interview with Shwani, 2014). Due to the constitutional disputes and different interpretations, the KP approved hydrocarbon Law no. 28 in 2007 that paved the way for the KRG to produce and sell oil. The federal government rejected the oil and gas law and all of the KRG's following petroleum actions (Natali, 2010, 110). Shwani said: 'The federal government has the general title and draws the general policy, but the implementation is for the federal region and governorates' (author's interview with Shwani, 2014). The KRG can implement the policy, but questions arise when the implementation contradicts Baghdad's interests. The Shia-led government disagrees with Shwani's interpretation and argues that the federal government has the sole power to control the KR-I's international oil and gas management and its external activities. The petrol energy conflicts have clashed on international platforms. For example, to block the KRG from directly exporting oil, the Iraqi Oil

Ministry filed a lawsuit against it in the US-Texas District Court regarding a vessel carrying more than US$100 million worth of crude oil anchored off the Texas coast. On 29 October 2015, the lawsuit was dismissed.

During negotiations, Erbil and Baghdad stick to certain constitutional articles and interpretations. Both interpret the same articles in their own favour. Shwani said: 'This is a consensus constitution, *Dastoor Tawafiqi*; it was written by the politicians and depicts and expresses the politicians as representatives of their component; Kurds, Arab Sunni, Arab Shia in the period of writing it' (author's interview with Shwani, 2014). As the constitution has its limitations key political figures in Baghdad and Erbil have the ability to compromise. There is wide consensus that the Iraqi constitution has significant loopholes and allows for different interpretations due to its ambiguity and lack of detail. Therefore, the constitution cannot solve the dilemma of division and competition in Iraq's foreign policy in any matter, whether diplomatic or economic; nor does it have the mechanisms to unify the KRG's foreign relations and policy with the federal government. The Iraqi constitution and Baghdad are failing to constrain the KRG's de facto development and aspirations in foreign affairs.

## *The emerging nature of the KRG's foreign policy*

Post 2003, the KRG's foreign policy priorities are to gain recognition for its rights to independently manage issues, including the economy, such as developing the hydrocarbon sector, selling its oil and trade cooperation; security cooperation with states and purchasing military hardware; increasing diplomatic cooperation with various foreign actors; having peaceful and prosperous relationships with neighbouring countries; having a strategic relationship with the United States, Turkey, Iran, Russia and European countries and institutions; familiarizing the KRG with the international arena; and promoting the KR-I's rights for independence (statehood) –after the 2017 referendum this priority has been stalled. Despite domestic disagreements between the KDP and other Kurdish parties regarding lack of transparency and distribution of powers and roles, there is relative consensus on a number of principles of foreign policy priorities. Most of Erbil's foreign policy priorities clash with Baghdad's interests.

The KR-I, similarly to other sovereign statehood-seeking entities such as Taiwan, Somaliland, Abkhazia, the Turkish Republic of Northern Cyprus and Nagorno-Karabakh, faces a crisis of legitimacy. Self-justification then becomes a foreign policy priority, reflecting both the lack of confidence in the state itself (e.g. the Iraqi state) or the indifference of the outside world (Voller, 2013, 77). Two of the KRG's foreign policy priorities are justifying separation or more devolution of power and earning sovereignty. The KRG's justifications before the referendum include: Baghdad not implementing the Iraqi constitution; despite some tactical and short-lived deals the power-sharing agreement failed to a considerable degree; Baghdad's centralized policies; marginalization of Kurds; unfair distribution of revenues and cutting the KRG's budget; and sectarian violence, which is drawing

Iraq into civil war, including the threats of Daesh and the Shia militias. The KRG uses its need for material resources to survive and Baghdad's incompetence to justify its formation of independent foreign policy. After Kurdistan's referendum, the KRG stopped its rhetoric for independence as a foreign policy priority and reached out to Baghdad.

To achieve its priorities the KRG has laid out strategic goals, including initiating and accepting relationships with states and lobbying in the major superpowers. Some of these goals do not match, and even antagonize, the federal government's foreign policy. The KRG set up external ties and is lobbying for economic, security and political issues that are somewhat problematic for Baghdad-Erbil relations. For example, Germany and Hungary and secretly, for a short time after the fall of Mosul, the United States provided a direct supply of weapons to the KRG (author's interview with Qadir, 2015). Nonetheless, most weapons are shipped via Baghdad, and the Kurds argue they have not been receiving all the allocated weapons particularly during the war against Daesh. Moreover, the KRG complained that Baghdad did not pay the Peshmerga salaries. It lobbied externally for military aid, and in July 2016 they signed a memorandum of understanding with the US Defence Department that included provisions of military support such as salaries for the KRG's forces.

The KRG has also found buyers for Kurdistan's oil, such as Hungary (Raval, 2015), which it previously struggled to sell because Baghdad threatened to sue and blacklist foreign buyers (Lister, 2014; Whitcomb, 2014). The KRG bypassed Baghdad in developing the energy petroleum sector, signed contracts with transnational corporations (energy/oil and gas companies based in the West, Middle East and Russia) and sought foreign buyers, which it argues is its constitutional right. The KDP perceives that the control of its natural resources, including exports, provides it with the capabilities to act as a prosperous quasi-state and/or de facto state and to be an independent sovereign state in the future.

To fulfil its foreign policy priorities, before 2003, the KRG's elite built relationships with US congressmen, politicians, prominent journalists and academics. The Iraqi Kurds are lobbying in Capitol Hill and engaged in talks with the State Department and the White House (Rubin Report, 2016). In the 1990s, during Dr Barham Salih's time as head of the office of the PUK and the newly formed KRG (the United States did not officially announce the latter position), his acumen for networking and activities laid out the foundation for developing the relationship. Thereafter, Qubad Talabani became the KRG's first official representative in the United States in the unification administration in 2006, where he successfully built on Dr Barham's foundation. The KRG Liaison Office, currently headed by Sami Abdul Rahman, has a role in promoting and developing the KRG's ties with the executive branch and the US Congress (KRG-I Representatives in the US, 2015). The Iraqi Kurdish elites were able to achieve support from a wide spectrum of US politicians and members of congress. Post 2003, the KRG systematically hired various lobbying, public relations, consultancy and law firms, and spent around US$1 million each year from 2010 to 2014, according to Foreign Agents Registration Act (FARA) filing (Pecquet, 2015a).[9]

The KRG has broad US political connections and groups that support its aims. For example, the Kurdish-American Congressional Caucus, founded by Congressmen Lincoln Davis (D-TN) and Joe Wilson (R-SC), was created in the US House of Representatives; its membership has increased from fourteen in 2008 to more than sixty. The establishment of a bipartisan congressional caucus on 25 May 2008, which promotes and endorses Iraqi Kurds' interests to the US administration, has also enhanced relations between the United States and the KRG (Shareef, 2014, 117). Numerous Kurdish organizations promote the KR-I in the United States in different sectors, such as the United States Kurdistan Business Council (USKBC). The KRG's efforts have succeeded to a certain degree in gaining supporters and sympathy among some US policymakers and lawmakers. Multiple bills in favour of directly supplying arms to the KRG were introduced in the US Congress and received considerable support; however, they did not gain enough approval until December 2015, when the House Foreign Affairs Committee unanimously voted to arm the Kurds directly (Pecquet, 2015b; Bill H.R. [1654] 2015). These bills angered the federal government and the Shia political factions.

Similarly, the KRG is lobbying in the UK via its representatives, who engage in various activities related to public relations and diplomacy. The KRG has close ties with UK members of Parliaments in the All-Party Parliamentary Group (APPG) on Kurdistan. This group has helped the Kurdish cause and promoted the KRG's efforts in the UK. Additionally, at the beginning of 2016, the Parliamentary Friends of the Kurds, an all-party caucus within the Canadian parliament, was created. This includes fourteen parliamentarians who support the KR-I and coordinate with the KRG (Kurdistan 24, 2016a). During the war against Daesh – the KRG was a major actor on the ground – the KRG's foreign relations received more and more logistic and material support from foreign state leaders, officials and parliamentarians (Gulmohamad, 2014a). States moved away from their state-centric approach in their interactions with Iraq (Mansour, 2016a).

Turkey has played a major role in the KRG, as it is the economic lifeline and the international gateway to the KR-I. A mutual economic benefit was key to rapprochement between Erbil and Ankara as Turkish companies invested in the region and trade has flourished. The friendly relationship between the KDP and Turkey's Justice and Development Party (AKP) has a political dimension; both parties had secured prosperous relationships until Kurdistan's referendum when their rapport weakened as the KDP leader refused Turkey's request to back down on the referendum. Iran is relevant but less economically strategic compared to Turkey for the KRG, despite trade and the future oil and gas projects between the KR-I and Iran as well as Iran's geopolitical importance and proximity to the KR-I. From some Kurdish perspectives, the Shia-led government in Baghdad is a partner of Tehran, and the Iraqi Kurds come second to Baghdad. The relatively stable relationships with the KR-I's neighbours and ties with Western countries' bodies have in turn benefited the KRG to survive its economic and political hiccups and can be considered as accomplishments in some of the KRG's foreign policy priorities.

The KRG does not have a sovereign state's privileges; as such, it finds it hard to solve economic, security, military and foreign relations challenges. Hardships have materialized regarding the drop in oil prices, Baghdad and Erbil's disagreements and the war on Daesh, which caused the KRG to experience unprecedented waves of external refugees from Syria, but mainly Iraqi IDPs totalling nearly two million (Prendergast, 2016) as well as the mismanagement of the KRG's revenues. Iraq and the KRG are rentier economies steeped in systematic corruption and nepotism with massive public services employees that lack effective performance. Since 2013, the KRG has been sucked into a severe economic and financial crisis, resulting in a huge debt of more than US$17 billion that has crippled the region's development (Manis, 2016, 7). The KR-I does not possess reserves, whereas Iraq has US$50 billion (Knights, 2016). Deputy Prime Minister Qubad Talabani said:

> What makes us [the KRG] different from the fallout of the drop of oil prices from other states' commodity economy, is that we are not a country, so as a sub-sovereign we don't have the levers to manage our economy in a way that a sovereign country does ... We are not in charge of monetary policy we cannot print or devalue. (Wilson Center, 2016)

This underlines the limitations of the KRG's financial and economic policies, particularly during the crisis. The government's burden resulted in its inability to regularly pay civil servants' and Peshmerga salaries, the halt of many public infrastructure and development projects and its inability to support the KR-I's private banks and pay the oil companies. Consequently, it reduced the cash flow to the KRG's foreign relations lobbying machine. The restrictions the KRG faces have hindered its functions, particularly in finding a buyer for its oil at a price similar to that of other states and purchasing weapons. Moreover, the KRG cannot independently and directly receive large loans or financial aid packages from the majority of international institutions, such as the World Bank or the International Monetary Fund (IMF) (Knights, 2016). Therefore, it is lobbying the United States and Europe to receive its share directly or trying to convince them to pressure Baghdad – which was expected to receive a US$15 billion loan, mainly from the IMF (as well as other institutions and donor states) – to transfer its share. With Baghdad's consent at the end of 2016 the World Bank is assisting the KRG to reform and develop its economic and infrastructure sectors, including the possibility of providing small loans (Sulaivany, 2016). The KRG's financial condition worsened particularly after Baghdad retook Kirkuk in October 2017 and the Kurds lost the oil wells which were among its key sources of revenues. In 2018, the relationship slowly began to improve, and in a fragile deal Baghdad sent the KRG's public employees' salaries.

The KRG cannot develop or resolve significant internal and external challenges itself. It has therefore resorted to invigorating its foreign relations officials who have visited superpowers' capitals and requested financial support. Despite the governmental and political setbacks in the KR-I, their voices have been heard to a degree. Due to the KRG's courageous role in fighting Daesh, there was a lot of sympathy for them and some support materialized; the United States paid the Peshmerga's salaries. The KRG is trying to focus its foreign policy on common interests and the security, economic and political support to fill the gaps caused by not being a sovereign state. Its foreign policy faces challenges to gain support from sovereign states.

The KRG's post-referendum foreign policy objective is to restore confidence with Baghdad and regional powers. The halting progress in foreign relations was evident when the internal political deadlock remerged in the KR-I in 2015 and continued, between the KDP on one side and the PUK and Gorran on the other. This led to divided low-level foreign policy messages and different foreign policy priorities. The internal tensions have halted the building of unbiased institutional bodies in the KRG's foreign affairs. This will derail the KRG's long-term aspirations. In the meantime, Baghdad, Tehran and Ankara benefit from the fragmentation in the KRG, as it finds allies in the KR-I.

## Conclusion

The KRG is compelled to have a foreign policy due to its distinctiveness from Baghdad in foreign relations, international interests, foreign policy priorities and objectives, and messages on the international platform. It has a de facto foreign policy, which it needs because the direction of its external relations has reached a broader scale and placed more emphasis on statehood (particularly before Kurdistan's referendum), more devolution of powers, the need for its survival and a decent livelihood. Post referendum, the KRG's foreign policy objectives are to: revive external ties especially with regional powers (Iran and Turkey) as well as with Baghdad; and invest not only in the Western states but look for additional friends, including Russia. The changing dynamics show the shifting priorities in foreign policy, for instance, from seeking statehood before the referendum to completely halting after the plebiscite.

The KRG's foreign relations have taken the lion's share of the Iraqi Kurd's state-building project. Mustafa said: 'The KRG utilises paradiplomacy, public diplomacy, political diplomacy, energy diplomacy, cultural diplomacy and sporting diplomacy. These are all tools that the KRG are using to pursue their objectives' (author's interview with Mustafa, 2014). The KRG's foreign policy also includes security and defence diplomacy.

Post 2003, the KRG has conducted foreign relations on two levels: first via the Presidency, the prime minister and his deputy, the DFR and its representatives via a number of advisors and bureaucratic bodies; second, via the political parties, mainly the KDP and PUK. These levels are not contradictory, as the KDP controls the major bodies and there is to a certain degree tacit agreement on some foreign policy issues between the main Kurdish parties. However, internal political differences cause divides to resurface between the KDP and other parties.

On the first level (government), the KRG's foreign policy has evolved and been projected to the outside world. Therefore, this level is the official and the most recognized face of the KRG. The president of the KR-I before his resignation in 2017 was the leading actor, followed by the prime minister; yet the current president, to a great extent, adheres to the former president (of the KDP) in formulating the KRG's foreign policy. The president, the prime minister and the DFR and its head conduct foreign relations. There has been coordination and cooperation between the major policymakers and implementers (the president, the prime minister and Council of Ministers, the DFR and its representatives and other governmental bodies, such as the KRSC). The KRG's representatives and officials engaged in the KRG's foreign affairs are far more coherent than the federal government's. Despite the political and bureaucratic division in the KR-I, there is awareness of common threats and the necessity to have a unified voice – at least on a number of issues in foreign affairs matters – and to represent a relatively united front to the outside world such as countering terrorism and building economic ties. After Kurdistan's referendum there has been increasing divergence between the major parties (KDP and PUK), and this has affected the KRG's effectiveness.

A major underlying reason for the agreement on the governmental level on most international interests and objectives is that the KDP controls all major bodies. The government elite and officers coordinate and synchronize – even those from the KDP and PUK. For instance, there is successful coordination between Prime Minister Nechervan Barzani (currently president) and his deputy Talabani on foreign affairs issues, and they do not contradict each other's foreign affairs statements.

On the second level (parties), unlike the first, there is almost non-existent coordination between the KDP and the PUK in foreign relations. These two levels overlap where there is coordination between the political parties and their officials in the KRG. The governmental foreign relations level matters the most in international relations. Domestically, the KRG is divided and incoherent – particularly on an administrative level, because administration is divided between the KDP and the PUK. This is in contrast to the formal foreign affairs that the KDP dominates. The parties' foreign relations do not clash with the KRG's foreign relations; their performances are complementary. However, the parties also pursue partisan interests to facilitate and manoeuvre the KRG's engagement with regional powers. For example, if the KRG has a dispute or misunderstanding with Iran, a number of the PUK officials will reach out to Iran in an attempt to solve the problem. Likewise, the KDP will do the same with Turkey. Post referendum, the KDP is also reaching out to Iran in order to mitigate the regional pressure and improve the bilateral relationship. Both parties are pragmatic and diplomatic in their external and regional approaches. Moreover, pragmatism remerged after the opposition and punitive measures of the regional powers. Each political party has its own priorities in foreign policy, particularly on regional issues such as how to deal with Syria and Baghdad.

The regional powers (mainly Turkey and Iran) appear to overtly and covertly intervene in order to pursue their interests in the KR-I. In some cases, this results in the widening of the divisions between the KDP and the PUK. At the same time, the KDP's and the PUK's relationships with regional powers have resulted in some stability, which has benefited the KR-I. After the Kurdish elites' rejection of Iran and Turkey's request to cancel the referendum, the latter have taken a distant and cautious stance towards the Iraqi Kurds. The KDP and PUK each have different ties with Kurdish parties in Turkey, Iran and Syria. There is regional competition between all Kurdish parties across the Middle East; some side with the PUK and others with the KDP.

There are two contradictory centres of governmental foreign policies: the federal government and the KRG. Post 2003, the KRG has experienced an evolution in foreign affairs that has placed the KR-I on the international map. Despite the KRG's hiccups and drawbacks, conducting implicit independent foreign relations and drawing up a foreign policy have been at the heart of the KRG's objectives. The Kurdish elite engaged primarily in Erbil focusing on state building to pursue the Kurdish aspiration for more devolution of powers. The Kurdish elites' purpose in Baghdad was to secure Kurdish rights and leverage in Iraq's new state structure and try to make Baghdad non-hostile towards their aspirations.

The KRG has developed relationships with state and non-state actors and gradually has been dealt with as a de facto entity. This narrative has been challenged since the KRG's referendum due to the lack of support from the international community. The international community, particularly the Western powers, accept the KRG's role in international affairs to the extent that it maintain its form as a non-sovereign entity. The KRG's ties reach beyond the region to governments, lawmakers (parliamentarians), political parties, lobbying firms, transnational organizations and corporations, think tanks and universities. It lobbies in Washington, DC, London and some European capitals, including Brussels; it has also begun to reach out to Russia. Since the KR-I's financial and security crisis, the KRG has invigorated its foreign policy but faced challenges, mainly due to its non-sovereign status. Since 1991, the Kurdish elite and major parties have sought to project themselves to the outside world as pro-West and an ally of the Western states – but not at the expense of their relationships with their neighbours. As such, this became a delicate part of their foreign relations and policy strategy.

The KRG has a set of foreign policy priorities that reflects the interests of the region. Post 2003, it tried to adopt foreign policy priorities and approaches, constructed relationships with external actors and lobbied to achieve its priorities, some of which it has attained relatively successfully. After the rise of Daesh, the KR-I's foreign policy priorities could be considered as four interrelated priorities: reaching out to the international community, security, economy (finance, trade, petrol energy) and lobbying for independence; the latter priority was salient until the referendum.

Finally, many Kurdish officials argue that they act within the framework of the Iraqi constitution. Nevertheless, Kurdish decision-makers – particularly those affiliated to the KDP – have stated on many occasions that they are not ready to sacrifice the interests of the KR-I for the Iraqi state. However, since the ramifications of the Kurdish referendum the KDP has been interested in investing in Baghdad. Publicly, the KRG's foreign relations and policy priorities first seek to serve the region as a de facto entity. The KRG has drawn a de facto foreign policy with identified objectives that (intentionally or not) do not match Iraq's foreign policy. Coordination between the federal government's (I-MOFA) and the KRG's (DFR) foreign affairs bodies has been difficult.

Since 2003, the KRG and Baghdad have had different foreign policy orientations with various degrees of disparity. Following Jalal Talabani's stroke and the rise of Daesh, the divergence between the KRG and the federal government has increased. This has reflected on foreign relations. The elites in Erbil and Baghdad interpret the Iraqi constitution in their own favour and cherry-pick articles from the constitution. Increasingly the KRG's external activities have become more noticeable in the KRG's laws and KR-I's draft constitution, which gives more power and superiority to its institutions in conducting foreign relations. The KRG's limited foreign relations include limited diplomatic representations and services, trade and cultural, educational and tourism activities, which are legitimate approaches for a non-sovereign entity, and through them the KRG has managed to obtain certain international interests and does not contradict the Iraqi constitution. However, the KRG's foreign policies for independence before the referendum contradict the Iraqi constitution (particularly from the Iraqi and a number of external states perspectives not Erbil's). Moreover, the superiority of the KRG's laws for the Kurdish policymakers and different interpretations of and loopholes in the Iraqi constitution regarding control of energy have further widened the splintered foreign policies of Iraq. The KRG is a nascent governmental structure that has to further develop its governmental organizations' responsibilities, duties and laws; the region's draft constitution; and its political system (e.g. presidential, parliamentary or hybrid).

## Chapter 4

### THE FEDERAL GOVERNMENT'S KEY FOREIGN POLICY PRIORITIES

*Introduction*

The priorities represent interests, have domestic dimensions and are essential for the regime's survival. In this chapter, I address the federal government's foreign policy priorities or imperatives and examine which, if any, have been achieved. The federal government's foreign policy imperatives are diplomacy, security and economy. Iraqi elites pay significant attention to security; moreover, insecurity has further weakened the government and governance. Baghdad's foreign policy priorities are: first, to restore Iraq's foreign relations and place in the international community; second, to build Iraq's security, including military, security capacity and capabilities and counter-terrorism; and third, to rebuild the economy, consisting primarily of oil and gas, which is in slow progress, and secondarily of trade and investment. These priorities are not listed in order of importance; rather, it is contended that they are interconnected and interdependent, with each strengthening or weakening the others. For instance, without diplomatic relationships with foreign entities, the two other priorities are not achievable; without minimum security, building the economy is not achievable. Although foreign policy imperatives have crystallized in the three aforementioned areas, there has been a focus on certain areas more than others depending on the political, economic, security and environmental challenges and necessities. For example, after Daesh's military defeat Baghdad began pursuing foreign aid and investment for reconstruction of the liberated cities in Iraq. Obtaining the international community's support in terms of financial aid would not succeed without having diplomacy as well as security that provides a comfortable environment for foreign aid and investments. Therefore, financial and humanitarian aid could fall under the category of economy as the three major domains include wide practical areas that fall within the scope of Iraqi foreign policy directions.

A number of observers and officials have indicated other foreign policy imperatives, for example, water competition (and its geopolitics). For years, water competition has affected bilateral relations and created tensions between Iraq, Turkey, Syria and Iran. Iraq faces an environmental catastrophe and the desertification of land. The significant reduction of water resources has affected drinking water and sustainable electricity. This has stirred Iraqis to protest against the government and their elites for lack of public services and corruption. The federal government's initiatives to mitigate the environmental challenges have barely materialized.[1] Until recently, Baghdad had not seriously pursued this imperative because it has been overwhelmed with its three main priorities.

Baghdad's foreign policy priorities have been a contested area between its core executive bodies and the Kurdistan Regional Government of Iraq (KRG), as well as within and between its key elites and Iraq's key political factions. The federal government has failed to achieve its security imperative. Lukman Faily (2016) agrees on the aforementioned priorities. However, he stated in an interview:

> Our [Baghdad's] foreign policy priorities are not cohesive or coherent ... There is no consistency to achieve certain goals and on certain policies ... Our priorities were such as not to have enemies and trying to interpret the constitution such as having good neighbourly relationships, and gaining countries' support but without knowing or having our SMART goals [Specific, Measurable, Agreed upon, Realistic, Time-based] we cannot achieve it. (Author's interview with Faily, 2016)

The federal government lacks a detailed foreign policy plan to pursue its interests. Since 2003, Iraq's foreign policy decision-makers have focused on remaking its image internationally, building military and security institutions and reviving oil revenues as the pillars for economic prosperity, state survival and state building.

The lack of security and political stability has overshadowed and exacerbated the absence of agreed-on foreign policy priorities between the elites. Each Iraqi political faction and their elites have their own set of foreign policy priorities and view most of them differently. Furthermore, two of Iraq's foreign policy priorities – diplomacy and economy – have been partially and poorly achieved. The divergence in ruling elites' and factions' foreign policy priorities not only demonstrates their interests and agendas but is also driven by representatives of ethnic or religious sects. The quota system (*al-Muhasasa*) and the political accord (*al-Tawafuq al-Syasi*) have partly reinforced the similar perspectives within each ethnic or sectarian political faction and among the elites. After the defeat of Daesh, Iraqi politics has gradually turned away from – but not eliminated – ethnic or sectarian tendencies. Although Baghdad has an incoherent foreign policy and its priorities have not been fully achieved, these priorities represent the elites' and partisan interests, as well as the imperatives for the regime to survive.

## Post-2003 foreign policy priorities

After 2003, Iraqi decision-makers realized the need to rearrange Iraq's foreign policy interests and priorities for the new state-building project and state survival. Achieving these priorities has been challenging due to the lack of a clear and agreed-on plan, insecurity, political instability, corruption, weakness in capacity, vulnerability, fragmentation of the federal government, the quota system and divisions within and between Baghdad and Erbil. Despite the presence of the United States and its involvement in building state institutions, the attributes and characteristics of Baghdad's foreign policy priorities or imperatives started to appear when the first Iraqi-appointed government, the Iraqi Interim Government (IIG), regained full sovereignty in June 2004.

In Washington, DC, in 2004, the IIG's prime minister Allawi said:

> The importance of maintaining the strength of the coalition and the support of the international community is helping us to succeed. We [Allawi and President Bush] discussed the plan that focuses on building democracy, defeating the insurgency, and improving the quality of life for ordinary Iraqis. Our political plan is to isolate the terrorists from the communities in which they operate ... Finally, our economic plan is to improve the everyday lives of Iraqis. (C-Span, 2004)

Allawi's speech at the White House focused on strengthening ties with the United States and coalition partners, which fits the first foreign policy priority diplomacy; counter-terrorism and building the security institutions, which fits with the second security; and building the economy, which is the third priority. The federal government's foreign policy became more apparent after the Iraqi constitution was passed in 2005. Despite various phases that Iraq went through between 2004 and 2019, its foreign policy imperatives have broadly remained diplomatic relations, security and economy.

*Restoring Iraq's foreign relations*

Iraq adopted a policy to recover its place and image on the international and regional stages by, first, focusing on regaining its seats in intergovernmental organizations (IGOs) and coming out of UN sanctions; second, amending its bilateral relationships with states and transnational bodies; third, not interfering in the internal politics of other states; and finally, having a peaceful approach in international relations, which is stipulated as a principle in the new Iraqi constitution (Article 8).

Diplomacy is Iraq's first foreign policy priority because unless it starts connecting and communicating with foreign entities through official channels, it is impossible to achieve its other priorities and interests. Iraq has restored many of its relationships and much of its international standing, and chapter seven of the UN's sanctions has been lifted (Salem, 2013). Former foreign minister Zebari said: 'Iraq's most important foreign policy priority was lifting chapter seven of the international [UN] sanctions' (Buratha News, 2009b). Iraq regained its seat in IGOs such as the Arab League, and in 2004 it entered the ongoing process (Iraq's working party members) for its accession into the World Trade Organization. Between 2003 and 2016 it set up more than eighty diplomatic missions around the world, which included forty-five ambassadors (I-MOFA, 2016b). Although Iraq recently increased its debt because of the fall in oil prices and war on Daesh, after 2003, it reduced its external debt from approximately US$133 billion in 2004 to US$33 billion in 2008 (Sassoon, 2009, 138). In 2008, Russia forgave Iraq its debt, while the Kingdom of Saudi Arabia (KSA) partially wrote off its debt and Kuwait did not. Although this might demonstrate a lack of affinity between Iraq and some regional countries, during al-Abadi's premiership Iraq's relationship improved with the aforementioned countries; in 2018, Kuwait allocated US$2 billion and the KSA US$1.5 billion as donations for Iraq's reconstruction at the summit in Kuwait.

Besides gradually reviving diplomatic ties with states and IGOs, Iraq's regional relationships have fluctuated and occasionally its elites' statements have clashed with those of Turkey and a number of the Arab states. Hoshyar Zebari's delivery of the official foreign policy statement in 2016 differed from previous practice: 'Although we had challenges with our neighbours due to Saddam's policies … One of the first issues [immediately post 2003] was to return Iraq to its place with Arab states' (Al-Rai Media, 2016). Iraqi elites intended to improve its relations in its immediate neighbourhood, but these efforts have been slowed by Sunni-dominated states' concerns about Shia militias, the Shia-led government and its close ties with Iran.

Iraq's diplomacy did not fail completely in the region; for example, it successfully played a mediating role between Iran and the West (regarding Iran's nuclear deal) and Syria and the West (the Geneva II conference). Iraq set up an official meeting in 2007 between Iran and US officials (the two ambassadors in the offices of the former prime minister al-Maliki) in Baghdad, which broke the ice between both countries (Semple, 2007). In 2009, the United States announced it would participate in P5+1 talks with Iran about the nuclear deal (Arms Control Association, 2016). In May 2012, at Iran's request, Baghdad hosted a meeting between Iran and the six world powers regarding the nuclear deal (BBC, 2012). With respect to Syria, Al-Mu'alim, Syria's foreign minister, said in Baghdad: 'The talks with Iraqi officials were positive and we decided to participate in Geneva II Talks and we discussed with al-Maliki the diplomatic preparations' (Al-Alam, 2013). These two issues underline Iraq's diplomacy initiative to resolve tensions with its current allies.

Contradictory and hostile statements from influential politicians and Iraqi officials (including al-Maliki), particularly towards regional powers (Turkey and the Arab Gulf States), have shown incoherence in Baghdad's foreign policy. The KRG's diplomacy priority serves the KR-I, rather than Iraq as a whole, and has disparate relationships with (and broadcasts divergent messages to) regional powers, including the aforementioned countries. In short, despite divisions in diplomatic messages between Baghdad and Erbil, the federal government's diplomacy priority reflects the urgency of emerging from isolation and improving its image regionally and globally. This priority has been poorly achieved as the relationships with many states, including Turkey and a number of Arab States, are fluctuating and not strategic.

*Iraq's security*

Iraq's security is about building its military capacity, securing its territories and combating terrorism, with the assistance of external powers. It reflects the security vacuum left by the US-led coalition's disbanding of Iraqi armed forces in 2003 and the need to ensure the regime's survival. Baghdad's foreign policy security priorities are formulated in three layers: first, developing its capabilities; second, securing and being able to protect the country's territories; and third, cooperating with external powers and entities in countering terrorism. To achieve these, foreign relations with other countries are essential.

Iraq's agencies (such as the Iraqi Ministry of Foreign Affairs (I-MOFA)) can pursue some security interests via their relationships with countries and transnational organizations. Baker Fatah, Iraq's ambassador to Sweden, said: 'Security is having the lion's share in Iraq's foreign policy priorities where Iraq has special circumstances [security dilemma]' (author's interview with Fatah, 2015). In 2017, the I-MOFA website indicated that its top foreign policy priority is Iraq's security, stability and integrity and protecting the country. It argued that the importance of security is due to Iraq's rapid transformation and decades of war during Saddam's era (Embassy of Republic of Iraq in the US, 2016). Former foreign minister Hoshyar Zebari stated:

> It is our fight [against terrorism] for survival. It [fighting terrorism] is our core national and regional policy [foreign policy]. We consider terrorism a threat towards regional peace and the peace of our people, we are working in close cooperation with the international community and our neighbours' countries to fight all sources and all manifestations of terrorism and where ever we find it. (Center for Strategic and International Studies, 2013)

In the same context, Falah al-Fayad, Iraq's former national security advisor and chairman of the Popular Mobilization Forces (PMF), argued that security affairs overshadowed Iraqi foreign policy (al-Kadhimi, 2013). The elites' views demonstrate that Iraq's security is a priority in the foreign policy context and the federal government's procedures to contain the situation. Thus, Baghdad's foreign policy is devised with security in mind.

Before the Iraqis were able to form or contribute effectively to controlling their security, the US-led coalition took the lead in building Iraq's military and security capacity. The first security measure that appeared during 2003 (the Coalition Provisional Authority (CPA) period) was married to the US-led coalition forces' reconstruction of the Iraqi Security Forces (ISF) and the mandate to defend Iraq's borders against external threats. Despite some progress in building the ISF and initiating the construction of vital security and military institutions, the CPA period did not provide a competent ISF.

The US-led coalition and Iraqi elite were engaged with the Multi-National Security Transition Command (MNSTC-I), which was formed in 2004 to rebuild the ISF. MNSTC-I focused on Iraq's Ministry of Defence and Ministry of Interior forces (Dodge, 2012, 117). Its primary goal was to build the Iraqi Army (IA) and police forces, which was extremely challenging. In June 2004, the IIG (headed by Ayad Allawi) requested and received NATO support in the form of training and other technical matters (NATO, 2014). The new Iraqi government made an effort to engage with international organizations to develop security and military capacity, but there was no long-term strategy to maintain the high quality of the ISF after US withdrawal. On 9 June 2006, Hoshyar Zebari thanked the Security Council and MNSTC-I on behalf of the Iraqi government for their contributions, and welcomed the continuation of their necessary presence for Iraq's security.

Organizations that practiced aspects of foreign relations were created to contribute to Iraq's security, including the Iraqi National Security Advisory (*Mustasharia al-Amn al-Watani al-Iraqi*), Iraq's National Security Agency (*Jihaz al-Amn al-Watani al-Iraqi*) and the National Security Council (formerly known as the Ministerial Committee of National Security, MCNS). Mowaffaq al-Rubaie, a Shia independent politician previously associated with the Islamic Da'wa Party, was the first national security advisor who Bremer appointed in 2004 (International Crisis Group, 2010). Subsequently, former prime minister al-Jaafari and then al-Maliki's first government again selected al-Rubaie (Al-Rubaie, qtd from al-Majdi, 2009). Al-Rubaie's successor is Falah al-Fayad who heads the Advisory and the Agency, and he is the chairman of the PMF. The National Security Advisory contributes to formulating Baghdad's foreign policy in the security imperative by advising the prime minister. Al-Fayad met with foreign security and military officials to develop military strategies in combating terrorism. Since the beginning of the war against Daesh, the Advisory and Agency have been more actively engaged with international powers. For example, al-Fayad regularly met with Brett McGurk, the US special presidential envoy, for the Global Coalition to Counter ISIL. In June 2014, the United States set up the Joint Forces Land Component Command (JFLCC) for conducting operations in Iraq to combat Daesh; this was the first military operational headquarters since the US withdrawal in 2011. The JFLCC, which expanded to include more than sixty coalition partners or countries, is authorized to conduct combined joint operations in Iraq.

In 2013, Safa Hussein, the deputy national security advisor, stated that there was consensus on principles stipulated in the constitution and national security strategy but that the differences were in the details. He also pointed out that Iraq did not have a very coherent foreign policy or policymaking process (Sirri et al., 2013, 15). Clashes between foreign affairs actors, such as the I-MOFA and the National Security Advisory, have been apparent and are bolstered by the quota system, elites and partisan interests. In 2013, al-Fayad criticized the I-MOFA, which he said was 'unable to craft a political policy that reflects the identity of the new Iraq', and indicated severe fragmentation between Iraq's major actors in foreign affairs (al-Kadhimi, 2013). The clashes with other institutions within the government reflect the government's incoherent approach to security in the context of foreign policy.

The CPA authorized the IGC to create the Iraqi National Intelligence Service (INIS) with functions similar to the CIA (Carcano, 2015, 246 and 247). According to the charter of the INIS, its purpose is to address threats to the national security of Iraq; terrorism and insurgency; proliferation of weapons of mass destruction; espionage, trafficking and other acts that threaten Iraq (Kahana and Suwaed, 2009, 145). In 2004, the US-led coalition helped set up the INIS, which is connected to the prime minister (Cordesman and Khazai, 2014, 52). It included some Iraqi former Ba'athist intelligence officers, many of whom left after the US withdrawal (Doran, 2016). The INIS plays a role in Iraq's external relations, as it has relationships with foreign intelligence agencies. It contributes to shaping foreign policy on security and counter-terrorism efforts by advising the prime minister. Other agencies conducting external relations include clandestine 'intelligence' and counter-terrorism agencies, such as the Iraqi Counter Terrorism Service (I-CTS). The creation of these reflects Iraq's security imperatives.

The security imperative of gaining control of Iraq's land, coastal borders and air space required strengthening the ISF and cooperating with external powers (International Crisis Group, 2010; Salem, 2013). There was no consensus among the political parties in Baghdad regarding the timing of US withdrawal. The ISF steadily took more control of its territories and faced challenges securing the porous borders with neighbouring countries, mostly along the Iraq-Syria, Iraq-Iran, Iraq/KR-I-Turkey borders and in the south along the Shatt al-Arab waterway. There are plenty of infiltration routes and waterway crossing points for terrorists, insurgents and criminals who facilitate the smuggling of weapons, ammunitions, improvised explosive devices (IEDs) and other contraband. Transnational violent non-state actors use Iraq's weak borders with Iran and Syria and, to a certain extent, with Turkey, Jordan and Saudi Arabia. The Iraqi Shia-led government's policy to cooperate with regional powers to counter terrorism and secure the borders has failed. Since Daesh gained control of western Iraq and eastern Syria, it demolished many frontiers between the two countries and merged the land into one territory. In 2018, the federal government initiated a security fence (work in progress) in Anbar between Iraq and Syria largely to prevent militant fighters infiltrating and launching attacks from Syria into Iraqi territories.

Using foreign relations to purchase weapons played a fundamental role in building military capabilities. The IIG began purchasing weapons in 2004; building firepower was one of Baghdad's security priorities. Weapons were purchased from countries such as the United States, the UK, Iran, Russia, Poland, the Czech Republic and China. In 2013, former foreign minister Zebari said: 'Iraq is in the process of purchasing [US]$10 billion worth of military equipment, mainly from the United States and other countries. We pay for it from our revenue' (Center for Strategic and International Studies, 2013). According to the Inter-Agency Information and Analysis Unit, Iraqi expenditure in 2013 was US$118 billion; comparing this figure with the military allocation hardware Zebari mentioned clarifies its importance (Joint Analysis Policy Unit, 2013). Post 2003, Iraq's military purchasing was usually from the United States, but the Iraqi government has gradually diversified its sources, particularly after 2012, and started to look to the east.

Corrupt deals were revealed in a number of the purchases; numerous officials in the governments of Allawi, al-Jaafari and al-Maliki spent millions of dollars on extremely poor-quality weapons (al-Shaf'i, 2005; Mahasna, 2005). The purchase of weapons from Russia and Eastern Europe, unlike those from the United States, did not include delays, bureaucratic complexities or usage restrictions (e.g. against civilians). The Kurds and some Arab Sunni elites opposed these deals, including purchasing fighter jets from the United States, which they believed emboldened the Shia-led government against them (Allawi et al., 2011). The Kurds recall Saddam's regime, which used massive firepower and chemical weapons against them. The KRG fears the central government will use force to settle disputes. Externally, Kuwait opposed these deals, as Saddam used Iraq's military machine against them. Major Iraqi leaders and factions did not reach consensus or secure trust on developing Iraq's military and security capabilities.

Iraq's bilateral relationships have somewhat contributed to the security and military sectors. Key Iraqi leaders viewed maintaining US support as essential for its security needs. Critical bilateral agreements included the 'Status of Force Agreement' (SOFA) and the US-Iraqi Strategic Framework Agreement (SFA), which were initially signed in 2008. In the wake of the rise of Daesh, the SFA was tested, and Iraq's ruling elite urged the United States for more military and security collaboration. The Iraq-Iran bilateral relationship also focuses on developing Baghdad's security and clandestine collaborations in the form of intelligence sharing and military and security advisers. Iran has systematically engaged with Iraq's various security agencies. Their collaboration intensified after the rise of Daesh, which poses an existential threat to Iran. Hashd al-Sha'abi, in which there are Iranian proxies, has indirectly influenced Iraq's policymaking. While Iraq has been a leading actor in the US-led global coalition against Daesh, it is also in another anti-Daesh alliance with Russia, Iran and Syria. Iraq officially expanded its clandestine cooperation beyond the United States and Western powers in 2015, when it announced a joint shared intelligence cooperation centre in Baghdad between Iraq, Iran, Russia and Syria, mainly against Daesh and other terrorist groups.

This underlines both the federal government's proactive foreign policy to defeating Daesh and its engagement with a broad range of countries, including contentious bedfellows. Baghdad's security imperatives reflect and encompass the United States' initial influence and Iran's increasing infiltration and influence through its agencies, proxies, agents and allies. While the influence of the United States diminished after its withdrawal, the role of the Shia militias' Iranian proxies increased and competition between Iraqi executive security actors escalated. The US leverage returned on a lesser scale to Iraq with the war on Daesh. Therefore, Iraq's foreign relations are influenced by the security interests of both Iran and the US-led coalition. The short-lived common interests between Iran and the United States gradually evaporated when Daesh was militarily defeated in Iraq and President Trump's anti-Iran's regime policy included withdrawing from the nuclear deal. Some of Iraq's key elites, such as former prime ministers al-Abadi and al-Mahdi, recognize that the US relationship is essential in military and security areas. Therefore, the relationship with the United States is military and strategic, whereas the alliance with Iran is political, regional and clandestine.

One of Baghdad's security priorities was blocking the KRG's access to state-issued end-user certificates for obtaining and purchasing heavy weaponry (Knights, 2015a, 26). Mustafa Said Qadir, the former minister of Peshmerga, said: 'The KRG is drawing its own security plan and policy' (author's interview with Qadir, 2015). The KRG's security needs and plans sometimes clash with the federal government's interests and have reflected on the foreign policy interests of the KRG and Baghdad. The differences emanate from competition to control a number of factors, including disputed areas; various constitutional interpretations, distrust and the will of Kurdish elites and factions to maintain an independent Kurdish security establishment. During the war on Daesh and under Prime Minister al-Abadi, there has been room for cooperation between Baghdad and the KR-I's forces (Peshmerga), including channelling some weapons the anti-Daesh US-led global coalition delivered to the Kurds. However, this coordination is more of a tactical reaction against Daesh than a political reconciliation.

Since the rise of Daesh, gaining external military aid and increasing security and intelligence cooperation with anti-Daesh coalitions have driven Baghdad's foreign policy security imperatives. Support has come from various governments; on 10 June 2014, al-Maliki called the UN, EU and Arab League to fight Daesh (Hussain, 2014). Alongside foreign officials, former prime minister al-Abadi stated in 2015 and 2016: 'Our priority is to defeat Daesh' (Middle East Eye, 2015; Kurdistan 24, 2016c; Prime Minister Press Office, 2017). Since 2014, through its foreign policy, Iraq has requested military, security and humanitarian aid and foreign (US-led coalition) air support to regain control of its territories and shared intelligence to execute counter-terrorism operations.

However, the federal government failed to translate Iraq's gains from its bilateral relationships into a successful domestic policy. This is because of the incoherent and divided government and the lack of a common vision between Iraq's elites and factions. Some of Iraq's security approaches do not defend its security; rather, they benefit an individual, group, sect or political force. Al-Mutlaq, deputy chair of Iraq's Defense and Security Committee in the Iraqi Council of Representatives (ICR), said:

> The most important security approach drawbacks are the absence of a security vision, strategy and plan; not building competent independent security institutions; the influence of sectarian politics on security institutions; the absence of national will to take national decisions and the presence of external interferences, such as Iran, on these bodies. (Author's interview with al-Mutlaq, 2015)

Al-Mutlaq blames security shortcomings on poor governance, especially by the Shia-led government and Iranian interference in the security bodies (author's interview with al-Mutlaq, 2015). Iraq's security imperative remains engaged with extensively building security and military apparatus. After the United States' withdrawal, Baghdad's strategy to maintain and build a competent ISF, as well as to provide security and complete control of Iraqi territories, largely failed. Security challenges and needs have profoundly shaped Baghdad's foreign policy interests and direction.

*Iraq's economy*

The development and prosperity of Iraq's petroleum industry has been imperative for Baghdad's foreign policy. Attempts to stabilize relationships with the regional and international community have been essential to developing Iraq's economic and financial backbone. This foreign policy priority has not been achieved fully due to political and security instability in Iraq, lack of a strategic economic plan, corruption, poor infrastructure and the long-standing differences between Erbil and Baghdad. Moreover, Iraq's state-run and rentier economy relies on its oil revenues. This sector deteriorated throughout the period of the UN's sanctions and the US-led invasion. One of Baghdad's key priorities has been to restore Iraq's devastated economy and its oil infrastructure.

Oil revenues transformed Iraq's economy from a self-sustaining low-equilibrium system in the beginning of the 1940s into an export-directed, rapidly growing economy in the 1970s and 1980s (Kubursi, 1988, 283). Iraq's post-2003 economy grew because of oil: from approximately US$18.5 billion in 2005 to US$94 billion in 2012 from oil revenues – an annual GDP growth of 4.4 per cent and 13.9 per cent, respectively (EITI, 2015; Mackey, 2013; Trading Economics, 2016). More than 90 per cent of all Iraq's federal revenues rely on oil (al-Khatteeb, 2016). These numbers provide an indication of how Iraq's economy grew because of oil and how it is solidly related to oil revenues. According to the International Monetary Fund (2016), 94 per cent of Iraq's income in 2014 was from oil revenues.

The federal government has made some progress towards achieving this priority, in terms of rebuilding the oil and then gas infrastructure with national and international oil and gas industries. Post 2003, Iraq has gradually increased its oil production by proactively seeking to construct energy export terminals and engage with the international market to sell its energy. For example, the federal government has a joint project with Royal Dutch Shell and Mitsubishi to produce gas in Basra (*Financial Times*, 2011). This is one of the largest contracts Iraq has signed with transnational corporations. Diplomacy and balanced bilateral relationships are necessary for Baghdad to have secure international energy routes. However, this has not been an easy task due to Iraq's fluctuating relationships with most of its neighbours (excluding Iran).

Iraq's ambitious plans to diversify and expand its energy routes have faced hurdles. It is a semi-landlocked country; the only sea route is from Basra's oil terminals in southern Iraq through the Strait of Hormuz. The south of Iraq, particularly Basra, possesses more than 70 per cent of the oil reserves and wells across Iraq. The rest are mainly in the north (in Kirkuk and Nineveh) and in the KR-I, which has emerged as a new energy hub (International Monetary Fund, 2015; US EIA, 2016). Iraq began to build a new giant shipping port to export oil from the hub of Basra to the Persian Gulf and out through the Strait of Hormuz, which is obstructed by 'Mubarak', the large Kuwaiti port project nearby (around one kilometre). This led to low-level tensions between Iraq and Kuwait. However, Iraq's project has been slow and underfunded.

Other hurdles include the closing of pipelines, including Iraq's western pipeline to the ports of Banias in Syria and Tripoli in Lebanon, and one from Iraq to the KSA, which closed in the 1990s (Salem, 2013). Al-Abadi's government tried to encourage Riyadh to reopen the latter pipeline, and the KSA did not reject the idea. Additionally, the Kirkuk-Ceyhan (Turkey) pipelines have been disrupted many times by attacks and are prone to sabotage by the Kurdish Workers Party (PKK). The latter was a strategic pipeline for the KRG. Kirkuk was fully under the control of the KRG's major political factions for around three years; in October 2017, it was retaken by Baghdad's forces. Therefore, the main stable route for oil exports that the federal government controls is from the south. Iraq's bilateral relationships with neighbouring countries are essential to diversify existing routes. It has slowly attempted to develop oil and gas pipelines, especially with Jordan, Turkey, Kuwait, Syria (before the civil war), the KSA and Iran. For example, in 2013, Iraq and Jordan signed an agreement and announced a 1,043-mile-long pipeline to export oil and gas from Iraq's Basra port on the Persian Gulf to Jordan's Aqaba port in the Gulf of Aqaba on the Red Sea (Oil Price, 2013; *World Affairs Journal*, 2013).

Iraq has exported its oil mainly to China, India, the United States, South Korea, Italy and Greece (Observatory of Economic Complexity, 2016). It holds the world's fifth largest proved crude oil reserves (143 billion barrels) (US EIA, 2016). In 2018, Iraqi officials estimated that Iraq may top the world in oil reserves, and in 2014, it was listed among the top ten largest gas reserves (al-Khatteeb, 2013; Everington, 2018); it contains 126.7 trillion cubic feet (tcf) of gas reserves, representing 1.7 per cent of global gas. Half of the gas has flared, and Baghdad is working with the World Bank to reduce this (al-Khatteeb, 2013). The perception among Iraqi politicians and the public is that Iraq's richness in natural energy resources has contributed to it becoming a relevant international and regional actor. Therefore, the Iraqi government believes its role – supported by its natural resources – is important in the international theatre. Many officials have mentioned this perception in their statements (Center for Strategic and International Studies, 2013).

The Iraqi federal government, including the Ministry of Oil, mainly shape Iraq's oil and gas policy. The State Organization for Marketing of Oil (SOMO) is authorized to negotiate oil sales (SOMO Oil, 2013). Iraq is also a founding member of the Organization of the Petroleum Exporting Countries (OPEC), in which it surpassed Iran in 2012 to become the second largest oil producer. Although Iraq's post-2003 oil production was slow to recover, it was climbing. As a giant oil producer, Iraq has influenced the international market prices for decades (Jaffe, 2007, 1). In 2016, Baghdad succeeded in increasing its oil production to above-pre-2003 levels. This is despite political and security instability, the skills and brain drain, sabotage and slow rebuilding of oil installations (Gulmohamad, 2013; Egan, 2016). According to members of the Oil and Gas Committee in the

ICR, in 2015 (with the drop in oil prices (which began in 2014) and consequently in Iraqi revenues) the federal government encouraged local and national energy corporations to invest more and develop its oil infrastructure rather than foreign transnational companies, in order to keep the benefit within the country and reduce the production costs (Sky News Arabia, 2015a).

Besides oil being Baghdad's and Erbil's main source of revenue, they plan to develop and even export gas in the near future. However, until now gas has been mainly for domestic consumption, such as providing electricity (Bloomberg, 2016; US EIA, 2016). Oil has contributed far more to Iraq's economy than the primitive gas infrastructure. Motivated by low oil prices and aided by local and transnational corporations, Baghdad and Erbil have begun to focus on and invest in gas. Iraq's federal government invited national and international investment for these sectors (Salem, 2013). Both the federal government and the KRG seek to export gas, but hold different and uncoordinated plans and routes to sell it. In 2011, Iraq, Syria and Iran signed gas pipeline agreements (Kadhim and Nayla, 2010; Hafidh and Faucon, 2011), which did not go ahead because of the civil war. There are plans between Erbil and Turkey to export gas from the KR-I to Turkey (Webb, 2009; Ingram, 2019). The KRG had plans to export gas and oil – oil has already been smuggled by various smugglers – to Iran (Iraq Business News, 2010; Reuters, 2012b). Since 2017, Russia – especially Rosneft, a state-owned petroleum company – is increasingly becoming an important energy partner to the KRG; they have invested around US$3.5 billion in the KR-I's oil and gas sector. This angered Baghdad, and the federal government requested clarification of Rosneft's agreement with the KRG (Foy and Sheppard, 2017; Zhdannikov, 2017). Therefore, Baghdad's and Erbil's oil and gas policies have been divided.

In 2008, al-Maliki invited Russian corporations to invest in and explore the oil and gas sector. In 2009, he held talks with the Russian government and companies to produce oil and gas (Al-Jazeera Arabic, 2009). In 2013, in Moscow, al-Maliki asserted that the Iraqi government has begun an ambitious programme to develop oil and gas sectors and the doors are open for the largest international companies, including Russian transnational companies (al-Arabiya, 2013; Energy Daily, 2013). The federal government offered opportunities and privileges to Russia's industry and companies in this field as additional stimulus to improve the bilateral relationship beyond military deals and security, as the Russians had shown goodwill towards improving the relationship. Prime Minister al-Maliki believed this relationship would provide him with more room to manoeuvre during his interaction with the United States.

Disputes between Baghdad and Erbil have arisen over oil and gas revenue shares and control of resources, production and export. In 2013, the KRG finished its own unilateral pipeline to Turkey independent of Baghdad's control. According to the KRG, the KR-I possesses around forty-five billion barrels of oil reserves. The International Energy Agency estimates that the KR-I contains four billion barrels of proven reserves (US EIA, 2016). Therefore, there are wildly different estimates for oil and gas in Iraqi Kurdistan (al-Khatteeb, 2013). When the KR-I became an energy hub, differences in their foreign policies became more visible.

The KRG has unilaterally begun to develop contracts with giant transnational energy corporations – such as Exxon Mobil, Total, Gazprom and Chevron – to develop its oil wells, including extraction and production, and is also independently looking for buyers. The KRG taking control of its oil and gas sector has increased tensions between Erbil and the federal government. Aside from Baghdad's and Erbil's achievements in reconstruction and production, there is neither coherence nor coordination in foreign policy oil and gas imperatives between them. The aspect of the economic foreign policy imperative has partly been achieved because of the divisions between the political actors' interests, which are clearly reflected in the disparate foreign policies.

Post 2003, trade and investment have been the second aspect of Iraq's economic priority, fostering and adopting a relatively open-door policy. This approach is fundamentally different to that in Saddam's era, in which Iraq was the subject of severe sanctions and isolation for more than a decade. Post Saddam, the UN sanctions gradually lifted, providing an opportunity for investment and trade with IGOs (including the EU), transnational corporations, companies and states from around the world. For example, in 2015, the EU was Iraq's second biggest trade partner (behind China) and total bilateral trade was to the tune of 16.1 billion euros. The EU-Iraq partnership and cooperation agreement governed the EU's trade relationship with Iraq (European Commission, 2016). The ranking between the top four trade partners changes every year between the United States, China, the EU and India. The US-led coalition encouraged and guided the open-door policy (Salem, 2013). All Iraqi governments' and most ruling political parties' programmes have mentioned opening and expanding investment and trade during electoral campaigns.

Iraq witnessed a new era of restoring trade and investments – a neoliberal economy and relatively open-door laws for foreign investors – that required a new and sophisticated policy (similar to the 2006 law) to adopt and seize opportunities (Sirri et al., 2013). Post 2003, the private sector and foreign investment emerged as new actors in the Iraqi and Kurdish political economic theatre. However, the state's elites and political parties have sponsored banks and companies that dominate the economy for their personal and partisan gain.

Foreign direct investment (FDI) has gradually increased since 2003. For instance, in 2004, FDI inflow was 0.8 per cent of Iraqi GDP; in 2013, it was 2.2 per cent. Due to the poor business environment and rise of Daesh, this number declined slightly (International Trade Center, 2016); in 2017 and 2018, FDI picked up again. In parallel to the investment, the Iraqi government requested and was granted observer status in the World Trade Organization (WTO), in which it is now pursuing full membership status (Iraqi Ministry of Trade, 2016). Iraq and the UN Conference on Trade and Development collaborated in negotiation support for accession in the WTO (UNCTAD, 2016). Therefore, the UN assisted Iraqi trade policy, which is part of Iraq's economy foreign policy imperatives.

The Iraqi government has forged bilateral and multilateral trade agreements with countries that have been key trade partners and investors in Iraq. Between 2003 and 2013, Iraq took part in nine separate multiparty agreements and thirty-five other bilateral agreements worldwide (United States of America Department of Commerce, 2013). Trade relationships have been arranged via various bilateral agreements and understandings. Iraq has expanded its trade partnerships beyond major partners through various types of trade arrangements, for instance, with Japan and India. This foreign policy priority reflects Iraq's need to rebuild its infrastructure, meet consumer needs and fuel its new and emerging market and businesses after years of sanctions, embargos and isolations.

Post 2003, trade and investment with Iran blossomed on an unprecedented level; while trade and investment with the United States has been open, it has faced obstacles from populist domestic factions and insecurity. A number of Shia factions, including al-Sadr's movement, have rejected Iraqi-US trade agreements. The Iraqi government did not ratify a US-Iraq trade and investment framework agreement, negotiated in 2005, until 2013 – after the United States' withdrawal (Sirri et al., 2013). Iraqi foreign policy is the main tool to conduct and develop trade and, according to Article 110 of the Iraqi constitution, policy is exclusive to the federal government. The KRG has its own regional investment and business laws that it designed, passed and implemented. In the beginning of 2019, the KRG and Baghdad unified customs tariffs and set up a new system laying out a new taxation process. Although from 2019 Baghdad and Erbil have been working on some of the trade and investment laws, there has been a different business and investment atmosphere in the KR-I, as well as diplomatic and management leverages for the KRG's officials to engage with international corporations. Post 2003, the KR-I has thrived economically, and has been dominated by Turkish trade and investment and flooded with the latter's and Iran's commodities. The KR-I includes flexible regulations and laws for trade and investment. According to the Department of Foreign Relations (2015), 'The KRG maintains very liberal investment laws' and is the most secure region in Iraq, which has helped it to become a hub for foreign corporations and investment. This has shaped the distinctiveness of its trade policy. According to interviews with KRG officials – such as Tahir, the KRG's representative to the UK – the KRG has its own economic and trade policies.

This reflects reality, wherein the KRG pursues its own oil deals and bypasses Baghdad as well as multilevel trade and economic ties with Turkey. For example, the Turkish private sector has heavily invested in the KR-I. In 2009, there were 485 companies; in 2013, there were 1,500 (Cagaptay et al., 2015). Since February 2014, and despite some short-lived budget-sharing agreements, the federal government has cut and/or withheld the KR-I's budget. This has added to the deterioration of the economy in the KR-I. Similarly to oil and gas, there is no unified approach between Baghdad and Erbil regarding trade and investment. Iraq's post-2003 economic growth accelerated from 5.9 per cent in 2010 to over 8.4 per cent in 2012 (International Monetary Fund, 2013). The World Bank indicated high economic growth annually from 2008 to 2012, averaging 7 per cent (World Bank, 2015). The IMF and World Bank agree that the economic growth is due to the significant increase in oil production. Despite this growth, however, the multilayered challenges of security and political instability, involvement of politicians in trade and business, systematic corruption and divisions between Baghdad and

Erbil have obstructed progress. The foreign policy priority of improving trade and investment has been partly achieved – due to Iraq's energy oil reserves and production and focused, proactive engagement with the global economy – but it has also been hindered by the fragmentation of the state, elites' competition, insecurity, corruption and drop in oil prices.

## Conclusion

Iraq's state building and regime survival has compelled elites to focus on certain key imperatives that became foreign policy priorities. Despite the statements on the I-MOFA website, the secretary general of the Council of Ministers' programme (General Secretariat of the Council of Ministers, 2014) and Iraqi officials' political rhetoric for domestic consumption, and political parties' election campaign programmes with limited insights about foreign policy, there is no plan detailing the country's foreign policy priorities or how they are to be obtained. Nevertheless, fieldwork, monitoring of officials' statements and performance, and some literature have provided the evidence to identify the priorities and assess their importance. Elites determine foreign policy priorities based on what they view as necessary for government survival. Despite Baghdad's incoherent foreign policy, the foreign policy priorities are imperatives for state building and government survival.

Iraq has three major areas of foreign policy priorities: diplomacy, security and economy. These priorities are interconnected. Each supports (if it succeeds) or hinders (if it fails) the attainment of the others, which demonstrates their interdependence. For example, improved security would attract investment, which would improve the economy. However, one of the reasons why Iraq's foreign policy priorities have not been clearly achieved is because the federal government has no clear plan on how to pursue them. This is, in large part, the result of insecurity, and disagreements between key elites in Baghdad, as well as between Baghdad and Erbil, are serious impediments to progress.

The first imperative was to restore Iraq's diplomacy and relationships. It was critical to establish communication with external powers and foreign entities for bilateral relationships, cooperation, projecting interests, reaching goals and participating in regional and international gatherings. Baghdad's post-2003 diplomacy shows no hostility towards the international community and restored diplomatic ties with states and IGOs. However, it has experienced difficulties in its relationships with regional states. Iraq's diplomacy has been a bridge between Tehran and Damascus (since the civil war) and the Western powers. Iraq's diplomacy during al-Abadi's and al-Mahdi's governments revived Iraq's relations with Arab states, including the KSA, Qatar, the United Arab Emirates, Jordan and Egypt, while maintaining its strategic relations with Iran. Iraq's diplomacy does not, however, represent the KRG's interests, particularly on issues concerning security and economy. The schism was at its peak as the KRG began to lobby for the KR-I's referendum; yet after the referendum this has simmered down. Baghdad has not completely achieved a coherent diplomacy; it lacks broad domestic support and inclusiveness, consistent and coherent messages, professional cadres and an affable relationship with most regional powers.

Baghdad's second priority is security. This imperative was a critical part of the US-led coalitions and the ruling elites' state building. However, Iraq has largely failed to achieve this. As vital as security is to the government's survival, its security needs and interests are splintered between and within the federal government (e.g. the ISF and pro-Iran Shia militias) and the KRG (KDP's and PUK's Peshmerga). The set of priorities not only represents a specific ethnic or religious sect but also elites' and partisan interests. In other words, there is fragmentation within each ethnic sectarian component in viewing the priorities, although, post 2003, there were more similarities in some interests and foreign affairs tendencies within each ethnic and sectarian political component than with other components. During al-Abadi's and al-Mahdi's governance (particularly after Daesh's military defeat), the fragmentation within ethnic sectarian blocs has deepened, their similarities have faded and overlapping interests have emerged across communal lines.

The Shia-led government and the major Shia parties have systematically engaged in integrating their elements into the ISF. Excluding some (such as al-Sistani's and al-Sadr's loyal militias), they seek closer ties with Iran on all levels. Iraqi-Arab Sunni elites have grievances, as they do not have a say in Iraq's security and running their own security affairs. Moreover, many of them seek closer ties with the Arab states. The 2003 destruction of the Iraqi forces and subsequent failure to competently rebuild the ISF have exacerbated Iraq's failure to achieve other foreign policy priorities. This has been worsened by the former prime minister al-Maliki's accumulation of power and interference in Iraq's armed forces. The deepening of the divisions has hampered the achievement of its security imperatives.

Iraq's third foreign policy priority is the economy. Oil revenues in particular have been the driver of regime survival. Despite the increase in oil production and revenues, Baghdad's efforts to achieve this priority have been hindered because of internal divisions, instability and corruption. Iraq's bilateral relationships have endorsed the build-up of gas facilities. However, expanding export routes via neighbouring countries as an additional revenue resource is fraught with difficulties due to Baghdad's unstable relationships with regional states (excluding Iran). So, Iraq does not have a unified oil and gas policy or strategy because policy preferences are divided on many levels, including control of the facilities between Baghdad and Erbil.

Despite the significant post-2003 increase in trade and investment, Baghdad and Erbil did not coordinate policy until recently on some issues. Their trade and investment policies were divided, and each has its own laws and administration; nonetheless, post the 2017 referendum, there has been some synchronization on a number of laws. Key factors hindering cooperation, investment and trade are insecurity and instability, failure to impose order and the rule of law, poor infrastructure, corruption and nepotism. Iraq has partly managed to achieve its economic priority because Baghdad restored the oil sector and is developing the gas sector and issuing new, flexible laws to encourage foreign investment. However, it has failed to provide security and stability, which would encourage further foreign investment and increase trade. The government has focused only on natural energy resources instead of cooperating with foreign entities for agriculture, industry and innovation. Although Iraq's foreign policy began to focus on collecting support for reconstruction, it failed miserably to utilize this to address environmental degradation, including significant water scarcity, drought and pollution.

Analysis of Iraq's foreign policy priorities shows clearly that there is no unified national and state interest projected in foreign policy making. Rather, various key leaders represent the interests of elites, factions or subgroups. In short, Iraq's three main priorities have been contested and weakly pursued. Some, such as the security imperative, have been a significant challenge. Scrutinizing the foreign policy priorities exposes Iraqi elites' lack of agreement on approaches and principles to achieve their foreign policy priorities.

Iraq's neighbours have exploited the country's weakness, disorder, fragmentation, and political and security vacuum to further their own interests. Iraq has historically been a theatre for regional powers' competition; the weakening of defence and security capabilities has weakened it, rendering it vulnerable to interference from its neighbours and increases in their influence in domestic Iraqi politics and policymaking (Hudson Institute, 2016). Iraq's neighbours have worried that its weak security establishment will allow chaos to spill into their countries. They favour a weak Iraq (albeit not to the extent of collapse or disintegration or disorder) so as to better control and secure their own interests.

# Chapter 5

## REGIONAL INTERFERENCES AND INFLUENCES ON IRAQ'S FOREIGN POLICY POST SADDAM

*Introduction*

Iraq's neighbouring states interfere in and have an impact on its foreign relations and foreign policies. Iran is the most powerful external player in Iraq, followed by Turkey. Other neighbouring countries, such as the Kingdom of Saudi Arabia (KSA) and Syria (before the Civil War), have far less influence. Iraq's two non-Arab neighbours Iran and Turkey have the most influence on Baghdad and Erbil, respectively.

Mohamad Sabir Ismail, Iraq's ambassador to the UN in Geneva, discussed these external influences:

> If we like it or not, Iran has an influence on Iraq ... because of the common sect [Shia] and they [elites and their political parties] were in the past hosted and supported in Iran, thus of course there are affinities between them including Shia and Kurds. However, Turkey and Saudi also have an influence in Iraq but it depends on which component we talk about ... And because the Shia are the most powerful in Iraq, Iran is the most influential. (Author's interview with Ismail, 2014)

He indicates that major regional powers have different influences on different components in Iraq. Lukman Faily argues that all of Iraq's neighbours interfere:

> All our neighbours get involved and interfere in our internal affairs [policymaking] because of a lack of cohesion and clarity on how we want the relationship with them. They all get involved, even Kuwait, as they want to understand the relationship between Basra and Baghdad.... Iraq is a buffer zone for other neighbouring countries. (Author's interview with Faily, 2016)

Certainly, some interference and influence from a neighbouring state is more obvious and has more impact than from another. Influence and interference are not synonymous, as most countries try to influence each other. Interference indicates seeking involvement in other countries' or entities' internal affairs and trying to influence decision-making. Therefore, not all influence is interference, but all interference is an attempt to influence. Historically, various Iraqi groups have tended to sympathize with different regional alliances and enmities (Tripp, 2002, 174). Senior Iraqi officials have acknowledged external interferences, such as Prime Minister al-Abadi, who said: 'There are a lot of countries intervening in my country, there has been a lot of support [from external forces] to terrorists and militias in my country' (Deutsche Welle, 2016). Iraq's domestic political debate has featured in the Iraqi media and programmes regarding external interferences on Iraq's foreign policies. Cables obtained by Wikileaks exposed key Iraqi elites complaining about the interference from neighbouring countries as well as neighbours' suspicions about Iraqi leaders. For instance, on 15 March 2009, King Abdullah of the KSA told US diplomats and policymakers that he has 'no confidence in [Prime Minister Nuri al-Maliki] is an Iranian agent' (Kechichian, 2012).

During Saddam's era one of Iraq's complications was unsettled identity, which distinctively and problematically connects Iraq's fragmented society with the regional environment (Tripp, 2002, 177). Iraqi Arab Shia and Arab Sunni actors draw in external forces in the process of Iraqi state building, from which they receive abundant support (Haddad, 2016). The Kurds also garner support from external forces to consolidate their position.

Although the influence of the US and Iraqi policymakers' consideration of the US-Iraqi relationship is critical, previously the regional powers' influence and interference have not been thoroughly examined. Not all regional states are equally influential in Iraqi politics or in formulating foreign policy; nor do they influence the same Iraqi political elites or factions. For example, in 2013, Foreign Minister Zebari said: 'There are two [major] countries that have an influence in Iraqi Sunni communities – Saudi Arabia and Turkey for different reasons ... With Turkey we experience many problems primarily because the lack of respect by the Turkish politicians for dictating what an elected Iraqi government should do' (Center for Strategic and International Studies, 2013). External actors seek to influence Iraq's foreign policy outcomes to suit their interests. Iraqi internal actors facilitate their allied neighbouring states' interference/influence on foreign policy, as they have common interests. External actors' influence and interference have contributed to Iraq's foreign policies becoming splintered and incoherent because of the fragmentation of its foreign policy making institutions and process. Iraq's policymaking is not made only domestically; it is also shaped by regional powers' interference, influence and pressure.

## *Iranian interference in Iraq*

Iran's foreign policy regarding Iraq is oriented towards building a secure environment at its borders (Bargezar, 2007) which could be utilized for Tehran's security, economic and political interests and also as a foreign policy channel to other states. Iran has had an influence on segments of Iraqi Shia communities since the Iranian Revolution in 1979. Covert Iranian aid for Baghdad's opponents increased in 1980, in response to the Iraqi regime aiding Iran's opponents (Halliday, 1986, 96). Iranian interference also included the formation of what is now known as the Islamic Supreme Council of Iraq (ISCI) and its previous armed wing, the Badr Brigade, in 1981. However, Iran's influence was challenged during the 1980–8 Iran-Iraq War, when the Arab Shia in the south of Iraq did not rebel against Saddam as Khomeini expected. In 2003, the US-led coalition's invasion of Iraq threatened Iran's national security but also provided a historical opportunity for the Iranian leadership to maximize Iran's power in Iraq. Since 2003, Iran has tried to influence Iraq's new government. Iranian influence and leverage in Iraq between 2003 and 2016 can be divided into four stages (Juneau, 2015, 124–33).

First, the period immediately after the toppling of Saddam represented a stage of threat and opportunity for Iran. Old friends became the vital power structure, but the proximity of US forces to Iran's borders was perceived as a threat. Iran was puzzled and began formulating two contrasting policies; this period was short as it included the Coalition Provisional Authority (CPA) and subsequently Ayad Allawi headed the Iraqi Interim Government (IIG); there was no democratically elected government and the constitution was not yet passed.

Second, since 2005, Iran further strengthened its ties with its Iraqi allies and invested in Iraq. Iran's interference in Iraq shows contradictory policies. Iran consolidated ties with old Iraqi friends and supported the Shia-led government and radical Shia armed groups. It covertly supported some Sunni jihadists and insurgents in Iraq; this declined in the following phase (Roberts, 2007; Eisenstadt et al., 2011).

Third, since 2009, Iran's allies in Iraq became more divided; they also began to demonstrate independence and concentrated on the distribution of Iraq's oil wealth. Iran increased its support for Shia militias loyal to Tehran. Al-Maliki kept a balance between Iraq's relationships with the United States and Iran. Meanwhile, competition within the Shia house surfaced in relation to Iran, demonstrating Iran's inability to control all Iraqi Shia factions. This is illustrated by emerging differences within the Shia elites and factions regarding what they think Iran's role in Iraq should be. After the US withdrawal in 2011, Iran's tacit, tactical support for Sunni radicals in Iraq diminished.

Fourth, since the fall of Mosul and other territories to Daesh in 2014, Iranian interference has faced both opportunities and challenges. The challenges included al-Abadi's government, al-Sadr and Ayatollah al-Sistani having similar objectives, such as strengthening Iraqi nationalism away from Iran and limiting powerful pro-Iran militias. The division between Qum and Najaf has become part of the rivalry between Tehran and Baghdad. Some Shia political figures temporarily counteracted their pro-Iran rivals in Iraq (e.g. al-Sadr mobilized his loyal militias as a counter-weight against pro-Iran militias) (Spyer and al-Tamimi, 2014). Opportunities for Iran include the rise of Daesh, during which Iranian clients and agencies (via pro-Iran Shia militias) have proliferated. Pro-Iran Shia militias seized the opportunity of the collapse of state military apparatus and al-Sistani's fatwa (*Wajib jihad al-Kafai*) on 13 June 2014 (Sistani, 2014; Gulmohamad, 2015). Former US ambassador Jeffery described Iran's influence during the rise of Daesh thus: 'Iranian influence in Iraq is higher than the United States' (Atlantic Council, 2016). The Iranian military and security advisors with the Iraqi Security Forces (ISF) illustrate the continuation of formal intelligence and military cooperation between Baghdad and Tehran.

The competition between Iran and the United States took a new direction with the rise of Daesh, which resulted in tacit and unintended common interests that diminished with Daesh's military downfall and Trump's presidency, despite both sides supporting different Iraqi Shia factions. Ali al-Najafi, Grand Ayatollah Sheikh Basheer al-Najafi's son, said: 'If the US took its security agreement with Iraq seriously there would be no need for Iran to intervene and Iraq would not ask for the help of Iran's experts. We think Iraq should be independent and have respectful relations with other countries' (qtd in Steele, 2015). Iraqi Holy Shia Shrines militias cooperate with the US-led anti–Islamic State (IS) coalition; they tacitly oppose the Iranian expansionist approach in Iraq and thus strengthen al-Sistani.

During al-Maliki's tenure, Iranian leverage was such that Iran used Baghdad's airport without being subject to restrictions or searches. The free-use protocol permitted Iranian military aid to be transferred to Baghdad, to the Popular Mobilization Forces (PMF) or resumed flights to Damascus. A change took place in mid-August 2015, when al-Abadi ordered that Iranian planes be subject to Iraqi laws (Middle East Brief, 2015). This was the result of the mild competition between al-Abadi and Iranian leverage.

Iranian's limitations or obstacles in Iraq have deep roots in modern Iraqi history, which Iraqi actors have revived. Besides ethnic and religious differences between the Kurds and Arab Sunnis and the distinctive regional interests of Shia Iran, there is divergence between Iranian elites and Iraqi Shia communities. These differences are ideological (doctrines regarding governance), cultural and political and can be felt in all phases of Iranian influence.

There are differences between the two Shia religious establishments in Iran and Iraq. The Iraq-based highest Shia cleric (*marjaia*) Grand Ayatollah Abu al-Qasim Al-Khoei and his successor Grand Ayatollah al-Sistani, along with his peers, adopted the 'Quietist' and *Nathariat al-Husbaih* Islamic Shia tradition.[1] They oppose Ayatollah Ruhollah Khomeini's 'Guardianship of Islamic Jurists' (*Wilayat al-Faqih*), doctrine that is entwined in Iran's political system. 'Khamenei wants to dominate Shia Iraq completely as a colony of Iran ... Khamenei's representatives in Iraq try to change Iraq to support Iran in all political stances in the region' (Mamouri, qtd in Washington Institute, 2017). Mahmoud Al-Mashhadani, former Speaker in the Iraqi Council of Representatives (ICR), acknowledged Iran's influences in Iraq: 'I went to Iran to talk about Iraq's strategic agreement with the US ... one who denies Iran's significant influence on the Iraqi political scene is a man who does not understand politics' (Al-Jazeera Arabic, 2008). Al-Mashhadani indicates Iran's influence on Shia political parties in Iraq, and consequently on their representatives in the ICR (Al-Jazeera Arabic, 2008). However, post Saddam, some Shia Islamist factions distanced themselves from Khomeini's doctrine (viz.

the Da'wa Party, Muqtada al-Sadr and ISCI), which made it challenging for Iran to have full control over Iraqi Shias.

Iran is lobbying strategically in Iraq via its supporters, allies, proxies and clients; yet, it has faced resistance from some Iraqi Shia factions. Non-pro-Iran Iraqis view Iranian policy in Iraq as serving Iranian hardliners' narrow national and security interests. Therefore, Iran's significant influence and interference are not unchecked. Iran views Iraq's foreign policy orientation as important for its interests in Iraq and the region. For Iran, Iraq is another critical corridor to the Arab world. In March 2015, Ali Younesi, one of President Rouhani's top advisors on Ethnic and Religious Minorities Affairs, said that 'Baghdad is now the capital of a Persian Empire'; this led to critical responses from Iraq and beyond and Younesi later modified his statement and argued that he was referring to the cultural and economic similarities and cooperation with Iraq (Al-Arabiya News, 2015; Dabashi, 2016, 38). Iraq's foreign policy is not a duplicate of Iran's. Iranian interference in Iraq's affairs should not overshadow the fact that Iraq has conducted some foreign policy matters that were not in Iran's interests, such as Iraq's Strategic Framework Agreement (SFA) with the United States. In generic terms, the Shia-led government backs Iran's regional positions and relations, in which there are common interests and perspectives, such as appealing for Shia grievances and supporting the Shia masses in the region, for instance, in Yemen, Lebanon, the KSA and Bahrain. In relation to the cultural, economic and security sectors, many Shia (and some Kurdish) politicians have demonstrated Iran's benign intervention in Iraq. According to Kamran Karadaghi, the former Iraqi president's chief of staff: 'Iran knows how to deal with the Iraqi elite professionally, which is coupled with their knowledge of Iraq's culture more than the Americans. This provided Iran with exceptional status and weight in Iraq' (author's interview with Karadaghi, 2015). While Iran occasionally pressures Iraqi actors by, for example, using proxies in Iraq to obtain their goals, in some ways, Iran utilizes gentle communication methods and revives memories of shared struggles (during Saddam's era) when interacting with the Iraqi political elite. Iran's proactive attitudes in Iraq include providing their old friends and allies with various types of assistance, such as logistical support.

*Iran's influence on Iraq's military and security apparatus*

Iran has funded, trained, equipped and indoctrinated numerous Iraqi Shia militias and armed groups, one of them being Badr, ISCI's former armed wing, that goes back to the beginning of the 1980s. Post 2003, Iran – partly through Shia militias – began infiltrating Iraq's security structure and establishment. Iran's military, security and clandestine strategy and network in Iraq can be considered as Iran exercising hard power (Bongers, 2013, 146). Between 2003 and 2005, 16,000 personnel from Iran-backed Shia militias were incorporated into the new ISF. The Badr Organization has strong historical ties with the Iraqi Revolutionary Guards Corps – Quds Force (IRGC-QF) and has provided most of the personnel to the ISF (Eisenstdat et al., 2011). The Iraqi National Intelligence Service's (INIS) first leader, Mohammed al-Shawani, a Sunni who had strained relations with some prominent Shia members, left in 2009, after clashing with al-Maliki. An al-Maliki loyalist replaced him, and INIS eventually built a relationship with Iran (Dodge, 2013, 205; Cordesman and Khazai, 2014, 52).

Iranian involvement in Iraq is not monolithic; it has emerged from various Iranian institutions and individuals, such as the Ministry of Intelligence and Security, the Ministry of Foreign Affairs, the Supreme National Council and – significantly – from Qasem Soleimani, the major general and commander of QF. To streamline operations in Iraq, IRGC-QF created a unified command, known as Ramazan Corps, and divided Iraq into approximately three geographical regions (Roggio, 2007). The aforementioned Iranian bodies engaged in Iraq show the multilayered involvement in Iraq's political, economic, military, security and intelligence structure.

Soleimani (until his death) was the most powerful Iranian figure in Iraq's security affairs; he has a tangible influence on Iraq's military strategies, particularly in frontline battles wherein Iraqi forces and Hashd al-Sha'abi are fighting Daesh. Hashd al-Sha'abi (PMF) became the most powerful paramilitary umbrella in Iraq's military structure. The PMF can be divided into two blocks of militias: pro-Iran; and the other block, including pro-Sistani and pro-Sadr armed groups, that does not consider itself as pro-Iran. Iran utilizes the pro-Iran militias within the PMF as a parallel security apparatus to the Iraqi Army and Iraqi Counter Terrorism Service – the Golden Division which has close ties with the United States.

Dozens of pro-Iran Shia militias in Iraq are considered the most powerful forces within the PMF, and follow the Iranian supreme leader's doctrines and take their instructions from Iranian hardliners and their security circles. Powerful organizations in the PMF, such as the Badr Organization (headed by Hadi al-Amiri) and Asaib Ahl Al-Haq (AAH) and its leader (Qayis al-Khazali) have very close ties with the Ramazan Corps. Al-Khazali was initially considered to be one of the senior officers or agents of the Ramazan Corps, and the United States refers to his group as the direct 'arm action' of the QF (Roggio, 2007; Nader, 2015). In a televised interview, al-Amiri threatened to pressure al-Abadi and his government if they did not agree with his policies regarding US military operations in Iraq (Parker, 2015). As such, AAH, Badr and other pro-Iran militias have become part of Iraq's political and security governmental structure. Iran gained political and security advantages via its armed proxies. Consequently, this might indirectly and directly influence decision-making processes in Iran's favour. However, while Iran's proxies in al-Abadi's and his successor's governments should be taken into consideration, their influence should not be exaggerated in foreign policy making. While the federal government expressed affinities and solidarity with Shia figures and parties in the Middle East, the Iraqi pro-Iran Shia militias have publicly announced their willingness to support the Shias and have threatened the Arab Gulf monarchies for suppressing their Shia populations (al-Arabiya, 2016; Baghdad Post, 2016; Al-Khaleej Online, 2016b). This underlines the radical approach of those actors compared to the federal government. Although the federal government has not adopted exactly the same rhetoric as pro-Iran Shia militias, Baghdad has been pressured by their rhetoric and has been careful in its statements to not antagonize them.

Former prime minister al-Abadi supported pro-Sistani armed groups in the PMF. Pro-Sistani armed groups, known as Holy Shia Shrines militias or A'tabat Forces, answer to al-Sistani and not Khamenei (Habib, 2015; Mamouri, 2015; Gulmohamad, 2016b). They neither possess strong political motivations nor hold the *Wilayat al-Faqih* doctrine (Gulmohamad, 2016a). Since the rise of Daesh, pro-al-Sadr militia – to a considerable degree – adhere to the federal government in Baghdad. Dissolving the militias and integrating them in the ISF and strengthening the Baghdad-headed federal government forces will limit the influence of Iran's influence.

Iranian hardliners and their powerful proxies (such as Kataib Hezbollah and AAH) have perceived the United States' return to Iraq to fight Daesh as an obstacle to their ascendance. The Iraqi pro-Iran and Muqtada's militias threatened to kill the US advisors in Iraq if they, for example, established fixed military bases and armed the Kurds and Arab Sunnis without the Shia-led government's consent (Knights, 2015b). This has pushed the federal government, including al-Abadi, to be more cautious (at least publicly) with the United States.

Iran through the Lebanon's Hezbollah supported Iraq's pro-Iran Shia militias. There are a number of Lebanese Hezbollah's skilled fighters in Iraq, alongside the PMF and ISF, providing advice and other forms of support usually for the militias (Spyer and al-Tamimi, 2014; Levitt, 2015). According to Abu Mahdi al-Muhandis, a leader of the PMF stated that Kataib Hezbollah in Iraq and AAH have a relationship with the Lebanon's Hezbollah, including training (*Al-Khabar*, 2015). On 16 February 2015, Hassan Nasrallah, leader of the Lebanese Hezbollah, revealed their presence in Iraq to fight Daesh, which the media subsequently reported (*National*, 2015). Lebanon's Hezbollah's involvement in Iraq can be understood in the context of cooperation and interference. Hezbollah is an Iranian non-state client in the region; it coordinates with Iranian IRGC elements in Iraq and assists Iran.

During the existential threat that Iraq faced against Daesh, both Shia and Kurdish leaders acknowledged the support – ammunitions to armed groups and to a certain degree bombing Daesh – that Iran provided. Iran's strategic interests include maintaining its proxies and allies, including pro-Iran militias in the PMF within the Iraqi state as a parallel security apparatus.

*Iranian soft power in Iraq*

Many Iraqi political elites have perceived Iranian soft power as useful, supportive and necessary for post-Saddam Iraqi state building. Iran's activities have manifested in many areas (e.g. politics, social and educational programmes, investment in energy and trade and so on), most notably in a number of active land-crossing borders, religious activities and tourism, including hundreds of thousands Iranian pilgrims travelling to Shia holy shrines in Najaf and Karbala annually.

Iran spends millions of dollars reconstructing Iraqi Shia holy shrines, engaging in infrastructure investment projects and providing energy (Loi, 2011; Trend News Agency, 2014). Observing Iranian economic influence on Iraq shows a gradual and significant increase in trade partnership between both countries: from under US$400 million in 2004 to US$4 billion in 2009 (Marr and Parker, 2011, 32) and US$12 billion in 2013 (al-Hassoun, 2014; *Financial Tribune*, 2015). In 2015, Iraq was one of Iran's top five trading partners (Esfandiary and Tabatabai, 2015). Their trade cooperation has been growing steadily; Iran began to funnel more investment in the Arab and Kurdish regions in Iraq as they became one of its top economic priorities, particularly after the US withdrawal from the Joint Comprehensive Plan of Action (JCPOA). Iran pursues access to Iraq's hard currency as the latter's revenues have increased since oil production rose.

Economic penetration is clearly a major pillar of Iran's policy towards Iraq (Juneau, 2015, 120). Iran's strategic economic policy towards Iraq can be depicted as economic diplomacy that serves its long-term interests to foster its relationships and impact on Iraq's internal political dynamics (Habibi, 2010; Kebriaeezadeh, 2015). Iran has the most diplomatic representations (eleven consulates and an embassy) that are scattered throughout Iraq. Iraq and Iran signed a number of bilateral agreements in multiple sectors, including between governments, chambers of commerce, energy sectors and universities. Iranian involvement in Iraq was not entirely detrimental. This was part of Iraq's open-door policy to Iran, which had political repercussions and served Tehran's interests. Iraq's infrastructure, poor facilities and incapacity to provide basic services opened the door for Iran's engagement in these sectors. The economic interdependence and cultural exchange between Iran and Iraq (Shia region) inevitably resulted in political gains for Iran.

Another level of Iranian engagement is Shia religious literature, which has flowed into southern Shia regions through the organization of book fairs, and media outreach through television and radio (Juneau, 2015, 121). Religious tourism and education (such as Iranian educational schools and cultural centres throughout Iraq) have substantially increased and now constitute a major instance of cultural diplomacy; the Imam Khomeini Cultural-Sports Centre in Diyala provides one such example. An unprecedented level of cultural interchange between the two countries helped to secure Iranian influence in Iraq.

Iran interferes in Iraqi seminary (*al-Hawza*) and Shiite Marjia circles; Khamenei was preparing a new *marjaia* to succeed Grand Ayatollah al-Sistani, who is viewed as a hindrance to the expansion of Iranian influence. With Iranian support and finance, Iraqi-born cleric Ayatollah Mahmoud Hashemi-Shahroudi (who died in December 2018) extended his network throughout the Shia community in Iraq, including in Najaf (Arango, 2012; Esfandiary and Tabatabai, 2015). Shahroudi was considered to be in Khamenei's close circle and posed a challenge to the non-cleric democratic system in Iraq. He had a good rapport with former prime minister al-Maliki (Hendawi and Abdul-Zahra, 2012). However, Ayatollah Shahroudi was a weak candidate as he had insufficient support among the Shia seminary in Najaf and spent insufficient time in Najaf to build a network and influence. Despite

Khamenei's efforts to influence Shia seminary in Najaf, it is a closed system that is challenging for him to penetrate (Washington Institute, 2017). Iran's blueprint for Iraq's future highest *marjia* matches that of al-Maliki's and the interests of the pro-Iran Shia militias.

Geography (a 905-mi-long porous border), common religious sect (Shia Islam) and security, economic, cultural and personal ties paved the way for Iranian influence (Gulmohamad, 2014b). After the rise of Daesh in the wake of ISF weakening, the emboldening of the pro-Iran Shia militias, the feeble Iraqi institutions, the Iranian support through its proxies became vital in the face of the existential threat of Daesh. While Baghdad assembled a fragile bridge between the two rival bedfellows, since the US withdrawal from the JCPOA, Baghdad has been in a dilemma to formulate an unbiased policy. Despite Iran's limitations, its soft power has extended its spheres of influence.

*Iran and Iraqi Kurdish and Arab Sunni factions*

Iran's interference in the Kurdistan Region of Iraq (KR-I) is tacit and less obvious than its influence on Iraqi Shia factions. The Kurdistan Democratic Party (KDP) and especially the Patriotic Union of Kurdistan (PUK) have a good relationship with Iran. The PUK-controlled areas border with Iran; in this context geopolitics matter, and the PUK has a relationship with Iran which shapes its decision-making with respect to Iran. Yet, after Kurdistan's referendum, the KDP and Iran have become close as well. Historically, the two Iraqi Kurdish parties and Iran have switched between affinity and tension. For example, in the 1980s, the KDP had closer ties with Iran than the PUK, as the latter was allied with the Kurdish Democratic Party of Iran (KDP-I) (Stansfield, 2003, 90). The two parties have historical ties that go back to before the Iranian Revolution in 1979. Iran tried to manipulate the Kurds in its political bargaining and games in both Iran and Iraq, to direct certain issues to their interests. The 373-mi-long border between the KR-I and Iran and mutual economic and political elites' interests have influenced the relationships between Iran and the Kurdish parties, especially the PUK.

Iranian influence and soft power includes cultural diplomacy: the relationship of the Kurdish language to Farsi (Persian), tourism and the popularity of Iranian music among the Kurds. Economic ties also play a significant role in their relationship. Iran is the KRG's second largest trade partner; for example, mutual trade generated US$4 billion in 2013 (Ingram, 2015). Several economic and trade agreements have been signed in various sectors. Their ties include construction and energy (oil, gas and electricity). Iran serves as another trade corridor for the KR-I, particularly for the PUK-dominated areas, adding to its political leverage in the KR-I and on the PUK.

The KR-I's referendum in 2017 brought both Tehran and Baghdad even closer as there were significant fears such as the control of oil-rich Kirkuk which has geo-economic and geostrategic importance. Thus, Iran, in coordination with Baghdad, responded by putting economic pressure on the KR-I. In addition to the key role of pro-Iran militias within the PMF in seizing Kirkuk from the Kurdish authorities on 16 October, Iran, with Baghdad's consent, shut down border crossings with the KR-I, such as Parviz Khan. Iran gradually opened them as they are lucrative trade border crossings for both sides.

The KRG has a formal representative in Tehran: Nazim Omer, from the PUK party. This is alongside many Kurdish parties' representatives, including the KDP and Islamic Union. As each Kurdish party has a slightly different relationship with Iran, Iran considers itself the occasional arbiter when tensions between Kurdish parties emerge, but it also tries to keep them divided if it suits its interests. The Shia-led government does not view the close ties between the KR-I and Iran as constituting interference in its internal affairs. Iran is firmly and publicly against Kurdish independence; meanwhile, it has interests that lead it to help maintain the KR-I's stability. Iran's ties with Kurdish parties build amicable relationships. Openly avoiding Iran's animosity is one of the KRG's political parties' national security interests. Limiting the Kurdish aspirations in Iraq for independence by the Iranians must be viewed through the prism of not only unifying Iraq but also curbing Iranian-Kurdish ambitions and activities for an independent state, or any sort of autonomy that has remerged over the past years. Despite Iran's pressure on Iraqi Kurdish parties, it does not dictate the decision-making of the KRG. The KDP and PUK take Iran into account in their decision-making, particularly in issues related to Iran. During Daesh's attacks on the KR-I in 2014, Iran helped the Peshmerga forces by providing some ammunition and weapons for which Kurdish officials formally thanked them. Although Iraqi Kurds appreciate Iran's support in pushing back Daesh and they are open to a friendly rapport, they are concerned about Iran's increasing leverage in Iraq.

Even though Iraqi Arab Sunni elites and factions are divided, they depict Iran as a threat and reject its engagement. Former vice president al-Hashimi (Arab Sunni) stated that Iran has taken over Iraq. Sheikh Jamal Khamis, a Sunnis tribal leader, said Qasim Soleimani and Islamic State of Iraq and Syria (ISIS) are the same and Iraqi Sunnis would refuse to fight ISIS if the alternative would be the prospect of living under Iranian hegemony. Sheikh Nawaf Hemoud al-Maghames, a Sunni tribal leader who tried to garner support for Iraqi Arab Sunnis from the Arab Gulf states, also pointed to the increasing role of Iran and the IRGC in Iraq (Younis, 2017, 123). These statements underline the perception held by many Arab Sunnis that Iran is a detrimental actor in Iraq and a threat to their security and interests. However, Iran has begun to build ties with some Arab Sunni figures, who became increasingly divided, including new emerging politicians to further secure its interests and appoint friendly Arab Sunni politicians in critical positions, who would not pose challenges for its policy in Iraq. For example, in 2018, a number of Iraqi Arab Sunni politicians, such as Jamal Karboli and businessman Khamis Khanjar (previously an enemy of al-Maliki), had shared interests with *Fatah*, a pro-Iran faction and militia led by Badr's leader al-Ameri, that formed pro-Iranian bloc *al-Bina* coalition in the ICR. Muhammad al-Halbusi, an Iraqi Arab Sunni lawmaker from Anbar, was supported by the Badr-led coalition to be Iraqi Speaker in 2018. Iran's interests in Iraq are to project power into Iraq, while checking the increasing influence of the United States, KSA, Turkey and other Arab states.

## Turkey and Iraq: Fluctuating relations

Turkey is the second most powerful regional actor in Iraq; their influence has been particularly felt in Erbil. Baghdad's and Ankara's regional policies and ruling political parties' ideologies and personalities have played a role in their relationship. Turkey maintained the operation of its embassy in Baghdad before and after the US invasion (Habeeb, 2012, 74). Post 2003, consulates opened in Mosul, Basra and Erbil, demonstrating Turkey's interests in Iraq (Republic of Turkey, Ministry of Foreign Affairs, 2015). In 2009, Erdogan and al-Maliki signed energy deals and attempted to cooperate on water sharing and fighting the Kurdish Workers Party (PKK). However, the effect of these deals faded due to accusations of sectarianism, Turkish interference in Iraq and different positions arising from the Syrian Civil War. Accusations were particularly fierce between Erdogan and al-Maliki and continued with Prime Minister al-Abadi.

Turkey's hosting of the fugitive former Iraqi vice president al-Hashimi worsened the bilateral relationship. During his premiership, al-Maliki called Turkey an 'enemy state' that interfered in the domestic affairs of its neighbour (Barkey, 2013; Cordesman and Khazai, 2014, 149). Erdogan responded: 'Al-Maliki should know this – if you start a period of conflict in Iraq with a sectarian struggle, it will be impossible for us to remain silent.' Al-Maliki's office stated that this was 'interference' in Iraq's affairs (Burch, 2012). The Iraq-Turkey relationship did not progress during al-Abadi's tenure, mainly because of the Turkish military presence in northern Iraq and KR-I, interference, support of a number of Arab Sunni figures and close ties with Erbil from 2007 until Kurdistan's referendum. The Shia-led government perceives Turkey's interests in Iraq as an attempt to control the energy-rich KR-I, Kirkuk and Mosul. Turkey's closest allies among Sunni leaders are, namely, the two brothers Atheel (the former Mosul governor) and former vice president Usama al-Nujaifi. Usama and Atheel established a higher coordination committee for Sunni factions and have connections with Turkish authorities (Ali and van den Toorn, 2015). Iraqi Shia policymakers publicly revealed the perception that Turkey utilizes the Sunnis and the Kurds against Iraqi interests. Iraqi officials view Turkey's policy as the rebirth of Ottoman domination, led by Erdogan in the region to subdue Mosul province.

The clashing policies of AKP and Baghdad towards the Syrian Civil War have worsened their already feeble rapport. Erdogan's and al-Maliki's policies stemmed from viewing each other through sectarian lenses, which deepened personal animosities. Former prime minister al-Maliki's allied pro-Iran Iraqi Shia militias are fighting alongside Assad's regime. For example, the AAH has sent fighters to Syria; their force is called Liwa Kafeel Zainab (Jihad Intel, 2015; Mapping Militants Organizations, 2015). Erdogan supports opposition groups, such as the Turkey-backed Free Syrian Army and Ahrar al-Sham, which fights Assad and his allies, including the Iraqi Shia militias (Heller and Stein, 2015; Cafarella, 2016; Alfoneh, 2017). The two leaders' opposing foreign policies in Syria damaged the bilateral relationship.

The relationship between Baghdad and Ankara further deteriorated in 2016, particularly when Erdogan insulted al-Abadi and the Turkish parliament extended its military involvement in Iraq. Subsequently, pro-Iran Iraqi Shia militias threatened to attack Turkish troops if they did not withdraw and/or participate in Mosul's liberation (al-Salhy, 2016; Mostafa, 2017). Military confrontations have not occurred between Baghdad and Ankara, although in 2016 and previous years Ankara and Baghdad summoned each other's ambassadors and condemned each other government's approaches, the diplomatic bilateral relationship survived.

During al-Abadi's tenure the hope of a stable relationship quickly evaporated; the regional struggle, the Turkish military presence in Bashiqa, the rise of Iranian proxies in Iraq and Baghdad's rejection of Turkey's participation in Mosul added to the strain. Erbil-Ankara energy and security ties, sectarianism, Turkey's interference in Iraq and elites' conflicting perceptions and interests shape Baghdad's policy towards Ankara. This has also had consequences on trade, investment and business between Baghdad and Ankara. Erbil has exceeded Baghdad in this respect, as Turkish business is more welcome. However, Kurdistan's referendum became a catalyst for rapprochement between Baghdad and Ankara as the latter are threatened by Kurdish ambitions for independence. Baghdad and Ankara's relationship stabilized and they coordinated to implement punitive measures against the KRG. For example, for a period of time Turkish airspace closed for all flights to and from the KR-I and Baghdad and Ankara's military forces held military drills at the Iraqi Kurdish-Turkish borders (Smith, 2017). Subsequently, the fragile relationship between the then prime minister al-Abadi and President Erdogan improved. Al-Abadi visited Ankara in August 2018 to discuss some of the contentious issues, such as operations against the PKK and Iraq's water crisis as Turkey has built a massive dam (*Daily News*, 2018; *Daily Sabah*, 2018). The revitalization of the relationship has not minimized the differences and critical pending issues between Ankara and Baghdad.

*The developing rapport between Turkey and the Kurdistan Regional Government*

Before the amicable relationship between Ankara and Erbil, Erdogan had been sceptical of engaging with Iraqi Kurds. He warned the Kurds not to play with fire in 2004 when he perceived the Kurdish parties (KDP and PUK) were close to the annexation of Kirkuk. Between 2005 and 2007, Ankara, particularly the Turkish military circles, viewed the KR-I from a counter-security perspective mainly because of the PKK. However, Erdogan's domestic politics had a more conciliatory tone about Iraqi Kurds and Erdogan led cautious talks to contact Iraqi Kurdish leaders. When the KRG managed to have a unified government and the Iraqi constitution recognized the KR-I in 2006 and Kurdish officials got senior critical positions in Baghdad (Kumral, 2016, 190, 191 and 192) the chances of rapprochement were imminent. This was particularly evident when Erbil sought a friendly relationship with Turkey and Turkey reciprocated (Cagaptay, 2017, 333).

Turkey and the KR-I's relationship should be analysed within the context of economics, geopolitics, security and the military, in which Turkey and the KRG's actors (mainly the KDP) are engaged. A limited, unofficial liaison has existed between the KDP, PUK and Turkey since the 1990s. A decade of distrust ended in 2007, when a rapprochement emerged after Kurdish initiatives and the first diplomatic Turkish delegations visited the KR-I in 2008. After an official meeting between Masoud Barzani and the former prime minister Ahmed Duvatogule, a Turkish consulate was opened in Erbil in July 2010 (KRG Cabinet, 2009). Ankara and Erbil's close ties have further contributed to the fluctuating Iraqi-Turkish relationship. When the KRG conducted its independence referendum in September 2017, its relationship weakened considerably but has been sluggishly recovering since 2018.

Turkey and the KR-I's relationship can be assessed in three areas: the economy, politics and security. Economically, Turkey is the KR-I's largest trade partner. The bilateral economic relations have covered almost all sectors in the KR-I – from energy (oil and gas, their extraction and developing strategic energy pipelines) to electricity, infrastructure, goods, healthcare, education, transport, agriculture, banking, tourism and small-to-large businesses. Turkish exports to KRG-governed areas in 2007 were US$1.4 billion; in 2013 they were US$8 billion, placing the KRG as Turkey's third largest export market (Cagaptay et al., 2015).

Turkish companies benefit from not only the KR-I's oil but also its gas sector; Turkish company Genel Energy has been developing gas fields, and it is expected that the gas will be exported into Europe via Turkey (Hacaoglu and Firat, 2014). Turkey saw the KR-I as a potential alternative to Russia for energy. In 2006, the KRG rewarded Turkish energy corporations for oil explorations to develop the Shiwaskok oil field for Genel Energy (Wahab, 2006). Turkish energy corporations such as Dogan Energy and Petoil also operated in the KR-I (Marco Polis, 2012; Iraq Business News, 2015). Baghdad was indignant about transnational energy corporations investing in the KR-I without its approval. From the KRG's perspective, the budgetary penalties Baghdad enforced on the KRG by cutting or limiting its 17 per cent share have justified independently exporting oil and monetizing routes through Turkey. The pressure Baghdad exerted backlashed by pushing the KRG closer to Turkey (Wahab, 2014). The central government's foreign policy towards Turkey was inflamed by accusations of interference in Erbil.

The strategic oil pipeline between the KR-I and Turkey is autonomous from the federal government. It lies in Taq Taq, close to Erbil, and even has its own independent metering station, which was completed in 2013 (Natali, 2013; US EIA, 2015). This is the second pipeline between the two countries, connected to Ceyhan and on the Iraqi-Turkey border (Natali, 2013). The older Kirkuk-Ceyhan pipeline is often disrupted, and the Kurdish factions controlled Kirkuk until October 2017 when it was retaken by Baghdad. The latter is enhancing its capacity with transnational energy corporations such as British Petroleum. A third new pipeline to export natural gas between Iraqi Kurdistan and Turkey is under development. These developments represent a deeper economic and energy integration stage between Erbil and Ankara. The fact that much of this is considered as interference attests to the divergence of economic policies between the KRG and the federal government. Turkey augmented the division in Iraq's foreign policies between

Baghdad and Erbil. It seeks to create a sphere of influence in the KR-I to further fulfil its interests. The mutually beneficial relationship provides the KRG with access to an economic power that consequently consolidated the KRG's political status and provided it with flimsy economic autonomy.

Masoud Barzani's visit to Diyarbakir alongside Erdogan in November 2013 had symbolic repercussions in Turkey and for the KRG's relationship and was part of their successful public relations. Erdogan sought to gain more Kurdish voters in 2013 by inviting Barzani into Diyarbaker and undermining the pro-Kurdish parties in Turkey (Winter, 2013, 32; Gunter, 2014, 23). Political, economic and security interests were embedded in their ties and cannot be analysed separately. One of the vital issues for Ankara and Erbil is the PKK as it poses a security and political challenge to Turkey and to the KDP, and as a result, the KDP does not resist Ankara's military operations against PKK (al-Arabiya, 2012; Korutürk, 2015).

Turkey's military intervention in Iraq goes back to the 1980s, when Saddam's regime and Ankara ratified a formal security cooperation agreement to attack or bomb the PKK in Iraq (al-Laythi and Zayer, 2012; Barham Salih, qtd in Sky News Arabia, 2015b). The Iraqi Kurdish Civil War in the mid-1990s facilitated Turkey's military presence in the KR-I, especially in the KDP-controlled areas. In 2015, Turkey had around three thousand troops in the KR-I, such as in Bamerni Airport and Kani Masi (Kasapoglu and Cagaptay, 2015). It has been shelling the PKK's bases and presence in the Qandil mountains in the KR-I and in other areas where they are allegedly operating, such as Choman and Rawaduz, which has resulted in civilian fatalities, damages and financial losses (Human Rights Watch, 2011; 2018). Although Baghdad's and Erbil's officials condemned the bombardment of civilians and the resulting damage (Pamuk and Kalin, 2015), the relationship between Erbil and Ankara continues.

In December 2015, Turkey sent reinforcements to Zilkan in northern Iraq, which already had forces there to train Peshmerga and Arab Sunni forces under the umbrella of 'National Mobilization' (*Hashd al-Watani*). Baghdad declared Turkey's actions to be a violation of its sovereignty, but Erbil did not object to Turkish troops (Ali and van den Toorn, 2015; Filkins, 2015; Knights, 2015b). Turkey's incursion was not only to fight Daesh. The KDP and Ankara were concerned about the rise of the PKK and Democratic Union Party (PYD) in fighting Daesh in Iraq, and their increasing popularity among a segment of Iraqi Kurdish society. The KDP and AKP enhanced their political rapprochement; the Turkish prime minister and president welcomed President Barzani to Ankara in 2015 and 2016 with Kurdish and Iraqi flags on the table – an uncommon gesture from Ankara. Despite Erdogan's public messages to cancel the referendum as well as Foreign Minister Cavusoglu and Chief of National Intelligence (MIT) Hakan Fidan being sent by Erdogan to Erbil in August and September 2017, respectively, to convince Masoud Barzani, he insisted on carrying out Kurdistan's referendum and the relationship became frigid (Uyanik, 2017).

Not all Iraqi Kurdish political factions depict Turkey as their political and security ally, although some of the PUK leadership openly disagree with former president Barzani's close ties with Turkey. The PUK and Ankara's relations are not as imperative as the KDP and AKP's. After the referendum Ankara opened its airspace to Erbil but not to the PUK's controlled areas (Sulaymaniyah International Airport) accusing the PUK of links with the PKK. President Salih and the PUK leaders sought to repair the relationship with Ankara and managed to persuade Turkey to open its airspace at the beginning of 2019. Traditionally, Ankara has tried to limit Iranian influence in Iraq, but after the KRG's referendum Ankara, Tehran and Baghdad united to implement punitive measures against the KR-I which were a setback for the KRG's regional relations. Ankara and Tehran do not want to destroy the entire political structure of the KR-I as the KDP and PUK have been friendly and cooperative neighbours.

In the rapport between the KRG and Ankara, economic, political, security and regional matters are interrelated. Interestingly, in 2016, Turkey approved the KRG's representations. This demonstrates slow diplomatic development compared to the significant mutual cooperation between Erbil and Turkey, highlighting Turkey's cautious political concessions to the KRG. Baghdad forthrightly resented Ankara's ties with Erbil and Arab Sunni factions, viewing them as interference in, and violation of, its sovereignty. Ankara's and Tehran's foreign policies towards Iraq and the KR-I are driven and shaped by security imperatives but also entail economic interest with lots of distrust on the part of Ankara.

*The Kingdom of Saudi Arabia and Iraq: An unstable shifting relationship*

Baghdad and Riyadh's fragile rapport includes resentment and suspicion, yet opportunities for détente have emerged since al-Abadi and Mohammad Bin Salman (MBS). Post 2003, the deceased king Abdullah reportedly criticized US officials for having 'allowed the Persians, the Safavids, to take over Iraq' (Betts et al., 2012, 187). Saudi rulers have perceived the changes in power and the political system in Iraq as a menace. The KSA is concerned about the influence of Iraqi Shia political factions and militias. The rise of the Shias would further provoke the Shia minority in the KSA – who have a tense relation with the monarchy and aspire to emulate the rise of the Iraqi Shia Arabs. The KSA views these as a threat to their national security (Stansfield, 2010a, 1407). Riyadh's fears have invigorated the KSA's foreign policy towards Iraq, and since 2015 when MBS took control of foreign policy making, a more engaging and broader approach has been pursued with various ethnic religious components in Iraq. MBS's foreign policy towards Iraq is considered pragmatic and conciliatory in comparison with a very different approach towards other regional states, such as the Saudi-led boycott of Qatar.

The KSA has been viewed as a defender of Sunni interests in Iraq (Alterman, 2007). In 2004, it proposed a plan for the creation of 'a Muslim international force' to help the UN and stabilize Iraq (Cordesman and Obaid, 2005, 2), which the United States and IIG rejected. This shows the KSA's attempt to obtain leverage in Iraq for its own ends. The KSA's position is clear: it asserts Iraq's unity as an Arab state free from Iranian influence (Cordesman, 2009, 26). Iraqi and Saudi government relations were very tense, especially between the KSA and the former prime minister al-Maliki's government (Stansfield, 2010a, 1407). Baghdad strongly believed that the Saudis had interfered with and provoked Iraq's Sunnis to oppose the Shia-led government. During his premiership, al-Maliki openly accused the KSA and Qatar of funding and supporting the Sunni insurgents; he believed they were deeply hostile towards the new Iraqi political system. Al-Maliki's discontent was pronounced when the Anbar rebellion began at the end of 2013. Al-Maliki said: 'They [the KSA and Qatar] have declared war on Iraq just as they have declared war on Syria' (MEMRI, 2014). Saudis believed the deterioration of Iraq's security was due to government discrimination against the Sunnis and the hostile military approach to dislodging Sunni demonstrations. The KSA sees the government's duty to be not blurring the line between the legitimate rights of the Sunnis and the extremists, such as Daesh.

The relationship between al-Maliki's government and the Saudi government was antagonistic; thus, Foreign Minister Zebari said in September 2009, 'There is a problem in Iraqi–Saudi relations' (Blanchard et al., 2009). Al-Abadi's government made some positive diplomatic progress; it sought to turn over a new leaf and normalize relationships with Riyadh. Iraq's and the region's instability hindered these efforts. In spite of attempts to rebuild ties after the toppling of Saddam, both sides were passive in approaching and understanding each other. In November 2014, Dr Wael Abdul Latif, a pro-Shia Iraqi politician and former minister, argued that the deterioration and ebb and flow of Iraqi and Saudi relations was due to some Iraqi government elites who represented Sunnis, such as a vice president or a minister, going to the KSA and sending messages that contradicted the Iraqi foreign minister's official message (Al-Fayhaa TV, 2014b). This symbolizes the incoherence of Iraq's foreign policies. The complexity of the feeble relationship involves dynamic changes of political power in Iraq and the fear of perceived Shiite expansion (*Al-Tamadud al-Shii*). The KSA's officials have bluntly accused Iran of detrimental interference in Iraq's affairs (Saadoun, 2016b). However, since 2015, increasingly more actors within Iraq and the KSA are seeking to improve bilateral relationships.

*The KSA's relationship with Sunni and Kurdish factions*

Especially before al-Abadi's government, the Shia-led government and Shia political elite constantly called on the KSA to stop supporting and financing the Sunni rebellion. Unidentified figures and wealthy individuals in the KSA are claimed to have provided financial and logistical support to some Sunni insurgent groups in Iraq (Kahl et al., 2008, 95; Baker and Hamilton, 2016). Iraqi officials stated that around US$25 million from the KSA funded top Sunni clerics in Iraq (Mansour, 2018). The KSA responded to the regional altercation by supporting some Arab Sunni forces in Iraq that oppose Iran (Gause, 2014, 191).

The KSA has had limited success, as their engagement in Iraq is far less than Iran's. The KSA has close ties with Iraqi-Arab Sunni elites, and tribes, which are spread across western Iraq and over the KSA's border. The Shammar tribe in Iraq extends into northern and central Saudi Arabia and the deceased king Abdulaziz

Abdullah had married a Shammar tribe member. These ties influenced how the KSA's rulers view Iraqi Sunnis, and Sunni leaders in other Arab countries pressured the Saudis to help Iraqi Sunnis (Ottaway, 2008, 241). When Ghazi al-Yawar, a prominent Shammar figure with close ties to the KSA's rulers, became Iraq's interim president, Riyadh unsurprisingly congratulated him. Other cross-border tribes, such as al-Anizah, have common interests and values. These cross-border links between the tribes could be described as 'tribal diplomacy' (al-Qassemi, 2012). The KSA provides intermittent funding and logistical support to Iraqi Sunni tribal leaders, and the Iraqi Sunni political elite encourage the KSA to develop close ties with Iraq. However, the KSA exerts limited influence on Iraq's tribes.

Former prime minister Allawi was believed to receive funding from the KSA for his political campaigns (Daragahi, 2014). Saudi diplomatic documents in Wikileaks show that Usama al-Nujaifi and Ayad Allawi received financial aid and privileges from the KSA (Hubbard, 2015; Rubin, 2015; Saleh, 2015). This caused an uproar in Iraqi media and politics. The KSA's financial aid also included the awakening movement (*Sahawat*) (Blanchard et al., 2009). Beyond the validity and integrity of the documents, this could be a realistic policy that the KSA adopted and Sunni leaders accepted. Al-Iraqiya gained the most seats in the Iraq national election in 2010; this was seen as a victory for the KSA and other Arab Gulf States who financed them (Mansour and Jabar, 2017, 9). Baghdad is aware that the KSA could have an influence on Iraqi Sunni elites due to the aforementioned links.

The aftermath of the attack on the al-Askari holy Shia shrine in Samarra resulted in Iraqi Shia militias retaliating against Sunni mosques and civilians. In February 2006, the Saudi imam of the Holy Mosque of Mecca granted support to the Iraqi Sunnis and condemned Shia attacks against Sunnis. The Saudi monarchy agreed with the imam (Alshamsi, 2011, 180). In October 2006, thirty-eight prominent Saudi religious figures signed a petition calling on Sunnis everywhere to oppose a joint 'Crusader [United States], Safavid [Iran] and Rafidi [derogatory term of Shiite] scheme' that targeted Iraqi-Arab Sunnis (Blanchard, 2008, 5). The Iraqi Shia and Shia-led government believe anti-Shia statements encourage instability and worsen bilateral relationships. Some Iraqi Shias see the KSA as promoting Wahhabism and Salafism among Iraqi Sunnis. However, Wahhabism and Salafism have some historical links to Iraq (Leaman, 2006, 283; McCants, 2015). While the KSA rejects these allegations, Saudi clerics such as Grand Mufti Shaykh Abd al Aziz have released religious judgements stating that travel to Iraq for the purpose of participating in violent activity is illegitimate (Blanchard, 2008, 5; Blanchard et al., 2009). However, Iraq has raised concerns over the hateful statements of some Saudi Sunni clerics and a number of Saudi fighters in Iraq who joined Daesh (Rogers, 2014; Bunzel, 2015; Atwan, 2015). The federal government in Baghdad's execution and torture of Saudi prisoners who were part of terrorist organizations, such as Daesh, without the KSA's approval/coordination has also added to the deterioration of the bilateral relationship between Baghdad and Riyadh (Saadoun, 2016a).

The KSA's ties with Iraqi Kurdish leaders and officials in Baghdad and Erbil are in a better condition than its ties with many of Shia-led government elites' tenures.

In 2010, the now deceased Saudi king Abdullah awarded Jalal Talabani with the King Abdullah Aziz Medal, and President Barzani also received an honour (*Asharq Al-Awsat*, 2010; *EKurd Daily*, 2010). According to documents Wikileaks released in June 2015, the KSA's Ministry of Foreign Affairs indicates the importance of having a close relationship with Barzani against al-Maliki. Another document reveals Saudi donations of US$500,000 to the Kurdish Islamic movement in Iraqi Kurdistan (*EKurd Daily*, 2015; Rubin, 2015). The Kurdistan Islamic Union (KIU; *Yekgirtu*) and Islamic factions in Iraqi Kurdistan had links with some figures in the KSA (Ali, 2015; Sherko, 2016). Several of the KSA's humanitarian NGOs (such as the International Islamic Relief Organization of Saudi Arabia) operate in Iraq, including in the KR-I (Egatha, 2016).

In 2015, the then president Barzani visited the KSA, where speculation about financial aid for the region was expected. Despite excellent relations with Iraqi Kurdish leaders and Riyadh's aim to have an internal ally to counterbalance pro-Iranian actors in Iraq, the KSA affirmed Iraq's territorial integrity and opposed Kurdistan's referendum. Unlike other Arab Gulf countries such as the United Arab Emirates, the KSA did not invest in the KR-I; its interests to invest in Iraqi Kurdistan's business, oil and infrastructure materialized when the bilateral relationship with Baghdad improved. In July 2018, an official Saudi delegation including the president of the Saudi Chambers of Commerce and businessmen visited the KR-I and met KRG officials and businessmen to explores investment opportunities.

*Slow progress in fragile diplomacy*

Iraq's diplomatic relations with the KSA were severed during the Iraqi invasion of Kuwait in 1990 until 2004, when bilateral ties were partially restored. Diplomatic relations somewhat resumed in 2012, when the KSA appointed a non-resident Saudi ambassador to Iraq, who was based in Amman (Intelligence Unit/*Economist*, 2015). Al-Abadi's tenure signalled mutual improvements; the former Saudi foreign minister Saud al-Faisil publicly welcomed al-Abadi's appointment in 2014. Iraqi officials visited the KSA, and al-Sistani called for Iraqi-Saudi rapprochement (Baghdad Akhbaria, 2014; Mamouri, 2014). Although the I-MOFA announced its readiness to prepare for opening a Saudi embassy in Baghdad during al-Maliki's tenure, al-Abadi's government stimulated the relationship.

The Iraqi government appointed Ambassador Rushdi al-Ani to the KSA, who arrived in Riyadh in September 2015. After twenty-five years, the KSA named its ambassador to Iraq, Thamer al-Sabhan, in June 2015. The ambassador, embassy staff and the officer in charge arrived in Baghdad in December 2015 (Ain Iraqi News, 2015; al-Bawaba, 2015). In that month, the Saudi embassy started diplomatic work in Baghdad, and in 2016 a consulate was opened in Erbil (Basnews, 2015; Mustafa, 2015). The opening of a consulate and an operating Saudi embassy in Baghdad after years of disrupted relations underlines the cautious diplomatic restoration, which both countries have described as delayed. Since 2003, many senior high-level Iraqi officials have visited the KSA, but fewer and lower-ranking Saudi officials have visited Iraq; however, in October 2017, Saudi oil minister Khalid Falih visited Baghdad for economic cooperation. This illustrates the KSA's hesitation and confined attitude towards developing relationships with the central government until the cautious shift in 2015. However, the KSA's first ambassador to Iraq since 1990, Thamer al-Sabhan, left the country at the request of the Iraqi government following diplomatic tensions and his statements regarding the PMF, which were seen as interference in Iraqi internal affairs (*Daily Star*, 2016). In November 2017, the KSA announced its new ambassador Abdul Aziz al-Shammari, who had been charge affairs of the Saudi embassy since October 2016.

Post 2003, Iraqi delegations to the KSA have mainly been divided between the Shia-led government, Sunnis and KRG officials. The split in Iraq's delegations and contradictory statements to the KSA have resulted in the KSA losing respect for the federal government, particularly during al-Maliki's government. This exposed Iraq's fragmentation and allowed the Saudis to match their interests with the Sunnis, Kurds and Shias – since MBS's rise to power – some Shia figures such as Haider al-Abadi and Muqtada al-Sadr and Prime Minister al-Mahdi have improved the bilateral relationship. Despite the improving rapport regionally, there is a significant divergence in the foreign policy interests of Riyadh and the Shia-led government in, for example, Syria, Yemen and Bahrain. Iraq's deep-rooted relationship with Iran is an obstacle to further develop the KSA and Iraq's bilateral relationship. Both have fundamental differences regarding who they believe should be in power, how the political system should be and which factions to back. Scrutiny of the conflicting actors in Syria shows that powerful Shia officials in Baghdad back Shia and Shia leaning armed factions, whereas the KSA supported some Sunni armed factions such as Jaysh al-Islam (Islamic Army). In the Arab League meeting in March 2015, Iraq officially rejected Saudi-led military intervention in Yemen. Shia-led government elites have overt relationships with Houthi leaders – the KSA's enemies – in Yemen, who visited Baghdad in 2016. As the threat of Daesh evolved since 2014, so did mutual national security threats, cooperation on which could have been a basis for mutual understanding as the KSA's counterterrorism policy recognized and participated in the war against Daesh.

Despite their disparate regional views, Prime Minister al-Abadi pursued reparation of the bilateral relationship and aimed to reduce animosities between Riyadh and Tehran, or at least to avoid allowing Iraq to become a theatre of conflict between them. Pro-Iran Shia militias in Iraq who are vehemently against the KSA have been antagonizing and trying to worsen the bilateral relationship between Baghdad and Riyadh. Although Iraq and the KSA share a 1,000-km border and both are major OPEC members, since 1990, for twenty-seven years, there was no direct trade; they traded via Jordan and Kuwait (al-Jumaili, 2016). This reduced the KSA's influence on Iraq's political dynamics, until al-Abadi's tenure. Both countries then began to prepare to open their land crossings for trade, for example, the Arar border crossing (which was previously open only once a year during Hajj), and have direct flights between Jeddah and Baghdad in 2017. Sixty Saudi firms participated in Baghdad's forty-fourth Baghdad International Fair in October 2017. Iraq and the KSA set up a cooperation council which held its first meeting on 22 October 2017, attended by leaders of both countries as well as the former US secretary of state Rex Tillerson. The purpose of this council is to develop relations and facilitate work on the common interests of both countries.

A dynamic of competition between Iraq and the KSA is petroleum energy. Friction over oil policy goes back to the end of the Iran-Iraq War, when Iraq expected the KSA to maintain high oil prices as Iraq was in huge debt (McMillan, 2006). In recent years, Iraq has competed with the KSA in oil production. The International Energy Agency (IEA) stated that Iraq had overtaken the KSA as the second largest seller after Russia in Europe (Lawler and Gamal, 2015; Trade Arabia, 2015). The giant oil producers' competition involves different visions regarding OPEC's policy, oil production levels, competitive pricing and the struggle to obtain shares in the international market (Zaaiter, 2012; Oil Price, 2015). Iraqi and Saudi oil policies became competitive. A narrow and temporary compromise on oil policy is likely to be achieved by negotiation as part of economic diplomacy and detente.

The fragile relationship between Iraq and the KSA is multifold and involves political and sectarian issues, combating terrorism, regional policy and natural resources. Before Prime Minister Abadi and MBS, the KSA's influence in Iraq was on Arab Sunnis and segments of Iraqi Kurds; since both leaders pursued the repair of the relationship and key actors such as Muqtada al-Sadar supported this, a new cautiously optimistic era of diplomacy has begun. However, Riyadh's involvement in Iraq was not strategic, and attempts to influence Iraq's foreign policy to their interests have not been fruitful so far and also lacked investment in many areas, including the economy.

## *Syria and Iraq: A shifting relationship*

Before and post 2003, the Baghdad-Damascus bilateral relationship was characterized by distrust and an unfavourable rapport. Since the onset of the Syrian Civil War they have become friends and to some extent allies. Saddam and former Syrian president Hafez al-Assad were from rival camps in the Arab Socialist Ba'ath Party *Hizb al-Ba'ath al-A'rabi al-Ishtiraki* of Iraq and Syria, respectively, and both competed for regional leadership. In 1979, Saddam thwarted a plan between former Iraq president Hassan Bakr and al-Assad for a union which would give the more experienced leader al-Assad the upper hand (Dawisha, 2009, 214). In August 1980, the bilateral relationship worsened and diplomatic relations were severed after accusations of plots against each other (Alasdair, 1992, 351), and when the Iran-Iraq War began Damascus sided with Iran. Damascus used to tacitly interfere in Iraqi politics and challenge Saddam's regime. It was not in their foreign policy interests to seek Saddam's removal from power, but they used the Iraqi opposition to weaken Saddam's regime. The Syrian regime had little interest in strengthening the Iraqi opposition (Scheller, 2013, 170) to the extent that the destabilization of Iraq would affect the region, including Syria. While Syria's Hafez al-Assad participated in US-led efforts to liberate Kuwait in 1991, his son, President Bashar al-Assad, opposed Iraq's invasion in 2003 and pursued an anti-US occupation rhetoric (171).

*Syria and Iraq post Saddam*

After overthrowing Saddam, the United States made non-negotiable demands for Syria to simply give up all its cards and limit its regional ambitions (Hinnebusch, 2014c, 228).[2] However, Syria conducted a two-faced foreign policy: overtly, it was bandwagoning with the United States' demands and diplomatically engaging with Iraq while covertly pursuing the destabilization of Iraq to hamper the US state-building project. Syria allowed Iraqi insurgent groups to operate and acted as a transmission belt for weapons and infiltrating terrorists to fuel the insurgency (Cordesman, 2006, 331). Syria hosted ex-Ba'athists (the wing of Izzat Ibrahim al-Douri and Ahmed Younis), senior ex-intelligence officers and Iraqi insurgent factions. For example, the Political Council for the Iraqi Resistance was conducting activities against Iraq and the US troops (Yacoubian, 2011, 152; Webb et al., 2014, 9 and 10). The Iraqi government and the United States depicted the Syrian sponsorship of the Iraqi opposition in Syria as blatant interference in Iraq's domestic affairs. Syria cautiously engaged with the IIG and restored full diplomatic ties in November 2004 (Prados and Sharp, 2005, 18).

The Syria-Iraq relationship see-sawed from 2003 until the Syrian Civil War. Embassies in both Baghdad and Damascus officially reopened in 2006, following a boycott that began during the Iran-Iraq War. Syrian policy towards Iraq repeatedly used the new post-Saddam Iraqi opposition in Syria to bolster its agenda for covert and clandestine activities in Iraq. Meanwhile, Syria pursued economic interests, including energy benefits, from Iraq. Bilateral relations began to improve when the two countries exchanged a series of dignitary visits, including former prime minister al-Maliki and former foreign minister Zebari. Nine memorandums of understanding and cooperation were signed in 2009, including a security file (terrorism), border control, trade and an energy pipeline (Al-Fayhaa TV, 2009; al-Alkim, 2012, 54).

However, after a series of devastating explosions in 2009, the relationship deteriorated. In September 2009, the Iraqi government said it had evidence of Syrian involvement in bombing in Iraq (Security Council Report, 2009). Al-Maliki sent a letter to the UN to nominate a senior international envoy to come to Iraq and evaluate the degree of interference. Both countries recalled their envoys after a short period. The federal government clashed internally over Syria's alleged involvement in the 2009 explosions. Iraq's Presidency Council rejected the government's internationalization of terrorism against Syria. Al-Maliki accused Iraqi ex-Ba'athists in Syria of involvement in the explosions and called for involvement of the International Criminal Court (Al-Arabiya, 2009; *Asharq Al-Awsat Arabic*, 2009). However, in October 2009, Iraqi former president Jalal Talabani addressed the General Assembly and again requested an investigation into foreign involvement in Iraq for bombing – without accusing any particular country, in contrast to al-Maliki (Security Council Report, 2016). Syrian interference in the new Iraq was a destabilizing factor, primarily in a security context. Iraqi ex-Ba'athists, elements in al-Qaeda in Iraq (AQI) and Iraqi insurgents had links to Assad's regime post Saddam (Mauro, 2009). Assad's regime turned a blind eye towards the infiltration of insurgents who were based in Syria to attack the US military and Iraqi government (Katzman, 2008; Mauro, 2009). Syria tacitly played a role in Iraqi politics, and during the parliamentary elections in 2010 it tried to find powerful political partners. Damascus got closer to some *al-Iraqiyya* leaders and brokered a meeting between Ayad Allawi and Muqtada al-Sadr. Ironically, before the Syrian Civil War, Bashar al-Assad was a part of the Iraqi political theatre siding with Iraqi Sunni actors who were supported by Turkey and a number of Arab Gulf States (Hinnebusch, 2014a, 20). The Syrian Civil War moved Assad's alliances in Iraq to the Shia.

*Syria and Iraq during the Syrian Civil War*

The Syrian uprising led to a shift in the relationship to the beginning of fresh rapprochement in Iraqi-Syrian relations. Al-Maliki changed his position to support the Syrian regime – partly because of his sectarian regional views, as allegedly Assad was combating Sunni jihadists. The Iraqi government gave moral support and turned a blind eye towards Iraqi Shia fighters going to Syria (Smyth, 2015), as well as to Iranian flights in Iraqi airspace that purportedly consisted of military equipment. Sunni regional powers placed Syria in a stranglehold; its survival relied on Hezbollah to the west, and Iran and Iraq to the east (Hinnebusch, 2014c, 230) and undoubtedly Russia's heavy military intervention further consolidated the regime. The Syrian Civil War was a catalyst for Iran-backed Iraqi Shia militias to send fighters to Syria, supposedly with the intention of defending al-Sayidda Zaynab Shrine (an important Shia site).

There has been a friendly shift – partly influenced by Iran – in Baghdad's foreign policy towards the Syrian regime since the beginning of the Civil War. Iraq abstained from voting for Syria's suspension from the Arab League in 2011. The change in Baghdad's strategic thinking towards Syria demonstrates the domination of Shia Islamists in Baghdad (al-Khoei, 2013). However, in 2012, Iraq voted in favour of the UN resolution to end the violence in Syria, while Iran was one of thirteen nations that voted against (United Nations, 2012). This is an example of Iraq demonstrating some independence in its foreign affairs.

Compared to al-Maliki, al-Abadi sought to pursue a less vocal and mediating diplomatic posture on Syria. He said: 'The current trend is that Daesh is the most dangerous group in Syria, not the regime' (Charbel, 2015). Al-Abadi's government channelled messages from the US-led coalition to Assad's regime about the fight against Daesh. He was under constant pressure from powerful pro-Iran Shia militias to take a closer position to Assad. Opening the intelligence-sharing centre, in which Syria was participating, was also a step towards a closer rapport with Assad. Baghdad's foreign policy towards Syria continues to be a subset of domestic politics, which does not favour Western interests in Syria (Mardini,

2015). Baghdad's stance on Syria is fundamentally different from that of Turkey and the KSA, which actively worked for regime change. Most of the Sunni elite and factions in Baghdad disagreed with al-Maliki's and al-Abadi's positions on Syria. Vice President al-Nujaifi said:

> The parliament was not consulted by the government to construct an approach towards Syria, the Iraqi political forces are divided between supporters and opponents of the Syrian regime that back the Syrian uprising ... I recommend that the Iraqi government avoid interfering in Syria ... no militias or arming of the Syrian regime. (Al-Jazeera Arabic, 2014)

Many Iraqi Sunnis want a regime change in Damascus and share similar grievances with the Syrian Arab Sunnis and rebels. AQI and other Iraqi Sunni militant groups began directing their efforts to Syria when the revolution started. Iraqi tribal Sunni and Shia Arab leaders in Iraq indicate that neither all Sunni tribes nor an entire clan is with Daesh or other militants in Iraq or Syria. The confederation of tribes extends into Iraq, Syria and other Arab countries and includes tribes such as the Baggara, Dulaim, Jabbour, N'eim, Qugaidat, Shammar and Tai'e. The Iraqi-Syrian tribes between the Tigris and Euphrates Rivers, known as the Jazirah (meaning 'island'), have maintained tribal ties (Knights, 2012). This demonstrates Iraq and Syria's Sunni kinship and sociopolitical and security links that connect both countries' populations.

The KRG's KDP-dominated foreign policy towards Syria is in line with the policy of the Arab states and Turkey, not with Baghdad's, and both the PUK and KDP played a role in Syria, particularly relating to various factions of Syrian Kurds: the PYD and Kurdish National Council, respectively. The lack of consensus among Arab Shia, Arab Sunni and Kurdish elites and factions shows the different agendas, interests and objectives towards Syria.

Before the Syrian Civil War, Assad's regime interfered in Iraq using Iraqi ex-Ba'athists, extremists and angry dissent to destabilize Iraq. In a striking reversion, elements of some Iraqi and Iraqi Kurdish factions became involved actors in the Syrian political scene. Baghdad's foreign policy during the Syrian Civil War sympathized with the Syrian regime, in which various Iraqi centres of power in Iraq (including Shia militias) played a remarkable role in shaping Baghdad's foreign policy towards Syria. The fragmentation of Syria exacerbated the divisions in Iraq's foreign policies, which has led to clearer but contradictory interests in Syria.

## *Conclusion*

On studying Iraq's interactions with Iran, Turkey, the KSA and Syria, the circumstances of their bilateral relationships and regional forces' internal allies in Iraq, we learn that external interference and influence on Iraq have both contributed to and exacerbated the fragmentation of its foreign policies. Safa

Hussein argues that regional actors justify their interference in Iraq's domestic politics via internal actors seeking external or regional support (Sirri et al., 2013, 15). Internal actors facilitate external states' influence and interference on Iraqi political, security and economic spheres that directly or indirectly affect foreign policy decision-making.

External interference and influence have contributed to the hindrance of state building and the thwarting of a coherent domestic and foreign policy. This external interference is also a result of the fragmented weak state of Iraq. Post Saddam, external influence and interference have been aggrandized and facilitated by distrust between Iraqi elites and political factions. The different political identities in Iraq have furthered the access of regional forces. In many cases, major Iraqi political factions and their figures have stronger relations with regional forces than with the federal government in Baghdad. Iraq has become a battlefield for external forces' rivalled interests and agendas. Iraqi relationships with external powers are for personal and partisan interests and seeking power, but they are also shaped by sectarianism, security, regional rivalry and economy. An Iraqi actor (an elite or a political faction) involved in foreign policy making may have ties and affinity with any one of the opposing powerful neighbouring countries. Accordingly, the actor might present a different formula and picture of how bilateral relationships, foreign relations and foreign policy are and should be.

Tangible interference in and influence on Iraq's domestic politics and policymaking, from the most to the least forceful, can be examined by the strength of external powers and internal allies and their impact on policymaking. The degree of external interference depends on the clout of the domestic actors, which eases penetration and the regional powers' strength and interests. Iran and Turkey have powerful internal allied actors with strong mutual interests. As a result Iran and Turkey are directly and indirectly the most influential regional states in the internal politics and external behaviour of the KRG and the federal government. Both states' strategic and powerful internal allies have contributed to them becoming the most potent external actors in Iraq. Their attempts at interference have further divided the ethno-sectarian political elites and factions therein. Iranian and Turkish interference leads to the conclusion that both countries check each other in Iraq. Traditionally, Tehran's and Ankara's approaches differ in terms of which sociopolitical component they target. Iran uses its religious relationship with the Shias and their fear of the return of the Sunnis to exert real power, both on security and throughout the state apparatus. It is increasingly utilizing Iraq's economic sphere, particularly since Trump withdrew from the nuclear deal. Turkey pursues an offensive economic and security policy (International Crisis Group, 2012) with the KRG. The AKP's economic policy is married with the KR-I. Ankara's political and security cooperation with some Iraqi Kurdish factions and Arab Sunni factions is there to serve their interests. Turkey has provided an opportunity for the KRG to thrive economically. Turkey and Iran seek to influence both Baghdad's and Erbil's foreign policies. Since September 2017, Ankara has tilted slightly towards the federal government in Baghdad and found common ground with Iran, particularly in restraining the Iraqi Kurds from achieving independence. Iran is the biggest stakeholder in Baghdad and the Shia areas and has increasingly sought to strengthen its ties with the Kurdish rulers and the KRG as well as begun to approach some of the Sunni Arab figures. While Turkey is the largest stakeholder in the KR-I and Sunni-dominated regions, it gradually seeks to improve its relationship with Baghdad. Although it maintains a close relationship with Erbil, they are also curbing the Kurds' ambitions of independence. Despite Iran's and Turkey's competing interests, both agree on the principle of a united and integrated Iraq and a power-limited KRG.

The KSA's influence on Iraqi Sunni actors should not be underestimated; they play a role in supporting Iraqi Sunni interests. The KSA and Turkey might have similar interests in Iraq by supporting Arab Sunnis (since MBS and Qatar's boycott they target rival Sunni factions), and they also have common interests in reducing Iranian leverage in Iraq, as this clashes with their interests. Since former prime minister Haider al-Abadi and MBS rose to power, Baghdad and Riyadh's relationship improved. The Iraqi Shia house has further fragmented and polarized between pro-Iran and the other Shia factions, such as Muqtada's faction which approached the Arab states including the KSA. Thenceforth, Riyadh has seized this opportunity and begun to focus on Baghdad and further improve its ties with Erbil.

Apart from Kuwait, none of the regional states desired the overthrowing of Saddam (Fawcett, 2013, 231). Post Saddam, each regional power has different degrees of interference and influence in Iraq's internal affairs. Post 2003, Iran is the most powerful external force in Iraq; it has an influence on all Iraq's vital sectors, politics and, to a certain degree, policymaking. Iran has expanded its spheres of influence in Iraq through its consistent, multilayer, in-depth strategy and use of its old and new Iraqi friends to gain internal leverage. It has clients and allies in Iraq's security and military apparatus, Iraqi Shia Islamic political parties and their armed wings (excluding al-Sistani and al-Sadr) and elements of Baghdad's governmental structure. Some Shia militias and groups who have political and ideological links with Iran have conducted de facto foreign relations and statements, which differ to al-Abadi's and Prime Minister al-Mahdi. The relatively modern orientations of Al-Abadi and his successor Adil Abd al-Mahdi are in contrast with pro-Iran Iraqi Shia militias. The latter oppose and threaten the engagement of the United States, Turkey and the KSA and encourage the involvement of Iran, Lebanon's Hezbollah and Russia in Iraq. Geopolitics plays a role, as Iran has a long border with Iraq. Furthermore, the shared Shia sect in the Sunni-dominated Islamic world has pulled them closer. The Shia-led government and Tehran have a common vision in regional affairs, such as in Syria and Yemen. While Iran has consolidated and is sustaining its relationships with Shia militias and their political wings, they have also approached the Kurds and recently some Arab Sunnis.

After the US withdrawal, Baghdad's foreign policy, particularly al-Maliki's, has been viewed as closer to Iran whereas al-Abadi and al-Mahdi have been portraying a relatively independent but weak foreign policy. The Shia-led government has driven this trajectory, rather than Iraq's entire elite or political factions as a whole. There are Iraqi officials, politicians and diplomats from various ethno-sectarian and political backgrounds, but the majority of Sunnis and Kurds disagreed with Iraq leaning towards the Iranians during al-Maliki's tenure. In interviews, they occasionally displayed contrasting views to those of the Shia-led government's orientations, as well as in public statements. Iran's influence and interference should not be overstated, as key decision-makers (such as al-Abadi and al-Mahdi) have a degree of independence. However, they take Iranian interests and inclinations into consideration in their foreign policy decisions, because Iran is of significance to Iraq and there are powerful Iranian allies in Iraq.

Iran's influence in the KR-I is limited, but to a certain extent tangible in defined issues and territories. It does not always succeed in achieving its goals. The PUK has been considered friendlier to Iran than other Kurdish parties, but after the referendum of 2017 the KDP and Iran began to improve their relationship. Iran's commitment to Baghdad and fear of Kurdish ambitions for independence has restrained Iranian leverage in the KR-I. Interestingly, the Shia-led government has not considered Iranian-Kurdish security ties as interference in Iraq's internal affairs. External interferences are a continuation of regional forces' ties with Iraqi political diaspora, which persisted after the toppling of Saddam.

Al-Maliki frequently accused all neighbouring and regional states (excluding Iran) of interference. In his era, major regional Sunni states were deplored with undiplomatic language for hosting exiled or opposition groups and organizing events regarding Iraq's internal affairs without Baghdad's consent. The Kurdish officials in Baghdad during al-Maliki's tenure, especially Iraq's former president Jalal Talabani, tried to take a moderate stance on regional and international issues. Their acumen, diplomatic behaviour and political weight usually protected them from political confrontations with al-Maliki.

Al-Maliki's and al-Abadi's governments depicted Turkey's close energy and political relationship with the KRG as interference in Iraq's internal affairs. As they have been sidelined, Baghdad denounced and rejected the energy ties between Ankara and Erbil. Baghdad views Ankara as a sectarian regional power that is encouraging the splitting up of Iraq and hankers for Iraq's resources. The Shia-led government depicts Turkey – especially Erdogan and the AKP – as exploiting Baghdad's inability to extend its authority and build economic and political ties with Iraqi Kurdistan. After September 2017, Turkey began to lean towards Baghdad while sustaining its beneficial relationship with the KR-I; likewise Erbil endures Turkey's relationship as it is vital for the KR-I. Turkey has actively supported a number of Arab Sunni political elites and factions; it has interests in the majority Arab Sunni regions in Iraq, including in determining the future of Mosul. Some Arab Sunnis, such as al-Nujaifi, see Turkey as a key external partner to balance against the Shia-led government's domination. However, Baghdad increasingly acknowledges the importance of Turkey's relationship to counterbalance the rise of the KRG as well as for water resources.

Regionally, al-Abadi was more accepted than al-Maliki; nevertheless, his political affiliations to the Da'wa Party somewhat slowed his progress in the view of many regional Sunni states. Since al-Abadi, Iraq's relationship with the KSA has progressed as Baghdad and Riyadh see the importance of the bilateral relationship, but it is fragile due to regional turbulence, the KSA's previous alleged support of the rebellious Sunni tribes and pro-Iran Shia militias' anti-KSA stance. Regional turbulence reflects on bilateral relationships; Baghdad portrays the KSA's anti-Houthi war in Yemen and its support of Sunni Islamist rebels in Syria as aggressive intervention. Meanwhile, the Shia-led government depicts Iran's military aid for Damascus and the Houthi as support for the victims of the Saudi-led Sunni states' military campaign. The relationship between Baghdad and Damascus changed from enmity before the Syrian Civil War to affinity after the war, and from Syrian interference to destabilize Iraq before the war to Iraqi support for Assad's regime and Iraqi pro-Iran Shia militias' interferences against the Sunni rebels since the war.

After al-Maliki, the federal government determined a path that leans towards utilizing diplomacy and soft power, projecting engagement and looking for common ground, including with regional states, combating terrorism and attracting the Western powers for military support. The complexity of Iraq's new political system, which is based on the quota system, has further bolstered external interference but secured each ethnic sectarian political faction to be a stakeholder in the state. Divisions between influential political elites in foreign affairs in Baghdad have manifested in more regional than international affairs. There are divisions among the Iraqi political class on which state is an ally, friend or enemy. The majority of Iraqi Islamic Shia parties see Turkey as an unwelcome meddling power, while a segment of the Kurds, represented by the KDP, sees Turkey as a counterweight to Baghdad – or at least, a closer partner than Baghdad, particularly before the referendum. Furthermore, a number of Iraqi Shia elites, for example, from al-Fatah alliance, see Iran as a strategic ally – or at least not a threat – to Iraq, while Iraqi-Arab Sunnis view the KSA or other Arab states as an ally.

Iraq is still debating the kinds of relationships it should have with regional and international forces. Examining its relationships with its neighbours shows fluctuations in different cases and over different time periods. Iraq's relationships with regional powers are not static and are significantly influenced by domestic politics, Iraqi elites, regional struggles and dynamics, in which non-state actors have increased their influence. As a result of external interferences and influences, sovereign decision-making regarding foreign policy is viewed as a non-independent process. Since the rise of tensions between Trump's administration and Iran, this matter has become a scorching subject that affects Iraq's security and stability. While Baghdad cooperates with Iran more than with any other regional state, some regional states have shown interest in constructive engagements as they might offer a way out of Iraq's lingering problems if Iraq and the neighbouring states find strategic common ground.

# CONCLUSION: THE CLOSING OF THE SAGA OF IRAQ'S FOREIGN POLICIES

Post 2003, foreign policy making denotes a new epoch in Iraq's politics. The tenuous process has endured setbacks and significant hurdles that have led to unconventional and weak policymaking. Iraq has splintered foreign policies. The two governments (the sovereign federal government in Baghdad and the non-sovereign Kurdistan Regional Government of Iraq (KRG) in Erbil) both formulate separate foreign policies. Foreign policy in Iraq is made purely by elites, backed by their political factions; these elites and factions use executive and/or bureaucratic bodies, including their resources and network. The federal government's foreign policy is incoherent, and a number of their foreign policy actors contradict the official foreign policy position (the contradictions slowly reduced after al-Maliki's premiership), whereas the KRG's foreign policy actors are relatively coherent but only at a governmental level. The KRG, on a partisan and security apparatus level, is uncoordinated and, to a certain degree, the Kurdish factions have competing external relations.

The Iraqi prime minister has the highest executive power; he orchestrates and leads the federal government's foreign policy making, while the KRG's president (until Masoud Barzani's resignation in November 2017) orchestrates and leads that of the KRG. In Baghdad, foreign policy making progresses through very weakly coordinated elites and core executive bodies, including the prime minister, president, foreign minister and Iraqi Ministry of Foreign Affairs (I-MOFA). The Iraqi Council of Representatives (ICR) and its Foreign Relation Committee (FRC) also have a degree of involvement; they can disturb or support executive actions. The position of Speaker of the ICR is allocated to members of the Arab Sunni political factions, which have increasingly engaged in foreign relations due to *al-Muhasasa*. Baghdad's prime minister is supported or constrained by key bureaucratic bodies, elites, prominent figures, the ICR and political factions (some of which possess militias). Discordant elites, poor bureaucratic performance and domestic instability shape the federal government's incoherent foreign policy. The constitutional powers and positions have laid out the generic framework for foreign policy making, but contradictions within it, lack of detail, different interpretations and cherry-picking by elites and political factions mean the constitution is unable to resolve the dilemma in policymaking. Schisms in foreign policy emerge from the interests of elites and parties, as well as ethno-sectarian and sectoral drivers, which have become increasingly divided within each communal component. When conducting foreign and bilateral relations, there is some space for bargains and compromises between elites and their political parties that has gradually led to cross-ethnic sectarian agreements purely based on interests and cutting deals. However, discussion between and within elites and their parties does not change their foreign relations and policy position unless their personal and partisan interests are achievable. As such, the Iraqi public's interest does not drive Iraq's foreign policies; this was more salient during al-Maliki's tenure. Although Iraq managed to restore its ties with global and regional powers and has relationships with adversarial bedfellows such as Iran and the Kingdom of Saudi Arabia (KSA), Baghdad is still trying to figure out its position on regional and international platforms and through its foreign policy to maintain government and state survival.

Ayad Allawi's government tried to mend Iraq's decades of isolation with openness towards both the Arab world and the West. Al-Jaafari's government represented the beginning of the Shia era in determining Baghdad's foreign policy. Al-Maliki attempted to project a vision of a strong, centralized government; he sidelined his opponents from the government and further deepened the splintering of foreign policies between Baghdad and Erbil. Haider al-Abadi's government tried to portray a more coherent foreign policy. Although, initially, al-Abadi's position was feeble domestically due to the lack of solid political backing from his faction, externally he was by far better received than al-Jaafari and al-Maliki. Al-Abadi's successor Adil Abd al-Mahdi inherited a position that has even less political backing.

Iraqi elites and political factions pursue their partisan and self-interests through their relationships with foreign states. Although al-Mahdi's government appears to be non-partisan and non-parochial, he is under tremendous pressure from partisan actors. Key elites and factions simultaneously influence Iraqi policymaking with their grassroots supporters and/or government networks, which include a considerable number of members in the federal government. Despite divisions within and between Shia elites and factions, they have more influence over the federal government's foreign policy than other political actors. The most influential faction post 2003 until the Iraqi election in May 2018 was the ruling Shia Islamic Da'wa Party, of which the former prime ministers were key members. Prominent Shia figures al-Sistani and Muqtada al-Sadr do not possess official positions but influence foreign policy making. Al-Sistani believes elites should be free to govern while he provides limited guidance and tries to play a conciliatory role; al-Sadr has populist views and seeks proactive political engagement from within and outside the government, and his political influence has increased considerably since his victory in the May 2018 election. Other political Shia factions engaged in foreign affairs include the Islamic Supreme Council of Iraq (ISCI), led by A'mmar al-Hakim (until 2017 when he founded the al-Hikma movement) who has moderate views and seeks a regional role supporting the federal government. Increasingly powerful pro-Iran Iraqi Shia factions with armed groups, such as the Badr Organization and Asa'ib Ahl al-Haq (AAH) and their political coalition al-Fatah, seek to reorient foreign policy according to their political and sectarian interests akin to Tehran. Arab Sunni political factions, such as the al-Nujaifi brothers, have their own agendas and objectives but recently some allied with conservative Shia camps, such as Karboli, and other Arab Sunnis allied with the so-called centrist Shia. Arab Sunnis have little to no influence over the Shia-led government; rather, they strongly illustrate the discrepancies in Iraq's foreign policy making. This includes their close ties with Arab Sunni states and Turkey, from which they gain logistic, and in some cases financial and military (viz. for Atheel al-Nujaifi's militias), support. Iraqi political actors have their own external ties and seek to steer Iraq's foreign policy behaviour or at least gain political and material support.

The KRG's foreign policy imperative reflects its political, security and economic interests. It needs a foreign policy as part of its independent governance and state-building project. It is projected from core executive bodies at the governmental level, namely, the president, the prime minister and the Department of Foreign Relations (DFR) and its head. The core executive bodies, including the deputies of the aforementioned posts and critical bodies such as the Kurdistan Region Security Council (KRSC), coordinate and perform adequately. The KRG's president has the highest executive authority and superiority in designing foreign policy, with input from the prime minister and the DFR's minister, who implements policies with limited diplomatic contributions, on which the president decides.

The Kurdistan Democratic Party (KDP) possesses the major positions in, and therefore controls, the core decision-making executive bodies (which includes the president, prime minister and minister of the DFR). The Patriotic Union of Kurdistan (PUK) is also involved and holds secondary posts with lesser powers in all executive bodies. The KDP and PUK have different priorities; for example, the KDP pushed for independence sooner than the PUK and favours closer energy ties with Turkey, while the PUK prefers to work through Baghdad. The KRG's two powerful political factions have different stances on foreign policy positions, particularly regionally; nevertheless, all key bureaucratic foreign policy positions adhere to the KDP's policy.

The KRG's foreign policy priorities primarily serve the interests of the Kurdistan Region of Iraq (KR-I) and other partisan interests. The KDP drives the KRG's interests and governmental representation and, in general, has the final word in foreign relations and policy. Its priorities include strengthening ties with the international community by being practical and realistic on all levels, including politics, the economy and security. It aims for peaceful and balanced relationships with neighbouring powers, as well as lobbying for the KRG's independence (this priority has stalled) and taking control of its own affairs in all sectors, particularly oil and gas, of which Baghdad disapproves. The KRG has the capacity to approach foreign policy priorities through its relatively coherent bureaucratic bodies, the factions' network with foreign entities, investing in lobbying in foreign capitals and possessing rich natural energy resources. However, the KRG faces challenges due to its non-sovereign status to achieve a number of its objectives, such as acceptance of the idea of future independence by sovereign states and receiving financial aid without the central government's permission.

The relationship between Baghdad and Erbil is fragile and characterized by feuds over control of natural resources, disputed territory, different interpretations of the Iraqi constitution and disparate positions on regional politics and security, including ties with states; these impact on foreign policy. The divergent foreign relations and foreign policies of the two governments have led officials from both governments to direct and redirect foreign policy behaviour according to their own interests and priorities. In foreign policy making specifically, Baghdad and Erbil's relationship is characterized by lack of coordination, bureaucratic confusion and domestic political tensions; however, there is some space for compromise where the KRG has managed to achieve some of its interests through Baghdad, such as the opening of consulates.

The KR-I's evolution has led it to pursue an increasingly independent foreign policy. Of critical significance is the KRG's shift from serving its own interests to lobbying for independence as a foreign policy priority and then after the referendum relinquishing the priority of sovereignty. Baghdad neither agrees with nor accepts the KRG's independent foreign policy; indeed, the Shia-led government's elites vehemently oppose Erbil's de facto foreign policy. Baghdad views the KRG's international activities as unfavourable at best and illegitimate at worst. The KRG does not necessarily seek to contradict Baghdad's foreign policy; rather, its foreign relations and foreign policy behaviour and a number of its objectives naturally differ from those of Baghdad and contradict the federal government. The strategic regional allies for the KRG (the KDP) and Baghdad (particularly al-Maliki and the powerful pro-Iran militias) somewhat differ depending on the factions' interests; Baghdad is allied with Iran and Erbil with Turkey; however, Erbil has gotten a bit closer to Iran especially after the referendum. Traditionally, Baghdad's and Erbil's trajectories differ, excluding in some circumstances. Before the referendum the scale of foreign policy divisions widened as a reflection of domestic tensions and instability – particularly since Baghdad cut off the KR-I's budget, its economy plummeted, the Daesh rose and the KRG officially called for independence via referendum.

Not every official, diplomat or political party (whether or not a part of the Erbil or Baghdad government) adheres to the Iraqi government's formal foreign policy positions. Iraq's splintered foreign policies are not analytical interpretations or explanations of divisions within the government; rather, they are practiced by key elites and their political parties.

The federal government's foreign policy priorities are interrelated and interdependent and reflect regime interests and survival. They focus on three areas: diplomacy, security and economy. The diplomacy priority aims to restore Iraq's place in the international community and present a different image than that during the Saddam era. Iraq has succeeded, to a certain degree, in achieving this – more at the international level than regionally. The security priority aims to utilize foreign relations as a tool to rebuild its security and military establishment, stabilize and safeguard the country and combat terrorism. Despite being able to provide some fragile security to certain areas, the federal government has so far generally failed to achieve this imperative. The economic priority first aims to use foreign relations and foreign policy to recover Iraq's economy, namely, by encouraging foreign transnational corporations to rebuild the oil and gas infrastructure and open new markets for Iraq's natural resources. Iraq has partly succeeded in this but disagreements have re-emerged between Baghdad and the regions, particularly the KRG (and, to a lesser extent, Basra). The second aim of the economy priority is trade and investment. Post Saddam, Iraq adopted an open-door policy towards foreign investment and transnational corporations, having been isolated for decades (particularly in the years of war and UN sanctions). Again, its achievements have been limited in this regard due to domestic instability, corruption and lack of infrastructure. All of the aforementioned priorities lack a concrete plan and elite consensus on how to approach and achieve them – both between the federal government and the KRG and within Baghdad. Although there are no unified foreign policy priorities between Baghdad and Erbil, and great distrust exists between the two sets of elites, the three priorities have been pursued by the elites in Baghdad as necessary objectives for survival and government operation.

Key Iraqi actors have alliances and common interests with regional actors (including material and political aspects), which they use to strengthen their domestic positions. As such, domestic and regional political, sectarian, economic and security dynamics are connected with, and shape, bilateral relationships with those countries. The links between Iraqi actors and external powers directly and indirectly influence the orientation of its fractured foreign policies. Iraq's weak and fragmented state and distrust between its elites (and their political factions) have paved the way for Iraqi actors and external alliances to forge relationships at the expense of other actors and the country. Powerful neighbours have therefore been able to project their own interests and gain receptive actors in Iraq.

Iran is the most powerful external force on Baghdad, and Turkey on Erbil (the ties were damaged after the referendum but gradually restored). Hitherto, Iran extended its influence on the KR-I's ruling factions and some Arab Sunni elites and factions. It has a strategic, multilayered rapport with the Shia elites and factions, considering not all Iraqi Shia elites and factions have same ties with Tehran. Turkey is more economically engaged with the KR-I; their relationship includes security and some political aspects with the KDP. Moreover, in Iraqi Kurdistan, the PUK has a relatively cordial relationship with Turkey but is not strategically similar to the KDP. The KSA has alliances in Iraq with Arab Sunni and Kurdish elites and factions and some Shia elites to counterweight the pro-Iran Iraqi Shia factions and Iran's influence. However, the KSA has far less leverage than Iran and Turkey, but since al-Abadi's and al-Mahdi's governments the KSA has increased its foreign policy engagement. Before the civil war, Syria covertly destabilized Iraq by its interferences, whereas since the civil war, Iraq's actors, namely, factions within the Popular Mobilization Forces (PMF), are operating in Syria alongside Assad's regime. Iraqi actors in policymaking have been disparate by exhibiting different positions and alliances with the aforementioned states. Iraqi elites and political factions are not puppets of regional powers (apart from a few) but rather have convergences of interests and, sometimes, similar visions and worldviews; for example, between al-Maliki and some of Tehran's key elites, who pull Iraq's foreign policies in different directions. Making foreign policies in Iraq remains a competitive process where many actors are involved – from core executive bodies (prime minister) and prominent figures such as Muqtada al-Sadr to external powers such as Iran. Therefore, the interests of the Iraqi population and the state are lost in foreign policy.

# NOTES

## Chapter 1

1 Sayyid Jawad al-Khoei said: 'This doctrine supports the idea that people should be responsible for electing their representatives' (American University of Iraq-Sulaimani, 2016).
2 'First, it shifted from a reformist Islamic organization to a revolutionary movement in the mid-1970s; second, it had to evacuate from Iraq to Iran after the Iranian revolution 1979; thirdly, it distanced itself from the Iranian authority in the late 1980s' (Dai, 2008, 238).
3 Besides the disagreement, the US administration followed al-Sistani's general map for the future of Iraq. This indicated good indirect cooperation between the United States and Najaf seminary post 2003 (Washington Institute, 2017).
4 In the first year of occupation Al-Sistani put pressure on the CPA to form a transitional government by forcing a compromise on the constitutional process when calling for a popular vote on the constitutional draft (Lukitz, 2011, 72).
5 Al-Sistani's conditions were safeguarding Iraq's interests, national sovereignty and national consensus and for the SOFA to be approved by the ICR (Cordesman and Ramos, 2008).

## Chapter 2

1 'Sovereign posts' is a common term used in politics in the Arab world to identify the most critical positions in the state.
2 Consociational is an idea and/or theory for governance designed to support political stability in deeply divided societies but only at the elite level (Bhandari, 2014, 191).
3 The IGC consisted of prominent individuals from Iraqi political factions. The CPA established it to facilitate the administration of Iraq and to present before it the voice of Iraqis (Buchan, 2013, 404).
4 Sunni negotiating figures such as Salih al-Mutlaq urged the UN, EU, the Arab League and the KSA to intervene and reject the constitution.
5 The US ambassador to Iraq Khalilzad stated that Bush 'doesn't want, doesn't support, doesn't accept al-Jaafari as the next PM' (Cordesman, 2008, 260).
6 Sdqian was the director of the Arabic Center for Iranian Studies in Tehran and closely connected to al-Maliki.

## Chapter 3

1 The KRG's foreign policy began since the unified cabinets in 2006.

2. For example, Sharif Pasha presented a map for greater Kurdistan in the Treaty of Versailles (1919).
3. In 2009, the Kurdistan National Assembly was renamed the Kurdistan Parliament.
4. The KDP pro-KNC is a rival to the PUK pro-PYD, and Baghdad supports Assad's regime, which opposes the two aforementioned Syrian Kurdish forces.
5. The KRG Peshmerga forces' intervention in Syrian Kurdistan (Rojava) in favour of the Kurds would not have been possible without the agreement of the president and Turkey's (AKP) leadership.
6. Although the laws from the Council of Ministers, ministries and other governmental or legislative bodies are valid, the draft constitution favours the president.
7. The KRG's Council of Ministers law no. 1 (2006) includes twenty-four articles that provide powers to the prime minister and the cabinet in the governance (KRG's Council of Ministers' Law, 2006).
8. The PUK has some ties with the Kurdish Democratic Progress Party (KDPP) in Syria and Komala in Iran.
9. For example, Greenberg Traurig, hired in 2007; QORVIS, hired in 2009; Squire Patton Boggs, hired in 2014; Dentons, hired in 2015. More than one firm has been hired each year; in 2014, four firms were hired (Pecquet, 2015a; United States Department of Justice, 2016).

## Chapter 4

1. Iraq submitted its Climate Action Plan ahead of the 2015 Paris agreement; Iraqi officials and diplomats have presented reports on Iraq's environmental condition at a number of environmental summits and events, such as the United Nations Security Council and UN's Environmental Assembly.

## Chapter 5

1. Quietism is a long-standing Shia tradition that discourages religious clerics from becoming directly involved in politics (Allawi, 2007, 30; Nazim, 2008, 316). *Al-Husbaih* theory or *Nathariat al-Husbaih* is a theory about prestigious religious figures issuing fatwas usually as guidance to help Muslims in their daily life that do not have a political nature.
2. The US demands included cooperation with the occupation of Iraq (Hinnebusch, 2014c, 22).

# REFERENCES

*Primary resources*

*List of interviews*

1. Dr Barham Salih (4 August 2014; Salih's Bureau in Sulaymaniyah, KR-I): deputy secretary general of the PUK; deputy prime minister of Iraq (2006–9); prime minister of the Kurdistan Regional Government (2009–12).
2. Nechervan Barzani (8 December 2014; the Prime Minister's Office in Erbil, KR-I): Kurdistan Regional Government's prime minister.
3. Dr Fuad Hussein (5 August 2014; Hussein's Bureau in Erbil, KR-I): Kurdistan Regional Government president Masoud Barzani's chief of staff and spokesperson (2005–present).
4. Dr Dhafer Al-A'ni (20 October 2014; the Iraqi Council of Representatives, Baghdad): Iraqi member of Parliament and member of the Foreign Relations Committee in the Iraqi Council of Representatives; spokesperson of the Al-Mutahidoon List and secretary general of the Al-Mustakbel National Gathering.
5. Abbas Al-Bayati (18 October 2014; the Iraqi Council of Representatives, Baghdad): Iraqi member of Parliament, member of the Foreign Relations Committee and Committee of Defence, a prominent Shia in the State of Law coalition.
6. Hassan Khudair Chuird Al-Hamdani (2 August 2015; the Iraqi Council of Representatives, Baghdad): chair of the Foreign Relations Committee in the Iraqi Council of Representatives (2013–16); Iraqi member of Parliament who was from al-Iraqiya List.
7. Hamid al-Ubadi Al-Mutlaq (2 August 2015; the Iraqi Council of Representatives, Baghdad): an Iraqi member of Parliament; deputy chair of the Committee of Defence in the Iraqi Council of Representatives (2013–present).
8. Baker Fatah (16 May 2015; Stockholm, Sweden): Iraq's ambassador to Sweden (2013–present); ambassador to Brazil (2010–13).
9. Mohamad Sabir Ismail (8 December 2014; Iraq's president's house in Sulaymaniyah, KR-I): ambassador to the United Nations in Genève and chief of Iraq's mission in the UN Genève (2011–16); formerly Iraq's ambassador to China (2005–10).
10. Kamran Karadaghi (27 February 2015; London, UK): advisor and chief of staff to Iraq's president Jalal Talabani (2005–7).
11. Najmaldin Karim (6 August 6 2014; Kirkuk governorate headquarters, Kirkuk, Iraq): governor of Kirkuk (2011–present); member of the PUK's political bureau.
12. Adnan Mufti (26 October 2014; Erbil, KR-I): member in the PUK's Political Bureau; speaker of the Kurdistan Parliament (2005–9).
13. Adel Murad (14 October 2014; Sulaymaniyah, KR-I): Iraqi ambassador to Romania (2004–9); co-founder of the PUK and head of the PUK Central Council.
14. Falah Mustafa (8 December 2014; Department of Foreign Relations in Erbil, KR-I): minister and head of the Kurdistan Regional Government's Department of Foreign Relations (2006–present).

15. Mustafa Said Qadir (30 May 2015; Sulaymaniyah, KR-I): minister of Peshmerga Affairs (2014–15).
16. Emad Ahmad Sayfour (2 December 2014; Sulaymaniyah, KR-I): Kurdistan Regional Government's deputy prime minister (2006–9); member of the PUK's Political Bureau.
17. Khalid Shwani (24 October 2014, Sulaymaniyah, KR-I; 16 July 2016, via phone): Iraqi president Fuad Ma'sum's spokesperson; chairman of the Legal Committee in the Iraqi Council of Representatives (2006–14); member of the PUK's Leadership Council.
18. Hussein Sinjari (19 April 2015; Erbil, KR-I): Iraqi ambassador to Romania (2013–present).
19. Abdul Bari Zebari (13 July 2016, via phone; 28 October 2014, the Iraqi Council of Representatives, Baghdad): the chair of the Foreign Relations Committee in the Iraqi Council of Representatives (2016–present).
20. Dr Dindar Zebari (6 August 2014; the Department of Foreign Relations in Erbil, KR-I): head of the Kurdistan Regional Government High Committee to Evaluate and Respond to International Reports (2014–present); the Kurdistan Regional Government's deputy minister of the Department of Foreign Relations (2006–14).
21. Karwan Jamal Tahir (29 June 2015; Department of Foreign Relations in Erbil, KR-I): the KRG high representative to the UK (2015–present).
Deputy Minister of Department Foreign Relations (2009–15).
22. Lukman Faily (25 November 2016; Manchester, UK): Iraq's ambassador to the United States (2013–16); Iraq's ambassador to Japan (2010–13).

*Speeches, statements and media interviews*

Al-Jaafari, I. (2014) Al-Iraqiya channel interview with Iraqi FM. 17 December. Available from: https://www.youtube.com/watch?v=zkqECj_P7p0.
Al-Yawer, G. (2004) The president speech: Future of Iraq. *C-Span*. Available from: http://www.c-span.org/video/?182229-1/future-iraq.
Brookings Institute (2015) Al-Jaafari speech: Iraq's foreign policy in turbulent region. 12 April. Available from: https://www.youtube.com/watch?v=hCAul3LAmDc.
Center for Strategic and International Studies (2013) Statesmen's forum: Iraqi foreign minister Hoshyar Zebari: A view from Iraq and the regio. 16 August. Available from: https://www.youtube.com/watch?v=3pSVeFwoFCQ.
Council on Foreign Relations (2014) Iraqi president Fuad Masum on ISIS and Iraq's challenges. 11 December. Available from: https://www.youtube.com/watch?v=hu8pg7BakWo.
C-Span (2006) Iraqi prime minister's address. 26 July. Available from: https://www.c-span.org/video/?193589-1/iraqi-prime-minister-address.
Deutsche Welle (2016) Interview with Haider Abadi: Conflict zone. 17 February. Available from: http://www.dw.com/en/haider-al-abadi-i-cannot-turn-the-country-upside-down-in-one-day/a-19045416.
France 24 (2015) Exclusive interview of Iraqi Shiite leader Moqtada al-Sadr. 16 June. Available from: https://www.youtube.com/watch?v=HPOBjVnxhNk.
France 24 Arabic (2014) Exclusive interview with the PM Nouri Al-Maliki. 8 March. https://www.youtube.com/watch?v=OYsU98rb8I8.
Jamal al-Din, A. (2015) Al-Arabiya channel interviewed Ayad Jamal al-Din. 4 December. Available from: https://www.youtube.com/watch?v=rVwBDn16LIk.
Washington Institute (2014) Falah Mustafa and Faud Hussein: Iraq's crisis and KRG. 11 July. Available from: http://www.washingtoninstitute.org/policy-analysis/view/iraqs-crisis-and-the-krg.

Washington Institute (2017) Interview with Mamouri: In after the Ayatollahs: The Middle East post-Khamenei. 7 February. Available from: https://www.youtube.com/watch?v=u-pomqXzFNI.

Wilson Center (2016) From ISIS to declining oil prices: Qubad Talabani on the Kurdistan Regional Government's challenges. Middle East Program, 14 April. Available from: https://www.wilsoncenter.org/event/isis-to-declining-oil-prices-qubad-talabani-the-kurdistan-regional-governments-challenges.

*Documents*

Bill H. R. ([1654] 2015) To authorize the direct provision of defense articles, defense services, and related training to the Kurdistan Regional Government, and for other purposes. 114th US Congress, 9 December. Available from: https://www.congress.gov/bill/114th-congress/house-bill/1654.

CPA (2004) Law of 2004 of administration for the state of Iraq for the transitional period. Refworld. Available from: http://www.refworld.org/docid/45263d612.html.

CPA (2014) Fact sheet: The annex to TAL. Available from: http://govinfo.library.unt.edu/cpa-iraq/government/Annex_Factsheet.html.

CPA Regulation 10 (2004) Members of designated Iraqi interim government. CPA, 9 June. Available from: http://govinfo.library.unt.edu/cpa-iraq/regulations/20040609_CPAREG_10_Members_of_Designated_Iraqi_Interim_Government_with_Annex_A.pdf.

Draft Constitution of Kurdistan Region-Iraq (2009). Kurdistan Parliament: Kurdistan Region of Iraq. 24 June.

General Secretariat of the Council of Ministers (2014) The strategies for the work of ministries for the period between 2014–2018. Prime Minister's Office. Available from: http://www.pmo.iq/pdf/2.pdf.

Iraqi Constitution (2005) The text of the constitution. Iraqi Federal Government. Available from: http://www.iraqinationality.gov.iq/attach/iraqi_constitution.pdf.

KRG's Council of Ministers' Law (2006) Council of Ministers of the KRG Law Number 1 for 2016. Dorar Al-Iraq, 22 June. Available from: http://wiki.dorar-aliraq.net/iraqilaws/law/20776.html.

Kurdistan National Assembly (2006) Amendment of the Kurdistan Region Presidents' Law. Kurdistan National Assembly, 24 January.

Rules of Procedures of the ICR (2006) Iraqi Council of Representatives rules of procedures. Iraqi Parliament. Available from: http://publicofficialsfinancialdisclosure.worldbank.org/sites/fdl/files/assets/law-library-files/Iraq_Rules%20of%20Procedure%20of%20Parliament_2006_en.pdf.

United States Department of Justice (2016) Semi-annual reports: FARA reports to Congress. Available from: https://www.fara.gov/annualrpts.html.

*Secondary resources*

*Academic and think-tank articles*

Ahmad, H., and S. M. Sabi' (2010) The interior determinations for Iraqi foreign policy: The political and constitutional determinations. *Journal of International Studies*, 46, 45–113.

Ahmad, A. M. (2017) Gamal Abdel Nasser's pan-Arabism and formation of the United Arab Republic: An appraisal. *Journal of Research Society of Pakistan*, 54(1), 107–28. Available from: http://pu.edu.pk/images/journal/HistoryPStudies/PDF_Files/8_V-30-No1-Jun17.pdf.

Alaaldin, R. (2017) The Islamic Da'wa Party and the mobilization of Iraq's Shia community, 1958–1965. *Middle East Journal*, 71(1), 46–65.

Ali, O. (2014) A reading on the Iraqi national assembly election results: National and regional implications. *ORSAM Review of Regional Affairs*, no. 3, 1 May. Available from: http://www.orsam.org.tr/index.php/Content/Assessments/28?s=orsam%7Cenglish.

Al-Khatteeb, L. J. (2013) Natural gas in the republic of Iraq. Harvard University's Belfer Center and Rice University's Baker Institute Center for Energy Studies, 18 November. Available from: http://belfercenter.ksg.harvard.edu/files/CES-pub-GeoGasIraq-111813.pdf.

Al-Khatteeb, L. J. (2016) Iraq's economic reform for 2016. Brookings Institute, 13 December. Available from: https://www.brookings.edu/opinions/iraqs-economic-reform-for-2016/.

Al-Khoei, H. (2013) Syria: The view from Iraq. European Council on Foreign Relations, 14 June. Available from: http://www.ecfr.eu/article/commentary_syria_the_view_from_iraq136.

Al-Qarawee, H. H. (2016) From Maliki to Abadi: The challenge of being Iraq's prime minister. Crown Centre for Middle East Studies, no. 100, June, 1–7.

Alsis, P., A. H. Cordesman, A. Mausner and C. Loi (2011) The outcome of invasion and Iranian strategic competition in Iraq. Center for Strategic & International Studies, 28 November. Available from: http://csis.org/files/publication/111128_Iran_Chapter_6_Iraq.pdf.

Alterman, J. B. (2007) Iraq and the Gulf states: The balance of fear. United States Institute of Peace, 1 August. Available from: http://www.usip.org/publications/iraq-and-the-gulf-states-the-balance-of-fear.

Bacik, G. (2012) Iraq after the US withdrawal: Al Maliki against Turkey. German Marshall Fund of the United States. Available from: http://www.gmfus.org/archives/iraq-after-the-u-s-withdrawal-al-maliki-against-turkey/.

Bargezar, K. (2007) Iran's foreign policy towards Iraq and Syria. *Turkish Policy Quarterly*, 6(2), Summer. Available from: http://www.belfercenter.org/publication/irans-foreign-policy-towards-iraq-and-syria.

Betts, R., M. Desch and P. Feaver (2012) Civilian, soldier and the Iraq surge decision. *International Security*, 36(3), 79–199.

Blanchard, C. M. (2008) The Islamic tradition of Wahhabism and Salafiyya. Congressional Research Service, 24 January. Available from: https://www.fas.org/sgp/crs/misc/RS21695.pdf.

Blanchard, C. M., K. Katzman, C. Migdalovitz and J. M. Sharp (2009) Iraq: Regional perspective and US policy. Congressional Research Service, 6 October. Available from: https://books.google.co.uk/books?id=LAxecf2QITIC&printsec=frontcover#v=onepage&q&f=false.

Bongers, R. (2013) Iran's foreign policy towards post-invasion Iraq. *Journal of Politics and International Studies*, 201(8), 124–60. Available from: http://www.polis.leeds.ac.uk/assets/files/students/student-journal/ug-winter-12/130213-win12-rob-bongers-4.pdf.

Brennan, R. R., C. P. Ries, L. Hanauer, B. Connable and T. K. Kelly (2013) Ending the US war in Iraq: The final transition, operational maneuverer war in and disestablishment

of United States Forces-Iraq. Rand Corporation. Available from: https://books.google. co.uk/books?id=8WcKAgAAQBAJ&printsec=frontcover#v=onepage&q&f=false.
Bruno, G. (2008) US security agreement and Iraq. Council on Foreign Relations, 23 December. Available from: http://www.cfr.org/iraq/us-security-agreements-iraq/p16448#p6.
Bunzel, C. (2015) From paper state to caliphate: The ideology of the Islamic State. Brookings Project on US Relations with the Islamic World, March. Available from: http://www.brookings.edu/~/media/research/files/papers/2015/03/ideology-of-islamic-state-bunzel/the-ideology-of-the-islamic-state.pdf.
Cagaptay, S., C. B. Fidan and E. C. Sacikara (2015) Turkey and the KRG: An undeclared economic commonwealth. Washington Institute for Near East Policy, 16 March. Available from: http://www.washingtoninstitute.org/policy-analysis/view/turkey-and-the-krg-an-undeclared-economic-commonwealth.
Chatham House (2013) Iraq's foreign policy in a changing Middle East. Workshop at Chatham House, February. Available from: https://www.chathamhouse.org/sites/files/chathamhouse/public/Research/Middle%20East/0213iraq_summary.pdf.
Cleave, Robert (2007) Conceptions of authority in Iraqi Shi'ism Baqir al-Hakim, Ha'iri and Sistani on Ijtihad, Taqlid and Marja'iyya. *Theory, Culture and Society*, 24(2), 59–78.
Cordesman, A. H., and J. Ramos (2008) Quietism and the US position in Iraq. Center for Strategic and International Studies, 19 June. Available from: http://csis.org/publication/quietism-and-us-postion-iraq.
Cordesman, A. H., J. Ramos and A. A Burke (2008) Sadr and the Mahdi Army: Evolution, capabilities and a new direction. Center for Strategic and International Studies, 4 August. Available from: http://csis.org/files/media/csis/pubs/080804_jam.pdf.
Dai, Y. (2008) Transformation of the Islamic Da'wa Party in Iraq: From the revolutionary period to the diaspora era. *Asian and African Areas Studies*, 7(2), 238–67. Available from: https://www.asafas.kyoto-u.ac.jp/dl/publications/no_0702/238-267.pdf.
Dawisha, A. (2005) Democratic attitudes and practices in Iraq, 1921–1958. *Middle East Journal*, 59(1), 11–30.
Dawisha, A. (2012) Post occupation Iraq: The brittleness of political institutions. Woodrow Wilson International Center for Scholars. Middle East Program, Occasional Paper Series, Spring. Available from: https://www.wilsoncenter.org/sites/default/files/Post%20Occupation%20Iraq%20FINAL.pdf.
Dodge, T. (2013) State and society in Iraq ten years after regime change: The rise of new authoritarianism. *International Affairs*, 89(2), 241–57.
Eisenstadt, M., M. Knights and A. Ali (2011) Iran's influence in Iraq: Countering Tehran's whole-of-government approach. Washington Institute for Near East Policy, Policy Focus 111, April. Available from: http://www.washingtoninstitute.org/uploads/Documents/pubs/PolicyFocus111.pdf.
Esfandiary, D., and A. Tabatabai (2015) Iran's ISIS policy. *International Affairs*, 91(1), January. Available from: https://www.chathamhouse.org/sites/files/chathamhouse/field/field_publication_docs/INTA91_1_01_Esfandiary_Tabatabai.pdf.
Fawcett, L. (2013) The Iraq war ten years on: Assessing the fallout. *International Affairs*, 89(2), 325–43.
Frankel, M. (2010) Threaten but participate: Why election boycotts are a bad idea. Brookings Institute, Policy paper (19), March. Available from: http://www.brookings.edu/~/media/research/files/papers/2010/2/election%20boycotts%20frankel/02_election_boycotts_frankel.pdf.

Geneva Center for the Democratic Control of Armed Forces (DCAF) (2009) Status of Forces Agreements Model: Agreement between the United States of America and the Republic of Iraq. Report 6.1.

Geranmayeh, E. (2014) Iran is not making U-turn in Iraq. European Council on Foreign Relations, August. Available from: http://www.ecfr.eu/article/commentary_iran_is_not_making_a_u_turn_in_iraq299.

Gulmohamad, Z. (2015) A short profile of Iraq's Shi'a militias. *Jamestown Foundation, Terrorism Monitor*, 8(13), 3–6. Available from: http://www.jamestown.org/single/?tx_ttnews%5Btt_news%5D=43805&no_cache=1#.VsYOWLxswdU.

Gulmohamad, Z. (2016a) Iraq Shia militias: Helping or hindering the fight against Islamic State. *Jamestown Foundation: Terrorism Monitor*, 14(9), 5–7.

Gulmohamad, Z. (2016b) Unseating the caliphate: Contrasting the challenges of liberating Fallujah and Mosul. *CTC Sentinel*, 9(10), 16–27. Available from: https://ctc.usma.edu/posts/unseating-the-caliphate-contrasting-the-challenges-of-liberating-fallujah-and-mosul.

Gunter, M. M. (1992) Foreign influences on the Kurdish insurgency in Iraq. *Journal of Conflict Studies/Conflict Quarterly*, 12(4), 7–24. Available from: https://journals.lib.unb.ca/index.php/JCS/article/view/15068.

Gunter, M. M. (2014) Turkish-Kurdish peace process stalled in neutral. *Insight Turkey*, 16(1), 19–26. Available from: http://file.insightturkey.com/Files/Pdf/insight_turkey_16_1_2014_gunter.pdf.

Habibi, N. (2010) Impact of sanctions on Iran–GCC economic relations. Middle East Brief Series, Crown Center for Middle East Studies, November, No. 45. Available from: http://www.brandeis.edu/crown/publications/meb/meb45.html.

Haddad, F. (2014) A sectarian awaking: Reinventing Sunni identity in Iraq after 2003. Hudson Institute, 4 August. Available from: http://www.hudson.org/research/10544-a-sectarian-awakening-reinventing-sunni-identity-in-iraq-after-2003Available from: http://www.understandingwar.org/sites/default/files/Backgrounder_ShiaMilitias.pdf.

Haddad, F. (2016) Shia-centric state building and Sunni rejection in post-2003 Iraq. Carnegie Endowment for International Peace, January. Available from: http://carnegieendowment.org/files/CP261_Haddad_Shia_Final.pdf.

Hammoud, M. A. (2015) Iraqi foreign policy. *Assabah al-Jadeed*, 17 April. Available from: http://www.newsabah.com/wp/newspaper/45110.

Hasan, H. (2018) Iraq's Dawa Party and electioneering: Division and survival. Atlantic Council, 9 January. Available from: http://www.atlanticcouncil.org/blogs/menasource/iraq-s-dawa-party-and-electioneering-division-and-survival.

Hinnebusch, R. (2014a) Syria–Iraq relations: State construction and deconstruction and the MENA states system. LSE Middle East Centre Paper Series/04, October. Available from: http://eprints.lse.ac.uk/60004/.

Hira, A., and K. Jabary (2013) The Kurdish Mirage: A success story in doubt. *Middle East Policy*, 20(2), 99–112. Available from: http://onlinelibrary.wiley.com/store/10.1111/mepo.12023/asset/mepo.12023.pdf?v=1&t=hxri7e9u&s=089ea976c13116e778af5e690548a15e42e1bf49.

Hudson Institute (2016) A view of the US election from Iraq. 4 November. Available from: http://www.hudson.org/events/1379-a-view-of-the-u-s-election-from-iraq112016.

Hudson Institute (2018) The future of Iraq. Hudson Institute/C-Span, 22 February. Available from: https://www.c-span.org/video/?441529-1/ambassador-speaks-future-iraq&start=2937.

Human Rights Watch (2011) Iran/Turkey: Recent attacks on civilians in Iraqi Kurdistan. 20 December. Available from: https://www.hrw.org/news/2011/12/20/iran/turkey-recent-attacks-civilians-iraqi-kurdistan.

Human Rights Watch (2018) Turkey/Iraq: Strikes may break laws of war. 19 September. Available from: https://www.hrw.org/news/2018/09/19/turkey/iraq-strikes-may-break-laws-war.

Ingram, J. (2019) KRG gas: Key producer eyes alternatives to Rosneft's stalled Turkey pipeline. *MEES*, 4 October. Available from: https://www.mees.com/2019/10/4/oil-gas/krg-gas-key-producer-eyes-alternatives-to-rosnefts-stalled-turkey-pipeline/59964d20-e6b9-11e9-bc74-551fc209d019.

International Crisis Group (2010) Loose ends: Iraq's security forces between US drawdown and withdrawal. Middle East Report no. 99, 26 October. Available from: https://d2071andvip0wj.cloudfront.net/99-loose-ends-iraq-s-security-forces-between-u-s-drawdown-and-withdrawal.pdf.

International Crisis Group (2012) Iraq's secular opposition: The rise and decline of al-Iraqiya. Middle East Report no. 127. Available from: http://www.crisisgroup.org/~/media/Files/Middle%20East%20North%20Africa/Iraq%20Syria%20Lebanon/Iraq/127-iraqs-secular-opposition-the-rise-and-decline-of-al-iraqiya.pdf.

International Monetary Fund (2013) IMF Country Report no. 13/217, 30 April. Available from: https://www.imf.org/external/pubs/ft/scr/2013/cr13217.pdf.

International Monetary Fund (2015) Selected issue: IMF Country Report no. 15/236, 14 July. Available from: https://www.imf.org/external/pubs/ft/scr/2015/cr15236.pdf.

Jaffe, A. M. (2007) Iraq's oil sector: Past, present and future. James A. Baker III Institute for Public Policy, Rice University, March. Available from: http://www.amymyersjaffe.com/content/pdf/IRAQnoc_iraq_jaffe-1.pdf.

Joint Analysis Policy Unit (2013) Iraq budget 2013. Joint Analysis Policy Unit, January. Available from: http://reliefweb.int/sites/reliefweb.int/files/resources/Iraq%20Budget%202013%20Background%20Paper.pdf.

Kahl, C., B. Katulis and M. Lynch (2008) Thinking strategically about Iraq: Report from a symposium. *Middle East Policy*, 15(1), 82–110.

Kasapoglu, C., and S. Cagaptay (2015) Turkey's military presence in Iraq: A complex strategic deterrent. Washington Institute for Near East Policy, 22 December. Available from: http://www.washingtoninstitute.org/policy-analysis/view/turkeys-military-presence-in-iraq-a-complex-strategic-deterrent.

Kassim, O. (2018a) Iraq's judiciary rules against Sunni politician ahead of Iraqi elections. Institute for the Study of War, 9 February. Available from: http://www.understandingwar.org/backgrounder/iraq's-judiciary-rules-against-sunni-politician-ahead-iraqi-elections.

Kassim, O. (2018b) Ayad Allawi sets conditions to recreate 2011 premiership bid. Institute for the Study of War, 9 March. Available from: http://www.understandingwar.org/backgrounder/ayad-allawi-sets-conditions-recreate-2011-premiership-bid .

Katzman, K. (2006) Iraq: US regime change efforts and post-Saddam governance. Congress Research Service, Reports for Congress, 13 January. Available from https://digital.library.unt.edu/ark:/67531/metacrs8109/m1/1/high_res_d/RL31339_2006Jan13.pdf.

Katzman, K. (2008) Al-Qaeda in Iraq: Assessment and outside links. Congressional Research Service, 15 August. Available from: https://www.fas.org/sgp/crs/terror/RL32217.pdf.

Katzman, K. (2010) Iran-Iraq relations. Congress Research Service, Reports for Congress, 13 August. Available from: https://www.fas.org/sgp/crs/mideast/RS22323.pdf.

Khadim, A. (2012) The Hawza and its role in post-war Iraq. Paper in the Annual Workshop of the Institute for Iraqi Studies. Available from: http://www.bu.edu/iis/files/2012/10/The-Hawza-and-Its-Role-in-Post-War-Iraq.pdf.

Knights, M. (2012) Syria eastern front: The Iraq factor. Washington Institute for Near East Policy, 6 July. Available from: http://www.washingtoninstitute.org/policy-analysis/view/syrias-eastern-front-the-iraq-factor.

Knights, M. (2015a) Devils you don't know. Washington Institute for Near East Policy, 8 September. Available from: http://www.washingtoninstitute.org/policy-analysis/view/devils-you-dont-know.

Knights, M. (2015b) The long haul: Rebooting US security cooperation in Iraq. Washington Institute, Policy Focus 137. Available from: http://www.washingtoninstitute.org/uploads/Documents/pubs/PolicyFocus137_Knights4.pdf.

Knights, M. (2016) Using international financial aid to improve Baghdad-KRG relations. Washington Institute for Near East Policy, Policy Watch 2588, 15 March. Available from: http://www.washingtoninstitute.org/policy-analysis/view/using-international-financial-aid-to-improve-baghdad-krg-relations.

Knights, M., L. Soper, A. Lembke and B. Salmoni (2011) The Iraqi Security Forces: A status report. Policy Watch 1814. Washington Institute, 13 June. Available from: http://www.washingtoninstitute.org/policy-analysis/view/the-iraqi-security-forces-a-status-report.

Kubursi, A. A. (1988) Oil and the Iraqi economy. *Arab Studies Quarterly*, 10(3), 283–98.

Latif, A. (2008) The Da'wa party's eventful past and tentative future in Iraq. Sada-Carnegie Endowment for International Peace, 19 August. Available from: http://carnegieendowment.org/sada/?fa=20930.

Levitt, M. (2015) Major beneficiaries of the Iran deal: IRGC and Hezbollah. Washington Institute for Near East Policy, 17 September. Available from: https://www.washingtoninstitute.org/uploads/Documents/testimony/LevittTestimony20150917.pdf.

Loi, C. (2011) US and Iranian strategic competition: Competition between the US and Iran in Iraq. Centre for Strategic and International Studies, 2 March. Available from: http://csis.org/files/publication/110302_Comp_between_US_Iran_in_Iraq.pdf.

Maggiolini, P. (2013) Iraq's foreign policy directions and regional developments: Where does Iraqi foreign policy start? Italian Institute for International Political Studies, no. 199, September. Available from: http://www.ispionline.it/sites/default/files/pubblicazioni/analysis_199_2013.pdf.

Manis, A. (2016) Averting an economic meltdown in the Kurdistan Region of Iraq: Aligning political objectives with economic necessities. Middle East Research Institute, July. Available from: http://www.meri-k.org/wp-content/uploads/2016/07/Averting-an-Economic-Meltdown-in-the-Kurdistan-Region-of-Iraq-Aligning-Political-Objectives-with-Economic-Necessities.pdf.

Mansour, R. (2014) Rethinking recognition: The case of Iraqi Kurdistan. *Cambridge Journal of International and Comparative Law*, 4(3), 1182–94. Available from: http://joomla.cjicl.org.uk/journal/article/245.

Mansour, R. (2016a) Mosul after the Islamic State: The Kurdistan region's strategy. Carnegie Middle East Center, 20 May. Available from: http://carnegie-mec.org/2016/05/18/mosul-after-islamic-state-kurdistan-region-s-strategy-mosul-after-islamic-state-kurdistan-region-s-strategy/iygh.

Mansour, R. (2016b) The Sunni predicament in Iraq. Carnegie Middle East Center, 3 March. Available from: http://carnegie-mec.org/2016/03/03/sunni-predicament-in-iraq/iusn.

Mansour, R. (2018) Saudi Arabia's new approach in Iraq. Center for Strategic and International Studies, November. Available from: https://csis-prod.s3.amazonaws.com/s3fs-public/publication/181105_RM_Gulf_analysis.pdf?AWXv0HPipY0ev0TR2M08l_PbRCQQSY99.

Mansour, R. (2019) Iraq's 2018 government formation unpacking the friction between reform and the status quo. LES Middle East Center, February. Available from: http://eprints.lse.ac.uk/100099/1/Mansour_Iraq_s_2018_government_formation_2019.pdf.

Mansour, R., and F. A. Jabar (2017) The popular mobilization forces and Iraq's future. Carnegie Middle East Center, April. Available from: http://carnegieendowment.org/files/CMEC_63_Mansour_PMF_Final_Web.pdf.

Mardini, R. (2012) Iraq's post-withdrawal crisis. Institute Study of War, 4 May. Available from: http://www.understandingwar.org/backgrounder/iraqs-post-withdrawal-crisis-update-20.

Mardini, R. (2015) Iraq's Abadi caught between global powers and domestic politics. Atlantic Council, 18 September. Available from: http://www.atlanticcouncil.org/blogs/menasource/iraq-s-abadi-caught-between-global-powers-and-domestic-politics.

Marr, P. (2004) Iraqi foreign policy. In L. Carl Brown (ed.), *Diplomacy in the Middle East: The International Relations of Regional and Outside Powers*. London: I.B. Tauris, 101–206.

Marr, P. (2007) Iraq's new political map. United States Institute of Peace, Special report 179, January. Available from: https://www.ciaonet.org/attachments/7162/uploads.

Martin, P. (2015) Turkey unilaterally deploys a battalion near Mosul. Institute for the Study of War, 6 December. Available from: http://iswresearch.blogspot.co.uk/2015/12/turkey-unilaterally-deploys-battalion.html.

Mason, R. C. (2008) CRS Report for Congress: Status of Force Agreement (SOFA): What is it and how might one be utilized in Iraq? Washington DC. Congressional Research Service, 15 March.

Mason, R. C. (2012) CRS Report for Congress: Status of Force Agreement (SOFA): What is it and how might one be utilized in Iraq? CRS Report for Congress, 15 March. Available from: https://fas.org/sgp/crs/natsec/RL34531.pdf.

Mauro, R. (2009) Has Damascus stopped supporting terrorists? *Middle East Quarterly*, 16(3), 61–7. Available from: http://www.meforum.org/2406/damascus-supporting-terrorists.

McCants, W. (2015) The believer: How Abu Bakr al-Baghdadi became leader of the Islamic State. Brookings Institute. Available from: http://www.brookings.edu/search?start=1&sort=&q=mccants.

McGarry, J., and B. O'Leary (2007) Iraq's constitution of 2005: Liberal consociation as political prescription. *International Journal of Constitutional Law*, 5(4), 670–98.

McMillan, J. (2006) Saudi Arabia and Iraq: Oil, religion, and enduring rivalry. United States Institute of Peace, Special report 157, January. Available from: http://www.usip.org/sites/default/files/McMillan_Saudi%20Arabia%20and%20Iraq_SR%20157.pdf.

Mohammed, H. K., and F. Owtram (2014) Paradiplomacy of regional government in international relations: The foreign relations of the Kurdistan Regional Government (2003–2010). *Iran Caucasian Centre for Iranian Studies*, 18(1), 65–84.

Nader, A. (2015) Iran's role in Iraq: Room for the US cooperation? Rand Corporation. Available from: http://www.rand.org/content/dam/rand/pubs/perspectives/PE100/PE151/RAND_PE151.pdf.

Nagan. W., and H. Hammer (2004) The New Bush National Security Doctrine and the rule of law. *Berkeley Journal of International Law*, 22(3), 375–434.

Norton, A. R. (2011) Al-Najaf: Its resurgence as a religious and university center. *Middle East Policy Council*, 18(1), 132–45. Available from: http://www.mepc.org/journal/middle-east-policy-archives/al-najaf-its-resurgence?print.

Obaid, N. (2006) Meeting the challenge of a fragmented Iraq: A Saudi perspective Center for Strategic and International Studies, 6 April. Available from: http://csis.org/files/media/csis/pubs/060406_iraqsaudi.pdf.

Piper, J. (2019) Iraqi businessmen hires former Trump aids as foreign agent. Open Secrets, 20 June. Available from: https://www.opensecrets.org/news/2019/06/iraq-businessman-hires-former-trump-aide-as-foreign-agent/.

Podeh, E. (2010) From indifference to obsession: The role of national state celebration in Iraq, 1921–2003. *British Journal of Middle Eastern Studies*, 37(2), 179–207.

Pollack, K. M. (2014) Iraqi elections, Iranian interests. Brookings Institution, 4 April. Available from: http://www.brookings.edu/blogs/iran-at-saban/posts/2014/04/04-pollack-iraq-national-elections-2014-iranian-interests.

Prados, A. B., and J. M. Sharp (2005) Syria: Political conditions and relations with the United States after the Iraq War. Congressional Research Service, 28 February. Available from: https://fas.org/sgp/crs/mideast/RL32727.pdf.

Prendergast, M. (2016) Slump hurts refugee schools in Kurdistan region of Iraq. UNHCR, 8 April. Available from: http://www.unhcr.org/uk/news/latest/2016/4/57077c986/slump-hurts-refugee-schools-kurdistan-region-iraq.html.

Rahimi, B. (2007) Ayatollah Sistani and the democratic of post-Ba'athist Iraq. United States Institute of Peace, Special report 187, June. Available from: http://www.usip.org/sites/default/files/sr187.pdf.

Raphaeli, N. (2004) The new leaders of Iraq: Interim president Sheikh Ghazi Al-Yawer. The Middle East Media Research Institute (MEMRI), Report no. 178. Available from: http://www.memri.org/report/en/print1149.htm#_edn1.

Reidel, B. (2016) Trump's Saddam: Terror killer or terror patron? Brooking Institute, 11 July. Available from: https://www.brookings.edu/opinions/trumps-saddam-terror-killer-or-terror-patron/.

Rogers, P. (2014) Is Islamic State here to stay. Oxford Research Group – Global Security Briefing, April. Available from: http://www.oxfordresearchgroup.org.uk/sites/default/files/ORGApr15IsIslamicStateHereToStay_0.pdf.

Romano, D. (2010a) Iraqi Kurdistan: Challenges of autonomy in the wake of US withdrawal. *International Affairs*, 86(6), 1345–59.

Rubin, A. H. (2007) Abd al-Karim Qasim and the Kurds of Iraq: Centralization, resistance and revolt, 1958–63. *Middle East Studies*, 43(3), 353–82.

Salem, P. (2013) Iraq's tangled foreign interests and relations. Carnegie Middle East Center, 24 December. Available from: http://carnegie-mec.org/2013/12/24/iraq-s-tangled-foreign-interests-and-relations.

Seloom, M. (2018) An unhappy return: What the Iraqi Islamic Party gave up to gain power. Carnegie Middle East Center, 19 November. Available from: https://

carnegie-mec.org/2018/11/19/unhappy-return-what-iraqi-islamic-party-gave-up-to-gain-power-pub-77747.

Shanahan, R. (2004) The Islamic Da'wa Party: Past developments and future prospects. *Middle East Review of International Affairs*, 8(2). Available from: http://www.rubincenter.org/2004/06/shanahan-2004-06-02/.

Sherko, F. (2016) In the regional power struggle, has Erbil decided to join the Sunni Bloc. Washington Institute for Near East Policy, 29 January. Available from: http://www.washingtoninstitute.org/policy-analysis/view/in-the-regional-power-struggle-has-erbil-decided-to-join-the-sunni-bloc.

Sirri, O., G. Stansfield and J. Kinninmont (2013) Iraq on the international stage: Foreign policy and national identity in transition. Chatham House, July. Available from: http://www.chathamhouse.org/sites/files/chathamhouse/public/Research/Middle%20East/0713pr_iraqforeignpolicy.pdf.

Smyth, P. (2015) The Shiite jihad in Syria and its regional effects. Washington Institute for Near East Policy, Policy Focus 138. Available from: https://www.washingtoninstitute.org/uploads/Documents/pubs/PolicyFocus138-v3.pdf.

Spyer, J., and A. J. Al-Tamimi (2014) Iran and the Shia militias advance in Iraq. Middle East Forum, December. Available from: http://www.meforum.org/4927/how-iraq-became-a-proxy-of-the-islamic-republic.

Stansfield, G. (2010a) The reformation of Iraq's foreign relations: New elites and enduring legacies. *International Affairs*, 86(6), 1395–409.

Stansfield, G. (2010b) Introduction to the political parameters of post-withdrawal Iraq. *International Affairs*, 86(6), 1261–7.

Stansfield, G. (2013) The unravelling of the post-first world war state system? The Kurdistan region of Iraq and the transformation in the Middle East. *International Affairs*, 89(2), 259–82.

Stein, A. (2014) Davutoglu, the AKP and the pursuit of regional order. Royal United Service Institute for Defence and Security Studies, Whitehall paper 83. Available from: https://books.google.co.uk/books?id=teEsCgAAQBAJ&printsec=frontcover#v=onepage&q&f=false.

Tonini, A. (2007) Propaganda versus pragmatism: Iraqi foreign policy in Qasim's years, 1958–63. *Review of International Affairs*, 3(2), 232–53.

Van Veen, E., N. Grinstead and F. El Kamouni-Janssen (2017) A house divided: political relations and coalition-building between Iraq's Shi'a. Netherlands Institute of International Relations, Clingdenael, CRU Report, February. Available from: https://www.clingendael.nl/sites/default/files/a_house_divided.pdf.

Voller, Y. (2013) Kurdish oil politics in Iraq: Contested sovereignty and unilateralism. *Middle East Policy*, 20(1), 68–82.

Wahab, B. A. (2006) How oil smuggling Greases violence. *Middle East Quarterly*, 13(4), 53–9. Available from: http://www.meforum.org/1020/how-iraqi-oil-smuggling-greases-violence.

Wahab, B. A. (2014) Iraq and KRG energy policies: Actors, challenges and opportunities. Institute of Regional and International Studies, American University of Iraq-Sulaimani, May. Available from: http://auis.edu.krd/sites/default/files/Iraq%20and%20KRG%20Energy%20Policies%20-%20Bilal%20Wahab.pdf.

Webb, S. (2009) Snap analysis: Iraqi Kurdistan to export gas to Europe, Turkey. Reuters, 17 May. Available from: https://www.reuters.com/article/us-iraq-kurds-nabucco-snapanalysis/snap-analysis-iraqi-kurdistan-to-export-gas-to-europe-turkey-idUSTRE54G0OI20090517.

Wicken, S. (2012a) Confidence vote against Maliki succeed this time? Institute for the Study of War, 21 December. Available from: http://www.understandingwar.org/backgrounder/political-update-can-no-confidence-vote-against-maliki-succeed-time.

Wicken, S. (2012b) Iraq's post-withdrawal crisis, update 15. Institute for the Study of War. Available from: http://www.understandingwar.org/backgrounder/iraqs-post-withdrawal-crisis-update-15.

Wicken, S., and J. Lewis (2013) From protest movement to armed resistance: 2013 Iraq update 24. Institute for the Study of War, 14 June. Available from: http://iswresearch.blogspot.com/2013/06/from-protest-movement-to-armed.html.

Winter, C. (2013) Turkey's strained Kurdish peace process. POMEPS Briefings 23 'Turkey's Turmoil'. *Project on Middle East Political Science*, 1–37. Available from: http://pomeps.org/wp-content/uploads/2014/01/POMEPS_BriefBooklet23_Turkey_web.pdf.

*Articles and political TV programs*

ABC News (2007) Iraq with CIA ties hires DC lobby firm. 17 December. Available from: http://blogs.abcnews.com/theblotter/2007/08/iraqi-with-cia-.html.

Abdelamir, A. (2014) Nujaifi discusses Iraqi crisis with US, officials, academics. *Al-Monitor*, 28 January. Available from: http://www.al-monitor.com/pulse/politics/2014/01/iraq-parliament-speaker-us-visit-maliki-anbar-crisis.html.

Abdullah, H. (2018) Iraqi resource: Al-Jaafari disagreed with Iraqi government for his condemnation against the US attack against Syria. *Akhbar al-Khaleej*, 17 April. Available from: http://akhbar-alkhaleej.com/news/article/1118718.

Abdulrazak, T. (2017) From top to bottom, Iraq reeks of corruption. *Arab Weekly*, 30 July. Available from: https://thearabweekly.com/top-bottom-iraq-reeks-corruption.

Aboulenein, A. (2017) Kurds will find it hard to implement independence, says Iraqi FM. Reuters, 13 September. Available from: https://uk.reuters.com/article/uk-mideast-crisis-iraq-minister/kurds-will-find-it-hard-to-implement- independence-says-iraqi-fm-idUKKCN1BO2IR.

Addustour (2004) Arrived in Manama and accused Iran in deteriorating Iraq's security. 2 November. Available from: http://www.addustour.com/13735/وصل+المنامة+واتهم+ايران+الياور+ينتقد+خطة+مهاجمة+الفلوجة+عسكريا+بالمساهمة+في+تدهور+الوضع+الامني+في+العراق3%.html.

Afaq TV (2014) Al-Maliki: We cannot be silent about Erbil becoming a base for conspiracy. Translated from Arabic by the author, 9 July. Available from: https://www.youtube.com/watch?v=yoICGVoQZF4.

Ain Iraqi News (2015) Saudi embassy in Baghdad started working. 23 December. Available from: http://www.alliraqnews.com/modules/news/article.php?storyid=24931.

Al-Ahed News (2016) ISCI rejects classification of Lebanese Hezbollah as a terrorist organization. 4 March. Available from: http://www.alahednews.com.lb/fastnews/323311/#المجلس-الأعلى-الإسلامي-العراقي-يستنكر-تصنيف-حزب-الله-تنظيما-إرهابيا/VxC5Rbw4n-Y.

Al-Alam (2013) Al-Mu'alm emphasize Damascus acceptance to participate in Geneva talks. 26 May. Available from: http://www.alalam.ir/news/1478127.

Al-Arab (2010) Al-Maliki's priorities are security and developing foreign relations. 22 December. Available from: http://www.alarab.com/Article/348022.

Al-Arab (2011) Muqtada with the rebellion in Syria and support Assad in power. 18 November. Available from: http://www.alarab.com/Article/412595.

Al-Arabiya (2009) Iraq's Presidency considered al-Maliki's position is illegal. 8 September. Available from: http://www.alarabiya.net/articles/2009/09/08/84357.html.

Al-Arabiya (2012) Baghdad moves to end Turkish presence in north Iraq. 2 October. Available from: http://www.alarabiya.net/articles/2012/10/02/241452.html.

Al-Arabiya (2013) Iraq's Maliki discusses oil project with Russian company. 1 July. Available from: https://english.alarabiya.net/en/business/energy/2013/07/01/Iraq-s-Maliki-discusses-oil-project-in-Russia.html.

Al-Arabiya (2014) Arab agreement on taking necessary steps to fight Daesh. 7 September. Available from: http://www.alarabiya.net/ar/arab-and-world/iraq/2014/09/07/وزراء-الخارجية-العرب-يصوتون-على-قرار-لمحاربة-داعش.html.

Al-Arabiya (2015) Sunni forces considers entering alliances with Russia and Assad is a treason. 18 October. Available from: http://www.alarabiya.net/ar/arab-and-world/iraq/2015/10/18/القوى-السنية-تعتبر-الدخول-في-تحالف-روسيا-الأسد-خيانة-.html.

Al-Arabiya (2016) Al-Sadr threatening the US troops if they participate in operation to liberate Mosul. 18 July. Available from: http://www.alarabiya.net/ar/arab-and-world/iraq/2016/07/18/الصدر-يهدد-القوات-الأميركية-المشاركة-في-عملية-الموصل.html.

Al-Arabiya News (2015) Iranian advisor clarifies 'Baghdad capital of Iranian empire' remarks. 13 March. Available from: https://english.alarabiya.net/en/News/middle-east/2015/03/13/Iranian-advisor-clarifies-Baghdad-capital-of-Iranian-empire-remark.html.

Alasdair, D. (1992) Syria and Iraq – the geopathology of a relationship. *GeoJournal*, 28(3), 347–55.

Al-Bab (2015) Iraqi National Accord. Available from: http://www.al-bab.com/arab/docs/iraq/ina02.htm.

Al-Bawaba (2010) Al-Maliki: Iraq will be against political axes. August 30. Available from: http://www.albawaba.com/ar/العراق/المالكي-العراق-سيكون-ضد-سياسة-المحاور?quicktabs_accordionar=1.

Al-Bawaba (2014) On ISIS, Maliki criticized by own Iraqi FM. 1 August. Available from: http://www.albawaba.com/news/maliki-isis-593803.

Al-Bawaba (2015) Saudi Arabia appoints first ambassador to Iraq in 25 years. 3 June. Available from: http://www.albawaba.com/news/saudi-arabia-appoints-first-ambassador-iraq-25-years-702862.

Al-Fayad, M. (2013) Kurdistan foreign relations chief: Federalism in Iraq is succeeding. *Asharq Al-Awsat*, 16 October. Available from: https://english.aawsat.com/maadfayad/interviews/kurdistan-foreign-relations-chief-federalism-in-iraq-is-succeeding.

Al-Fayad, M. (2014) Saleh al-Mutlaq: Iraq is going through hell. *Asharq Al-Awsat*, 23 August. Available from: http://english.aawsat.com/2014/08/article55335773/saleh-al-mutlaq-iraq-is-going-through-hell.

Al-Fayhaa TV (2009) Al-Maliki's visit to Syria. 18 August. Available from: https://www.youtube.com/watch?v=p-O6CmXgePw.

Al-Fayhaa TV (2014a) Discussions with the president Jalal Talabani. 23 March. Available from: https://www.youtube.com/watch?v=BYfR2erW4nE.

Al-Fayhaa TV (2014b) Special coverage for Iraqi-Saudi relationships. 13 November. Available from: https://www.youtube.com/watch?v=vuAdfmuOs6s.

Alfoneh, A. (2017) Iraqi Shia fighters in Syria. Atlantic Council, 4 May. Available from: http://www.atlanticcouncil.org/blogs/syriasource/iraqi-shia-fighters-in-syria/.

Al-Haddad, M. M. (2014) The most important issues that Ayatollah al-Sistani referred to with visited of the Gulf states. *Kitabat*, 20 August. Available from: http://kitabat.info/subject.php?id=49947.

Al-Hashimi, T. (2012) Weaponry deals with Russia, why now? *Asharq Al-Awsat*, 15 October. Available from: http://archive.aawsat.com/leader.asp?article=701246&issueno=12385#.Vzr2zWPmv-Y.

Al-Hashimi, T. (2015) Weeping over the unity of Iraq. *Middle East Monitor*, 7 May. Available from: https://www.middleeastmonitor.com/articles/middle-east/18482-weeping-over-the-unity-of-iraq.

Al-Hassoun, N. (2014) Iran-Iraq trade reached $12billion in 2013. *Al-Monitor*, 1 July. Available from: http://www.al-monitor.com/pulse/business/2014/07/iraq-iran-trade-increase-crisis-border-syria-jordan-turkey.html.

Alhurra Iraq (2014) Interview with the president of Iraq Fuad Masum. 4 September. Available from: https://www.youtube.com/watch?v=Rk4m43nrJp4.

Alhurra Iraq (2017) Conversation with president of Iraq Fuad Ma'sum. 28 September. Available from: https://www.youtube.com/watch?v=xO96cIl7zc0.

Alhurra Iraq (2018) Discussion with Iraqi vice president Usama al-Nujaifi. 13 February. Available from: https://www.youtube.com/watch?v=S-PaG5dHdc4.

Ali Ma' al-Haq (2017) The statement of Muqtada al-Sadr on the execution of Nimr al-Namir. 8 August. Available from: https://www.youtube.com/watch?v=3d3jq3SxjQM.

Ali, A., and C. van den Toorn (2015) Turkish boots on the ground, Institute of Regional and International Studies. American University of Iraq-Sulaimani, 15 December. Available from: http://auis.edu.krd/iris/iraq-report/turkish-boots-ground.

Ali, M. (2018) Iraq: Differences between al-Abadi and his foreign minister about Syria. *Al-Araby al-Jadeed*, 25 April. Available from: https://www.alaraby.co.uk/politics/2018/4/15/العراق-خلافات-بين-العبادي-ووزير-خارجيته-حول-الضربة-السورية.

Ali, R. (2015) Kurdistan and the challenges of Islamism: A conversation with Dr. Hadi Ali, former chairman of Kurdistan Islamic Union's Political Bureau. Hudson Institute, 14 August. Available from: https://www.hudson.org/research/11528-kurdistan-and-the-challenge-of-islamism.

Al-Jaafari, I. (2006) My vision for Iraq. *Washington Post*, 20 March. Available from: http://www.washingtonpost.com/wp-dyn/content/article/2006/03/19/AR2006031901003.html.

Al-Jaredah (2010) Document: State of law coalition 337 election program. Available from: http://www.aljaredah.com/paper.php?source=akbar&mlf=interpage&sid=15683.

Al-Jazeera (2011) Qatar to host crisis meeting on Syria. 17 December. Available from: http://www.aljazeera.com/news/middleeast/2011/12/20111221753317115452.html.

Al-Jazeera (2012) Baghdad hosts Arab League summit. March 28. Available from: http://www.aljazeera.com/news/middleeast/2012/03/20123289517350385.html.

Al-Jazeera Arabic (2008) Interview with Mahmoud al-Mashadani. 19 October. Available from: https://www.youtube.com/watch?v=vZTOfN3jcaY.

Al-Jazeera Arabic (2009) Al-Maliki invited Russian companies for investment in Iraq. 11 April. Available from: http://www.aljazeera.net/news/ebusiness/2009/4/11/المالكي-يدعو-الشركات-الروسية-للاستثمار-ببلاده.

Al-Jazeera Arabic (2014) Interview with Usama al-Nujaifi. Aljazeera Arabic TV, 2 February. Available from: http://www.aljazeera.com/programmes/talktojazeera/2014/01/osama-al-nujaifi-want-an-iraqi-solution-2014129143346410344.html.

Al-Jazeera English (2010) Inside Iraq: Iraq's political deadlock. 23 July. Available from: https://www.youtube.com/watch?v=eciTnpdoGxo.

*Al-Journal* (2017) The secrets of the struggle between al-Hakim and others in ISCI. 25 July. Available from: https://www.aljournal.com/الجورنال-نيوز-تكشف-أسرار-خروج-الحكي/.

Al-Jumaili, G. A. (2016) The horizon of the relationship between the kingdom and Iraq. *Al-Riyadh*, 12 November. Available from: http://www.alriyadh.com/993366.

Al-Jumaili, H. Q. (2010) Reading about the most important manifesto for the winners of the 2010 election. Unit for Research and Strategic Studies, Baghdad. Available from: http://www.iasj.net/iasj?func=fulltext&aId=25426.

Al-Kadhimi, M. (2013) Iraqi National Security Advisor says terrorism linked to havens in Syria. *Al-Monitor*, 25 February. Available from: http://www.al-monitor.com/pulse/originals/2013/02/iraq-national-security-advisor-interview.html#ixzz2RrhhS0WN.

Al-Kadhimi, M. (2014) Iraqi deputy prime minister: I was mistaken in joining government. *Al-Monitor*, 4 July. Available from: http://www.al-monitor.com/pulse/originals/2014/07/iraq-saleh-mutlaq-interview-mosul-crisis-army-solution.html.

*Al-Khabar* (2015) Interview with the commander of Hashd al-Sha'abi. 13 July. Available from: http://www.al-akhbar.com/node/237749.

Al-Khaleej Online (2016a) Al-Nujaifi refused alliance with Russia. 10 October. Available from: http://alkhaleejonline.net/articles/1444483080461829100/النج-يفي-يرفض-التحالف-مع-روسيا-تزيد-حدة-الصراع-في-العراق/.

Al-Khaleej Online (2016b) How Saudi Arabia deals with the repeated threats of Hashd al-Sha'abi. 9 November. Available from: http://alkhaleejonline.net/articles/1447066449128047300/كيف-ستتعامل-السعودية-مع-تهديدات-الحشد-الشعبي-المتكررة-ضدها/.

Al-Knani, A. (2012) Goals of Iraqi foreign policy from geopolitical perspective. *Kitaba*, 7 October. Available from: http://www.kitabat.info/subject.php?id=22922.

Allawi, A. A. (2013) Ayad Allawi's personal website. Available from: http://www.ayad-allawi.com/عن-علاوي/.

Allawi, A. A., O. al-Nufaifi and R. al-Essawi (2011) How to save Iraq from Civil War. *New York Times*, 27 December. Available from: http://www.nytimes.com/2011/12/28/opinion/how-to-save-iraq-from-civil-war.html?_r=3&scp=1&sq=iraqiya%20allawi&st=Search.

Al-Laythi, N., and K. A. Zayer (2012) Potential Iran-Iraq deal worries west, pressures Turkey. *Al-Monitor*, 4 October. Available from: http://www.al-monitor.com/pulse/security/01/10/iran-iraq-strategic-agreement.html.

Al-Mada Paper (2004) Allawi completed his visits to Saudi Arabia and Lebanon. July. Available from: http://almadapaper.net/sub/07-164/p01.htm.

Al-Mada Press (2013a) Reelecting Maliki for the Da'wa Party. 16 March. Available from: http://www.almadapress.com/ar/NewsDetails.aspx?NewsID=8433.

Al-Mada Press (2013b) Al-Nujaifi to Europe Union: Iraqi army use extreme violence against the demonstrations. 17 June. Available from: http://almadapress.com/ar/news/13740/النجيفي--للاتحاد-الاوربي--الجيش-الع.

Al-Majdi, A. (2009) Mowffak al-Rubaie: Our relationship with Iran is friendship and interests. Elaph, 26 June. Available from: http://elaph.com/ElaphWeb/AkhbarKhasa/2009/6/454910.htm.

Al-Maliki, N. (2013) Nouri al-Maliki: The US has a foreign policy partner in Iraq. *Washington Post*, 8 April. Available from: https://www.washingtonpost.com/opinions/nouri-al-maliki-the-us-has-a-foreign-policy-partner-in-iraq/2013/04/08/dcb9f8a6-a05e-11e2-82bc-511538ae90a4_story.html.

Al-Manar (2014) Iraq at war with Saudi Arabia, war without armies. 22 April. Available from: https://www.youtube.com/watch?v=ihEY5eQcX88.

Al-Masalah (2016) Al-Sadr calls people to demonstrate and condemn the execution of Nimr. 10 March. Available from: https://almasalah.com/ar/News/66946/الصدر-يدعو-لتظاهرات-غاضبة-ردا-على-إ.

Al-Mustaqbal (2007) Al-Maliki: We decided Iraq foreign policy. 12 March. Available from: http://www.almustaqbal.com/v4/Article.aspx?Type=np&Articleid=226949.

Al-Qarawee, H. (2014) Iraqi judiciary accused of bias, failure. *Al-Monitor*, 28 March. Available from: http://www.al-monitor.com/pulse/originals/2014/03/iraq-judiciary-accusation-politicized-maliki.html.

Al-Qassemi, S. (2012) Tribalism in the Arabian Peninsula: It's a family affair. *Jadaliyya*, 1 February. Available from: http://www.jadaliyya.com/pages/index/4198/tribalism-in-the-arabian-peninsula_it-is-a-family-.

Al-Rafidain (2015) ISCI: A good step for Iran, Syria, Russia and Iraq alliance. 6 October. Available from: http://alrafidain.org/قناة_الرافدين-عمار-الحكيم-تحالف-سوريا/.

Al-Rai (2016) Interview with Ammar Hakim. 6 March. Available from: http://www.alrai-iq.com/2016/03/06/198601/.

Al-Rai Media (2016) Conversation with Hoshyar Zebari. 31 December. Available from: http://www.alraimedia.com/ar/article/foreigns/2016/12/31/734676/nr/iraq.

Al-Salhy, S. (2016) Iraqi forces threaten to attack Turkish troops as Mosul battles looms. Middle East Eye, 6 October. Available from: http://www.middleeasteye.net/news/iraqi-army-militias-threaten-attack-turkey-if-it-does-not-withdraw-troops-1700165186.

Al-Shaf'i, M. (2005) Poland is angry about accusations about the quality of their weapons: Accusations against the Iraqi government on spending too much on weapons. *Asharq Al-Awsat*, 30 September. Available from: http://archive.aawsat.com/details.asp?article=326003&issueno=9803#.V9519Fd6rlI.

Alsharif, A. (2016) Saudis walk out of Arab League meeting after Iraqi minister's comments. Reuters, 11 March. Available from: http://www.reuters.com/article/us-mideast-crisis-arabs-idUSKCN0WD1J7.

Al-Sharqiya (2015) ISCI: A good step for Iran, Syria, Russia and Iraq alliance. 6 October. Available from: http://www.alsharqiya.com/news/?p=178454.

Al-Sumaria (2011) Exchanging accusations between Zebari and the Committee of Foreign Relations. 29 April. Available from: http://www.alsumaria.tv/news/41152/alsumaria-news/ar#.

Al-Sumaria (2012) Sami al-A'skari: The Baathists control Foreign Affairs Ministry and use its resources. 12 November. Available from: http://www.alsumaria.tv/mobile/news/66271/iraq-news.

Al-Sumaria (2014) Zebari calls al-Maliki to apologize to the KRG about his recent announcements. 13 July. Available from: http://www.alsumaria.tv/news/105448/زيباري-يدعو-المالكي-إلى-الاعتذار-لإقليم/ar.

Al-Sumaria (2019) Mohammed Ali al-Hakim foreign minister – episode fourteen. 24 May. Available from: https://www.youtube.com/watch?v=7FyrV0rN-Xs.

Al-Tamimi, A. J. (2014) Iraq: Who are As'ib Ahl al-Haq Islamists. *Islamic Gate*, 6 March. Available from: http://www.aymennjawad.org/14510/iraq-who-are-asaib-ahl-al-haq-islamists.

Al-Tawafoq (2010) Al-Tawafoq political program (338) 2010–2014.

*Alwasat News* (2012) Saudi and Qatari media attacks on al-Maliki. 6 July. Available from: http://www.alwasatnews.com/news/647733.html.

Al-Watani (2016) The political program for Iraqi National Accord. 3 January. Available from: http://www.al-watnia.com/#!prog/c1ebi; http://media.wix.com/ugd/424eda_6ad3520a344140238f19af7f754dfd6c.pdf.

American University of Iraq-Sulaimani (2016) A discussion with Sayyid Jawad al-Khoei. 12 April. Available from: http://auis.edu.krd/iris/events/discussion-sayyid-jawad-al-khoei.

Arango, T. (2012) Iran presses for official to be next leader of Shiites. *New York Times*, 11 May. Available from: http://www.nytimes.com/2012/05/12/world/middleeast/iran-promotes-its-candidate-for-next-shiite-leader.html?_r=1&ref=timarango.

Arms Control Association (2016) Timeline of nuclear diplomacy with Iran. Available from: https://www.armscontrol.org/factsheet/Timeline-of-Nuclear-Diplomacy-With-Iran.

*Asharq Al-Awsat* (2004) Al-Yawar and King of Jordan: Iran interferences in Iraq's election. 9 December. Available from: http://archive.aawsat.com/details.asp?article=270145&issueno=9508#.V0QXgWPmt-U.

*Asharq Al-Awsat* (2010) Visits to improve relations with Riyadh-Iraqi sources. April. Available from: http://english.aawsat.com/2010/04/article55251125.

*Asharq Al-Awsat* (2015) Iraq asks UAE to remove Badr Organization and Sadr militia from terror list. 4 February. Available from: http://english.aawsat.com/2015/02/article55341129/iraq-asks-uae-to-remove-badr-organization-and-sadr-militia-from-terror-list.

*Asharq Al-Awsat Arabic* (2009) Damascus: We will talk the necessary measures. 3 September. Available from: http://archive.aawsat.com/details.asp?section=4&issueno=11237&article=534441#.VSlml4dGjww.

Atlantic Council (2016) Launch of the Task Force Future of Iraq. 16 February. Available from: https://www.youtube.com/watch?v=yZEDHIiqNjI.

Ayman, A. (2004) Files and facts about Iran's role in Iraq. Mokarabat. Available from: http://www.mokarabat.com/s849.htm.

Baghdad Akhbaria (2014) Marjia in Najaf supports improving relationship with Saudi Arabia. 19 November. Available from: http://www.baghdadnp.com/news.php?action=view&id=25742.

Baghdad Post (2016) Kata'ib Hezbollah defies Iraqi PM, threatens Saudi border. 16 July. Available from: https://www.thebaghdadpost.com/en/Story/42762/Kata-ib-Hezbollah-defies-Iraqi-PM-threatens-Saudi-border.

Baghdad Post (2018) Qatar put pressure on Iraqi Sunnis to join Iran's allied al-Bina coalition. 4 July. Available from: https://www.thebaghdadpost.com/ar/Story/120450/قطر-تضغط-على-سنة-العراق-للانضمام-لـ-البناء-حليف-إيران.

Barkey, H. (2013) Turkey–Iraq relations deteriorate with accusations of sectarianism. *Al-Monitor*, 8 February. Available from: http://www.al-monitor.com/pulse/originals/2012/al-monitor/turkey-iraq-ties-sour-brover-syr.html.

Basnews (2015) Saudi Arabia to open consulate in Erbil. 16 December. Available from: http://www.basnews.com/index.php/en/news/middle-east/248600.

BBC (2012) Six world powers 'make Iran nuclear proposal'. 23 May. Available from: http://www.bbc.co.uk/news/world-middle-east-18170651.

BBC News (2006) Bush delays fresh Iraq strategy. 12 December. Available from: http://news.bbc.co.uk/1/hi/world/americas/6172103.stm.

Beinart, P. (2014) Obama's disastrous Iraq policy: An autopsy. *Atlantic*, 23 June. Available from: http://www.theatlantic.com/international/archive/2014/06/obamas-disastrous-iraq-policy-an-autopsy/373225/.

Berenson, A., and D. Filkins (2004) The reach war: The insurgents; rebel Iraqi cleric is told to give up or face attack. *New York Times*, 25 August. Available from: http://www.

nytimes.com/2004/08/25/world/reach-war-insurgents-rebel-iraqi-cleric-told-give-up-face-attack.html?_r=0.

Beth News (2016) Interview with Secretary General of Iraqi Islamic Party regarding Iraq and Saudi Arabia relationship. 7 January. Available from: http://www.bethpress.com/index.php/beth_press/indetails_close/22366/.

Bloomberg (2016) Iraq's Kurds to start natural gas exports to Turkey in 2019–2020. 15 January. Available from: https://www.bloomberg.com/news/articles/2016-01-15/iraq-s-kurds-to-start-natural-gas-exports-to-turkey-in-2019-2020.

Braun, S. (2017) Iraqi VP asks for arms, training for Sunnis in his country. *Times of Israel*, 7 November. Available from: https://www.timesofisrael.com/iraqi-vp-asks-for-arms-training-for-sunnis-in-his-country/.

Brown, M. E. (1979) The nationalization of the Iraqi Petroleum Company. *International Journal of Middle East Studies*, 10(1), 107–24.

Buratha News (2009a) Agents from the previous regime in court in the US. 10 January. Available from: http://burathanews.com/news/57434.html.

Buratha News (2009b) Zebari: Save Iraq from international sanctions is the most important foreign policy priorities. 13 October. Available from: http://burathanews.com/arabic/news/77300.

Buratha News (2014) Al-Muatin coalition electoral program: Ammar Al-Hakim. 5 April. Available from: http://burathanews.com/arabic/news/233596.

Burch, J. (2012) Turkey warns Iraqi PM over sectarian conflict. Reuters, 24 January. Available from: http://www.reuters.com/article/us-turkey-iraq-idUSTRE80N1V920120124.

Cafarella, J. (2016) How Turkey could become the next Pakistan. Institute for the Study of War, 19 July. Available from: http://iswresearch.blogspot.co.uk/2016/07/how-turkey-could-become-next-pakistan.html.

Calamur, K. (2017) Jalal Talabani: 'The rare politician who could talk to anybody'. *Atlantic*, 3 October. Available from: https://www.theatlantic.com/international/archive/2017/10/jalal-talabani-dies/541836/.

Charbel, G. (2015) Iraqi PM talks Iran, IS and Saudi Arabia. *Al-Hayat*, 15 April. Available from: http://www.alhayat.com/Articles/6925767/العبادي-لـ-الحياة-بغداد-خارج-خطر-داعش-والسنّة-أول-المتضررين.

CNN (2007) Former Iraqi leader returning to fight for our country. 27 August. Available from: http://edition.cnn.com/2007/WORLD/meast/08/26/allawi.returns/index.html?iref=nextin.

CNN (2008) Ayad Allawi on late edition. 27 August. Available from: https://www.youtube.com/watch?v=6a_F99eg5LM.

CNN (2015) Iraq's deputy PM: We worry about country post-ISIS. Amanpour, 24 May. Available from: http://edition.cnn.com/videos/world/2015/05/25/intv-amanpour-pleitgen-saleh-al-mutlaq.cnn.

CNN Arabic (2015) Al-Nujaifi bloc calls Baghdad to enter in Islamic coalition alongside Saudi Arabia. 16 December. Available from: http://arabic.cnn.com/middleeast/2015/12/16/iraq-saudi-maliki-alliance-military.

CNN Arabic (2017) Muqtada al-Sadr: I hope the Kurds adhere to the constitution. 15 October. Available from: https://arabic.cnn.com/middle-east/2017/10/15/sadr-kurdistan-referendum-kurds-iraq-constitution.

Cole, J. (2004a) Platform of United Iraqi Alliance. *Informed Comment*, 31 December. Available from: https://www.juancole.com/2004/12/platform-of-united-iraqi-alliance.html.

Cole, J. (2004b) Ghazi al-Yawer on Iraqi politics. *Informed Comment*, 1 June. Available from: http://www.juancole.com/2004/06/ghazi-al-yawar-on-iraqi-politics-here.html.

Council on Foreign Relations (2004) A meeting with Iraqi interim prime minister Ayad Allawi. 23 September. Available from: http://www.cfr.org/iraq/meeting-iraqi-interim-prime-minister-ayad-allawi/p7401.

C-Span (2004) US and Iraqi operations. 23 September. Available from: https://www.c-span.org/video/?183645-1/us-iraqi-operations.

*Daily News* (2018) Turkey, Iraq agree to be in full cooperation against PKK. 14 August. Available from: http://www.hurriyetdailynews.com/turkey-iraq-agree-to-be-in-full-cooperation-against-pkk-135799.

*Daily Sabah* (2018) Iraqi PM Haider al-Abadi visits Turkey with bilateral, regional matters on agenda. 13 August. Available from: https://www.dailysabah.com/diplomacy/2018/08/14/iraqi-pm-haider-al-abadi-visits-turkey-with-bilateral-regional-matters-on-agenda.

*Daily Star* (2016) Saudi replaces Iraq envoy who riled Shia militias. 16 October. Available from: http://www.dailystar.com.lb/News/Middle-East/2016/Oct-16/376646-saudi-arabia-reassigns-ambassador-to-iraq-after-controversy.ashx.

Damon, A., and M. Tawfeeq (2011) Iraq's leader becoming a new 'dictator' deputy warns. CNN, 13 December. Available from: http://edition.cnn.com/2011/12/13/world/meast/iraq-maliki/.

Daragahi, B. (2014) Iraqi elections overshadowed by claims of claims of corruption. *Financial Times*, 14 April. Available from: https://next.ft.com/content/8495e4a4-c188-11e3-97b2-00144feabdc0.

Daudey, A. (2006) Iraqi Sunni-Arab MP Saleh al-Mutlaq takes over Kurdish properties. *EKurd Daily*, 29 November. Available from: http://ekurd.net/mismas/articles/misc2006/11/government858.htm.

Department of Foreign Relations (2014) The Kurdistan Regional Government Department of Foreign Relations. 20 April. Available from: http://dfr.krg.org/p/p.aspx?p=25&l=12&s=010000&r=332.

Department of Foreign Relations (2015) The KRG's policies. 16 June. Available from: http://dfr.gov.krd/p/p.aspx?p=29&l=12&s=010000&r=336.

Ditz, J. (2014) Iraq opposition leader hires lobbyist to oppose US arms push. *Antiwar*, 27 January. Available from: http://news.antiwar.com/2014/01/27/iraq-opposition-leader-hires-lobbyist-to-oppose-us-arms-push/.

Doran, M. S. (2016) Iraq and campaign 2016. Hudson Institute, C-SPAN, 4 November. Available from: https://www.c-span.org/video/?417984-1/hudson-institute-hosts-discussion-us-policy-toward-iraq.

Egan, M. (2016) Iraq is pumping oil at record pace despite chaos. CNN Money, 7 June. Available from: http://money.cnn.com/2016/06/07/investing/iraq-oil-production-record-high-isis/.

Egatha (2016) External relations of IIROSA. Available from: http://www.egatha.org/eportal/index.php?option=com_content&view=article&id=12&Itemid=4.

EITI (2015) Iraqi Extractive Industries Transparency Initiative. Available from: https://eiti.org/iraq#overview.

*EKurd Daily* (2010) Saudi King Abdullah receives Kurdistan President Barzani. 13 April. Available from: http://ekurd.net/mismas/articles/misc2010/4/state3750.htm.

*EKurd Daily* (2015) Massud Barzani in Wikileaks' Saudi Arabia cables. 21 June. Available from: http://ekurd.net/massud-barzani-in-wikileaks-saudi-arabia-cables-2015-06-21.

Elaph (2004) Iranian and European discussions: Tehran is unfortunate for al-Yawar accusations. 9 December. Available from: http://elaph.com/Politics/2004/12/26466.htm.

Elaph (2016) Interview with Atheel al-Nujaifi. 5 January. Available from: http://elaph.com/Web/News/2016/1/1065249.html.

Embassy of Republic of Iraq in the US (2016) Foreign policy. Available from: http://www.iraqiembassy.us/page/foreign-policy.

Energy Daily (2013) Iraq's Maliki discusses oil project in Russia. 1 July. Available from: https://www.energy-daily.com/reports/Iraqs_Maliki_discusses_oil_project_in_Russia_999.html.

Euronews (2009) Nouri al-Maliki: 'Iraq is no longer a burden for its neighbours, the USA, or the UN Security Council'. 3 April. Available from: https://www.euronews.com/2009/04/03/nouri-al-maliki.

European Commission (2016) The EU and Iraq. 16 February. Available from: http://ec.europa.eu/trade/policy/countries-and-regions/countries/iraq/.

Everington, J. (2018) Iraq may have twice as much oil as previously thought, says minister. *Arab News*, 29 March. Available from: http://www.arabnews.com/node/1275391/business-economy.

Fairweather, J. (2004) New Iraqi president outspoken on US role. *Irish Times*, 2 June. Available from: http://www.irishtimes.com/news/new-iraqi-president-outspoken-on-us-role-1.1143041.

Fars News Agency (2015) Saudi deposited $575 million to ex-Iraqi speaker account after Mosul's fall. 23 June. Available from: http://en.farsnews.com/newstext.aspx?nn=13940402000971.

Fatha al-Hurriya (2012) Interview with Jalal Talabani. Al-Fayhaa TV. Available from: https://www.youtube.com/watch?v=OGcEKkeG2d4.

Fayad, M. (2011) Interview with Da'wa party historian. *Asharq Al-Awsat*, 17 April. Available from: http://archive.aawsat.com/details.asp?section=4&article=617586&issueno=11828#.VzWKiWPmtmA.

Filkins, D. (2015) What are Turkish troops doing in northern Iraq. *New Yorker*, 9 December. Available from: http://www.newyorker.com/news/news-desk/what-are-turkish-troops-doing-in-northern-iraq?mbid=social_twitter.

*Financial Times* (2011) Iraq signs $17bn gas deal with Shell and Mitsubishi. 27 November. Available from: http://www.ft.com/cms/s/0/ba07d154-192b-11e1-92d8-00144feabdc0.html?ft_site=falcon&desktop=true#axzz4fujv4FP7.

*Financial Tribune* (2015) New chapter in Iran-Iraq trade ties. 17 February. Available from: https://financialtribune.com/articles/domestic-economy/11434/new-chapter-in-iran-iraq-trade-ties.

Fordham, A. (2012) Iraq, Saudi Arabia show signs of improved relations after years of strain. *Washington Post*, 4 March. Available from: https://www.washingtonpost.com/world/middle_east/iraq-and-saudi-arabia-show-signs-of-improved-relations-after-years-of-strain/2012/03/04/gIQAXnxBrR_story.html.

Foy, H., and S. Sheppard (2017) Iraq demands clarification on Rosneft's Kurdistan contracts. *Financial Times*, 30 October. Available from: https://www.ft.com/content/1d425216-bd8c-11e7-b8a3-38a6e068f464.

France Diplomatie (2014) International Conference on Peace and Security in Iraq. 15 September. Available from: http://www.diplomatie.gouv.fr/en/country-files/iraq/events/article/international-conference-on-peace.

General Secretariat for the Council of Ministers (2014) Available from: http://www.cabinet.iq/PageViewer.aspx?id=4.

Glenewinkel, K. (2004) Iraqi National Accord (INA). Niqash, 6 November. Available from: http://www.niqash.org/en/articles/politics/1013/.

Glenewinkel, K. (2005) Iraqi Islamic Party 'IIP'. Niqash, 7 November. Available from: http://www.niqash.org/en/articles/politics/1013/.

Global Policy Forum (2008) Al-Maliki vows deal with US. Global Policy, June. Available from: https://www.globalpolicy.org/component/content/article/168/36327.html.

Gordon, M. R. (2010) Iran supplying Syrian military via Iraqi airspace. *New York Times*, 4 September. Available from: http://www.nytimes.com/2012/09/05/world/middleeast/iran-supplying-syrian-military-via-iraq-airspace.html?pagewanted=all&_r=0.

Gulmohamad, Z. (2013) The new phase in the Turkish-Iraqi relationship: Fluctuating between friendly and inimical. *Open Democracy*, 20 August. Available from: https://www.opendemocracy.net/zana-khasraw-gul/new-phase-in-turkish-iraqi-relationship-fluctuating-between-friendly-and-inimical.

Gulmohamad, Z. (2014a) Report: Iraqi Kurdistan's rise on the international scene amid the expansion of the Islamic state. Your Middle East, 30 November. Available from: http://www.yourmiddleeast.com/culture/report-iraqi-kurdistans-rise-on-the-international-scene-amid-the-expansion-of-the-islamic-state_28218.

Gulmohamad, Z. (2014b) The Washington and Baghdad relationship: Are the allies in the same orbit? E-International Relations, 12 April. Available from: http://www.e-ir.info/2014/04/12/the-washington-and-baghdad-relationship-are-the-allies-in-the-same-orbit/.

Habib, M. (2015) Some of them don't respect the government decisions: Disputes between the Shia factions that fights Daesh. Niqash, 20 June. Available from: http://www.niqash.org/ar/articles/politics/5033/.

Hacaoglu, S., and K. Firat (2014) Genel to produce Kurds' gas as Turkey said to ready pipeline. *Bloomberg Business*, 13 November. Available from: http://www.bloomberg.com/news/articles/2014-11-13/genel-agrees-to-develop-kurdish-gas-fields-for-export-to-turkey.

Hafidh, H., and B. Faucon (2011) Iraq, Iran Syria $10 billion gas-pipeline deal. *Wall Street Journal*, 25 July. Available from: https://www.wsj.com/articles/SB10001424053111903591104576467631289250392.

Hashisho, A. (2016) Arab league labels Hezbollah terrorist organization. Reuters, 21 December. Available from: http://www.reuters.com/article/us-mideast-crisis-arabs-idUSKCN0WD239.

Heller, S., and A. Stein (2015) The trouble with Turkey's favourite Syrian Islamists. War on the Rocks, 18 August. Available from: https://warontherocks.com/2015/08/the-trouble-with-turkeys-favorite-syrian-islamists/.

Hendawi, H., and Q. Abdul-Zahra (2012) Iran eyes spiritual leadership of Iraq's Shi'ites. *San Diago Union Tribune*, 5 April. Available from: http://www.sandiegouniontribune.com/sdut-iran-eyes-spiritual-leadership-of-iraqs-shiites-2012apr05-story.html.

Hubbard, B. (2015) Cables released by Wikileaks reveals Saudis' checkbook diplomacy. *New York Times*, 20 June. Available from: http://www.nytimes.com/2015/06/21/world/middleeast/cables-released-by-wikileaks-reveal-saudis-checkbook-diplomacy.html.

Hussain, A. (2014) Maliki calls international community to support Iraq's war against terrorism. *Iraqi News*, 10 June. Available from: http://www.iraqinews.com/baghdad-politics/maliki-calls-international-community-to-support-iraq-s-war-against-terrorism/.

I-MOFA (2016a) Iraq's ambassadors fifth conference hosts the spokesperson the Hashd al-Sha'abi. 17 December. Available from: http://www.mofa.gov.iq/ab/news.php?articleid=1371.

I-MOFA (2016b) Diplomatic mission abroad. Available from: http://www.mofa.gov.iq/ab/submenu.php?id=39.

I-MOFA's Law (2013) Ministry's Law. Iraqi Ministry of Foreign Affairs. Available from: http://www.mofa.gov.iq/ab/submenu.php?id=14.

Ingram, J. (2015) Iranian support for Iraqi Kurdistan president strengthens political stability and improves prospects for investment in energy, telecoms, construction. *IHS Jane's 360*, 9 August. Available from: http://www.janes.com/article/53488/iranian-support-for-iraqi-kurdistan-president-strengthens-political-stability-and-improves-prospects-for-investment-in-energy-telecoms-construction.

Intelligence Unit/*Economist* (2015) Saudi Arabia considers reopening Iraq embassy. 16 September. Available from: http://country.eiu.com/article.aspx?articleid=333509417&Country=Iraq&topic=Politics&subtopic=Forecast&subsubtopic=International+relations&u=1&pid=1323750916&oid=1323750916&uid=1.

International Monetary Fund (2016) Economic diversification in oil exporting Arab countries. April. Available from: http://www.imf.org/external/np/pp/eng/2016/042916.pdf.

International Trade Center (2016) Iraq: Evolution of FDI. Available from: http://www.intracen.org/layouts/CountryTemplate.aspx?pageid=47244645034&id=47244652068.

Invest in Group (2014) Diplomacy and politics. July. Available from: http://www.investingroup.org/publications/kurdistan/overview/diplomacy-politics/.

Iran Focus (2004) Surprise visit to Iran by Iraq vice president. 24 August. Available from: http://www.iranfocus.com/en/index.php?option=com_content&view=article&id=99:surprise-visit-to-iran-by-iraq-vice-president&catid=4&Itemid=109.

Iran Focus (2008) Iraq will not be used to harm Iran, PM vows. 8 June. Available from: http://iranfocus.com/en/index.php?option=com_content&view=article&id=15535:iraq-will-not-be-used-to-harm-iran-pm-vows&catid=7&Itemid=112.

Iraq Business News (2010) Kurdish crude oil still smuggled to Iran. 24 July. Available from: https://www.iraq-businessnews.com/2010/07/24/kurdish-crude-oil-still-smuggled-to-iran/.

Iraq Business News (2015) List of international oil companies in Iraqi Kurdistan. Available from: http://www.iraq-businessnews.com/list-of-international-oil-companies-in-iraqi-kurdistan/.

Iraqi Ministry of Trade (2016) World Trade Organization. Available from: http://www.mot.gov.iq/index.php?name=Pages&op=page&pid=150.

Iraqi Parliament Info (2016) Guideline for Iraqi parliament: Islamic Supreme Council of Iraq. Available from: http://www.iraqiparliament.info/node/822.

Irvine, R. (2017). MERI debate on the referendum for independence. Middle East Research Institute. Available from: www.jstor.org/stable/resrep13608.

James, G. (2013) Kurdistan Regional Government. *Middle East Economic Digest*, 22 February. Available from: http://web.b.ebscohost.com/ehost/detail?sid=224ddafe-86a2-4a57-90c8- fe9b158baa14%40sessionmgr112&vid=1&hid=128&bdata=JnNpdGU9ZWhvc3QtbGl2ZQ%3d%3d#db=buh&AN=86693719.

Jeffery, J., and B. Wahab (2018) Putting Iraq-KRG oil relations on solid legal ground. Washington Institute for Near East Studies, 19 July. Available from: https://www.washingtoninstitute.org/policy-analysis/view/putting-iraq-krg-oil-relations-on-solid-legal-ground.

Jeffrey, J. F. (2014) Behind the US withdrawal from Iraq. *Wall Street Journal*, 2 November. Available from: http://www.wsj.com/articles/james-franklin-jeffrey-behind-the-u-s-withdrawal-from-iraq-1414972705.

Jihad Intel (2015) Asaib Ahl al-Haq. Middle East Forum. Available from: http://jihadintel.meforum.org/group/86/asaib-ahl-al-haq.

Kadhim, A. (2017) A major crack in Iraqi Shia politics. *Huffington Post*, 24 July. Available from: http://www.huffingtonpost.com/entry/a-major-crack-in-iraqi-shia-politics_us_59766ab6e4b01cf1c4bb72bd.

Kadhim, A., and R. Nayla (2010) Iraq, Syria agree to build pipelines, official says. Bloomberg, 16 September. Available from: http://www.bloomberg.com/news/articles/2010-09-16/iraq-syria-agree-to-build-cross-border-oil-gas-pipelines-official-says.

Kebriaeezadeh, H. (2015) Economic diplomacy, Iran's new window to foreign relations. *Iran Review*, 18 September. Available from: http://www.iranreview.org/content/Documents/Economic-Diplomacy-Iran-s-New-Window-to-Foreign-Relations.htm.

Kechichian, J. (2012) Is Nouri Al Maliki an Iranian lieutenant? *Gulf News*, 12 March. Available from: https://gulfnews.com/opinion/op-eds/is-nouri-al-maliki-an-iranian-lieutenant-1.1303237.

Khedery, A. (2014) Why we stuck with Maliki and lost Iraq. *Washington Post*, 3 July. Available from: http://www.washingtonpost.com/opinions/why-we-stuck-with-maliki-and-lost-iraq/2014/07/03/0dd6a8a4-f7ec-11e3-a606-946fd632f9f1_story.html.

Korutürk, O. (2015) Former envoy: Turkey's presence in Iraq being question due to Ankara's policies. *Today's Zaman*, 9 December.

KRG Cabinet (2009) President Barzani, Turkey's foreign minister Davutoğlu hold historic meetings, announce plans to open consulate. 31 October. Available from: http://cabinet.gov.krd/a/d.aspx?s=02010100&l=12&r=223&a=32216&s=010000.

KRG-I Representatives in the US (2015) KRG-US relations. Available from: http://new.krg.us/relations/.

Krohley, N. (2014) Moqtada al-Sadr's difficult relationship with Iran. Hurst Publishers, 7 August. Available from: http://www.hurstpublishers.com/moqtada-al-sadrs-difficult-relationship-with-iran/.

KUNA (2006) Al-Maliki seeking trade and investments with Saudi. 2 July. Available from: http://www.kuna.net.kw/ArticlePrintPage.aspx?id=1619291&language=ar.

Kurdistan 24 (2016a) Canada wants to build relationship with Kurds. 26 March. Available from: http://www.kurdistan24.net/en/news/c38cd2fe-6d31-42d8-88fd-4ee137c604dd/Canada-wants-to-build-relationship-with-Kurds.

Kurdistan 24 (2016b) Kurdish NGO joins UN assemblies. 2 May. Available from: http://www.kurdistan24.net/en/news/8e8d4a52-0fb3-458f-ac23-cab43d5d37e0/kurdish-ngo-joins-un-assemblies.

Kurdistan 24 (2016c) Abadi reiterates priority to defeat IS. 20 January. Available from: http://www.kurdistan24.net/en/news/4317d04f-a4af-4671-8af9-a1cbef34cdd7/abadi-reiterates-priority-to-defeat-is.

Kurdistan 24 (2017) NRT TV owner lobbies against Kurdistan independence referendum. 25 July. Available from: http://www.kurdistan24.net/en/news/018b438c-13ac-4676-9ca9-981e0cec5336.

Kurdistan Parliament (2016) Available from: http://www.kurdistan-parliament.org/Default.aspx.

Kurdistan Regional Government (2005) Presidency law of the Kurdistan Region of Iraq. 12 June. Available from: http://cabinet.gov.krd/a/d.aspx?a=3633&l=14.

Kurdistan Regional Government (2014) Program of the cabinet. Available from: http://www.krg.org/p/page.aspx?l=12&s=000000&r=408&p=324&h=1&t=0.

Kurdistan Regional Government (2015) Fact sheet: About the Kurdistan Regional Government. Available from: http://cabinet.gov.krd/p/p.aspx?l=12&p=180.

Kurdistan Regional Government (2016) Fact sheet: About regional government. Available from: http://cabinet.gov.krd/p/p.aspx?l=12&p=180.

Kurdsat (2014) Inside Kurdistan extra with Hoshyar Zebari. 29 March. Available from: https://www.youtube.com/watch?v=EccJP-osvZU.

Lake, E. (2014) Iraq deputy PM asks Obama for election monitors. *Daily Beast*, 14 January. Available from: http://www.thedailybeast.com/articles/2014/01/14/iraqi-deputy-pm-asks-obama-for-election-monitors.html.

Latif, A. (2012) Iraq's Central Bank governor is removed under cloud. *Al-Monitor*, 17 October. Available from: http://www.al-monitor.com/pulse/business/2012/10/warrant-issued-for-iraqs-central-bank-governor.html.

Lawler, A. and R. Gamal (2015) Iraqi oil selling at $30 as OPEC readies for new battles. *Reuters*, 19 November. Available from: http://uk.reuters.com/article/uk-iraq-oil-idUKKCN0T80MB20151119.

Lister, T. (2014) Destination unknown: Will Kurds use oil to break free from Iraq? *CNN*, 24 June. Available from: http://edition.cnn.com/2014/06/24/world/meast/iraq-kurds-oil-sale/index.html.

Luizard, P. J. (2007) Islam as a point of reference for political and social groups in Iraq. *International Review of the Red Cross*, 89(868), December, 843–55. Available from: https://www.icrc.org/eng/assets/files/other/irrc-868_luizard.pdf.

Mackey, P. (2013) Iraq sees hefty return to oil growth in 2014. *Reuters*, 23 October. Available from: http://www.reuters.com/article/iraq-oil-idUSL5N0ID2K820131023.

Ma'd, F. (2009) Allawi: There is ambiguity regarding Iraq's policy towards neighboring countries. Archive *Asharq Al-Awsat*, 24 August. Available from: http://archive.aawsat.com/details.asp?section=4&issueno=11227&article=533058#.VwJkZbw4kdV.

Mahasna, S. (2005) Allawi: Iraqi Ministry of Defense has been subjected to a $1 billion corruption case. *Asharq Al-Awsat*, 20 September. Available from: http://archive.aawsat.com/details.asp?article=324330&issueno=9793#.V9516Fd6rlI.

Mahdi, O. (2004) Allawi admit the disagreements with Iran. *Elaph*, 2 August. Available from: http://elaph.com/Politics/2004/8/2930.htm?sectionarchive=Politics.

Mamoun, A. (2016) Iraqi Foreign Ministry summons UAE ambassador to Baghdad. *Iraqi News*, 27 February. Available from: http://www.iraqinews.com/baghdad-politics/148426/.

Mamouri, A. (2018) Khamenei, Sistani and fight for the soul of Shiite Islam. *Al-Monitor*, 25 April. Available from: http://www.al-monitor.com/pulse/originals/2018/04/dueling-ayatollahs-sistani-khamenei-shiite-iran-iraq.html#ixzz5Jj1rl9AP.

Mamouri, A. (2014) Qom, Najaf call for improved relations with Saudi Arabia. *Al-Monitor*, 17 December. Available from: http://www.al-monitor.com/pulse/originals/2014/12/iraq-najaf-qom-relations-rapprochement-saudi-arabia.html.

Mamouri, A. (2015) How to rein in Iraq's popular mobilization units. *Al-Monitor*, 8 September. Available from: http://www.al-monitor.com/pulse/originals/2015/09/iraq-popular-mobilization-militias-isis-iran-government.html.

Mapping Militants Organizations (2015) Asa'ib Ahl al-Haq. Stanford University. Available from: https://web.stanford.edu/group/mappingmilitants/cgi-bin/groups/view/143.

Marco Polis (2012) Kurdistan oil companies. 12 December. Available from: http://www.marcopolis.net/kurdistan-oil-companies-list-of-oil-companies-in-kurdistan.htm.

Masrawy (2016) ISCI rejects classification of Lebanese Hezbollah as a terrorist organization. 4 March. Available from: http://www.masrawy.com/News/News_PublicAffairs/details/2016/3/4/763266/-تصنيف-يستنكر-العراق-في-الإسلامي-الأعلى-المجلس
حزب-الله-اللبناني-كمنظمة-ارهابية

MEMRI (2014) Iraqi PM al-Maliki: Saudi Arabia and Qatar declared war on terrorism against Iraq. France 24 TV Channel. Available from: https://www.youtube.com/watch?v=aD-qMqp4XC8.

Middle East Brief (2015) Abadi versus Suleimani: Who will go first? Available from: http://mebriefing.com/?p=1901.

Middle East Eye (2015) Military officials Iraq likely to welcome 'no red line' Russian airstrike. 6 October. Available from: http://www.middleeasteye.net/news/military-officials-say-iraq-likely-welcome-no-red-line-russian-airstrikes-1790574154.

Middle East Institute (2015) Robert Ford on Prime Minister Abadi's visit to Washington DC. 17 April. Available from: http://www.mei.edu/profile/robert-s-ford.

Middle East Monitor (2015) Baghdad blasts Doha's 'Iraq reconciliation' conference. 7 September. Available from: https://www.middleeastmonitor.com/news/middle-east/20900-baghdad-blasts-dohas-iraq-reconciliation-conference.

Mostafa, M. (2017) Militia leader threatens to use force against Turkish troops in Iraq. *Iraqi News*, 11 January. Available from: http://www.iraqinews.com/iraq-war/shia-militia-leader-threatens-use-force-turkish-troop-iraq/.

Munther, A. (2005) About the Kurdistan alliance manifesto. Kurdistan Regional Government, 11 January. Available from: http://cabinet.gov.krd/a/d.aspx?l=14&s=01010300&r=249&a=360&s=010000.

Mustafa, H. (2015) After 25 years of boycott, Saudi diplomatic envoy arrives in Baghdad. *Asharq Al-Awsat*, 17 December. Available from: http://english.aawsat.com/2015/12/article55345875/after-a-25-years-of-boycott-saudi-diplomatic-envoy-arrives-in-baghdad.

Mustafa, S. (2017) Iraqi President issues a statement about Kurdistan's referendum to initiate dialogue. Al-Sumaria TV, 16 September. Available from: https://www.alsumaria.tv/news/215895/alsumaria-news/ar?fb_comment_id=1539696756089368_1539722416086802#.

Nasiria (2015) Foreign policy is the second stage on war on terror. 2 April. Available from: http://www.nasiriaelc.com/?p=44235.

Natali, D. (2013) How independent is the Iraqi-Kurdish pipeline to Turkey? *Al-Monitor*, 4 November. Available from: http://www.al-monitor.com/pulse/ar/originals/2013/11/iraqi-kurdish-pipeline-turkey-oil-policy-export.html.

*National* (2015) Hezbollah is fighting ISIL in Iraq, Nasrallah reveals. 17 February. Available from: http://www.thenational.ae/world/middle-east/hizbollah-is-fighting-isil-in-iraq-nasrallah-reveals.

*New Arab* (2017) Muqtada al-Sadr calls Bashar al-Assad to resign. 8 April. Available from: https://www.alaraby.co.uk/politics/2017/4/8/الأوان-فوات-قبل-للتنحي-الأسد-بشار-يدعو-الصدر-مقتدى

NBC News (2019) Iraq says it supports Syria's return to Arab League. 13 January. Available from: https://abcnews.go.com/International/wireStory/iraq-supports-syrias-return-arab-league-60345986.

Now (2007) Al-Maliki: We decided Iraq foreign policy. 4 March. Available from: https://now.mmedia.me/lb/ar/latestnews2ar/نقرره_نحن_لعرقي_لخرجي_لملكيلسيس.

Observatory of Economic Complexity (2016) Iraq profile. Available from: http://atlas.media.mit.edu/en/profile/country/irq/.

Oil Price (2013) Iraq Jordanian $18 billion pipeline-reality of fantasy. 15 April. Available from: http://oilprice.com/Geopolitics/Middle-East/Iraq-Jordanian-18-billion-pipeline-Reality-or-Fantasy.html.

Oil Price (2015) Competition with OPEC set to intensify amid low oil prices. 23 December. Available from: http://oilprice.com/Energy/Crude-Oil/Competition-Within-OPEC-Set-To-Intensify-Amid-Low-Oil-Prices.html.

O'Leary, B. (ed.) (2008) The Kurdistan Region: Investment in the future. Kurdistan Regional Government. Washington: Newsdesk Media. Available from: http://www.polisci.upenn.edu/ppec/PPEC%20People/Brendan%20O'Leary/publications/Invest_in_the_Future_2008.pdf.

O'Leary, B. (2018) Debate: Solving Baghdad-Erbil disputes constitutionally. Streaming online from Missouri State University, Middle East Studies Program, 5 October. Available from: https://www.facebook.com/studyMENA/videos/150327642578516/.

Otterman, S. (2004) Q&A: Iraq vs the Bremer Edicts. *New York Times International*, 8 July. Available from: http://www.nytimes.com/cfr/international/slot2_070804.html?pagewanted=1&pa.

Palmer (2013) Iraq to hire DC lobbyist. Politico, 13 February. Available from: http://www.politico.com/story/2013/02/iraq-to-hire-dc-lobbyist-087599.

Pamuk, H., and S. Kalin (2015) Iraq's Barzani condemns Turkish bombing, he says killed civilian. Reuters, 1 August. Available from: https://www.reuters.com/article/us-mideast-crisis-turkey-iraq-idUSKCN0Q635X20150801.

Parker, N. (2015) Power struggle: Power failure in Iraq as militias outgun state. Reuters Investigates, 21 October. Available from: http://www.reuters.com/investigates/special-report/iraq-abadi/.

Parliament Iraq (2015a) In the presence of the speaker of Council of Representatives convened a forum called the challenges of Iraqi foreign policy. 11 November. Available from: http://www.parliament.iq/details.aspx?id=26481&AlwType=News .

Parliament Iraq (2015b) The speaker received the FRC and emphasized developing relationships with international parliaments. 4 October. Available from: http://parliament.iq/details.aspx?id=50221&AlwType=Pre .

PBS News Hour (2015) Prime Minister Abadi: Iraq welcomes Russia in Islamic fight. 30 September. Available from: https://www.youtube.com/watch?v=klp25ogTzMs.

Pecquet, J. (2015a) Middle East lobbying: Kurdistan Regional Government. *Al-Monitor*, 16 August. Available from: http://www.al-monitor.com/lobbying/iraqi-kurdistan.

Pecquet, J. (2015b) House panel approves Peshmerga bill that Baghdad deems unwise and unnecessary. *Al-Monitor*, 9 December. Available from: http://www.al-monitor.com/pulse/originals/2015/12/congress-iraq-peshmerga-bill-baghdad-unwise.html.

PMO (2015a) Prime Minister Dr Haider al-Abadi's official website. Available from: http://www.pmo.iq.

PMO (2015b) The implementation and follow-up Committee for National Reconciliation. Available from: http://www.iraqnr.com/Home/.

Prime Minister Press Office (2017) H.E. Prime Minister Dr. Haider Al-Abadi receives a phone call from vice president of the United States Mike Pence. 7 April. Available from: http://pmo.iq/pme/press2017en/7-4-20171en.htm.

Qanat al-Dijla al-Fathaia B (2017) Discussion with the vice president Usama al-Nujaifi. 8 November. Available from: https://www.youtube.com/watch?v=EOWXpHdl-gA.

Qanat al-Furat (2019) Ayad al-Samarai. Qanat al-Furat TV, 20 August. Available from: https://www.youtube.com/watch?v=cNPPrlJRINo.

Qanat al-Tasi'a (2016) Interview: Asa'd Sulaiman: Iraq–Turkey's bilateral relationship. 11 October. Available from: https://www.youtube.com/watch?v=oIwpoC0JRuQ.

Radio Sawa (2007) Iraqi Islamic Party create a lobby in Washington DC to achieve a request from the US administration. 16 March. Available from: http://www.radiosawa.com/content/article/148142.html.

Rafat, S. (2004) Relationship between Arabs and Iran. Saaid. Available from: http://www.saaid.net/Minute/138.htm.

Raval, A. (2015) Israel turns to Kurds for three quarters of its oil supplies. *Financial Times*, 23 August. Available from: https://next.ft.com/content/150f00cc-472c-11e5-af2f-4d6e0e5eda22.

Relief Web (2008) Iran, Iraq sign MoU on defense co-op. 9 June. Available from: http://reliefweb.int/report/iraq/iran-iraq-sign-mou-defense-co-op.

Republic of Iraq, Ministry of Foreign Affairs (2015) Foreign Policy. Available from: http://www.mofa.gov.iq/en/submenu.php?id=28.

Republic of Turkey, Ministry of Foreign Affairs (2015) Relations between Turkey and Iraq. Available from: http://www.mfa.gov.tr/relations-between-turkey-and-iraq.en.mfa.

Reuters (2012a) Qatar says won't hand VP Hashemi over to Baghdad. 13 April. Available from: http://www.reuters.com/article/us-iraq-hashemi-qatar-idUSBRE8320R320120403.

Reuters (2012b) Iraq's Shahristani says Kurdish oil smuggled, mainly to Iran. 2 April. Available from: https://www.reuters.com/article/iraq-kurds-oil/iraqs-shahristani-says-kurdish-oil-smuggled-mainly-to-iran-idUSL6E8F22C320120402.

Reuters (2015) Shi'ite militias threaten Turkey over incursion into Iraq. 9 December. Available from: http://www.reuters.com/article/us-mideast-crisis-iraq-turkey-idUSKBN0TS21W20151209.

Reuters (2016) Iraq's Sistani condemns Nimr execution, Sadr organizes protests. 3 January. Available from: https://uk.reuters.com/article/us-saudi-security-iraq-idUKKBN0UH06L20160103.

Reuters (2017) Turkey, Iran, Iraq consider counter-measures over Kurdish referendum. 21 September. Available from: https://www.reuters.com/article/us-mideast-crisis-kurds-referendum-minis/turkey-iran-iraq-consider-counter-measures-over-kurdish-referendum-idUSKCN1BW1EA.

Review Kurdistan Region of Iraq (2013) KRG Department of Foreign Relations: Looking ahead. Kurdistan Regional Government, March, bi-monthly issue.

Roberts, K. (2007) US general says Iran backs Iraqi Shi'ites and Sunnis. Reuters, 19 April. Available from: http://www.reuters.com/article/us-usa-iraq-iran-idUSN1943087020070419.

Roggio, B. (2007) Iran's Ramazan Corps and the ratlines into Iraq. *Long War Journal*, 5 December. Available from: http://www.longwarjournal.org/archives/2007/12/irans_ramazan_corps.php.

Rubin, M. (2015) Saudi Wikileaks a reality check on Iraq. *Commentary Magazine*, 22 June. Available from: https://www.commentarymagazine.com/foreign-policy/middle-east/saudi-arabian-involvement-in-iraq/.

Rubin Report (2016) Interview with Bayan Sami Abdul Rahman: The Kurds: everything you need to know. 21 March. Available from: https://www.youtube.com/watch?v=Mt6UwbhMFBg.

Rudaw (2016) Shiite militias in Iraq threaten to fight Turkish forces during anticipated Mosul offensive. 5 October. Available from: http://www.rudaw.net/english/kurdistan/051020165.

Rudaw (2017a) The man who worked to win Iraq diplomatic credibility after 2003. 9 January. Available from: http://www.rudaw.net/english/middleeast/iraq/080120171.

Rudaw (2017b) Deputy PM Talabani asks Shiite cleric to mediate between KRG and Iraq. 11 September. Available from: http://www.rudaw.net/english/kurdistan/091120172.

Saadoun, M. (2016a) Executing of Saudi prisoners widens gap between Baghdad, Riyadh. *Al-Monitor*, 30 October. Available from: http://www.al-monitor.com/pulse/originals/2016/10/saudi-iraq-prisoners-terrorists-execution.html.

Saadoun, M. (2016b) Saudi ambassador's comments on Popular Mobilization Units stir ire of Iraqis. *Al-Monitor*, 11 February. Available from: http://www.al-monitor.com/pulse/originals/2016/02/iraq-saudi-arabia-ambassador-comments-pmus.html.

Saleh, I. (2015) Why Silence? Why local media have shut up about Iraq-Saudi Arabia Wikileaks scandal. Niqash, 9 July. Available from: http://www.niqash.org/en/articles/politics/5050/.

Salih, M. (2015) US military aid bills highlight Iraq's deep divisions. *Al-Jazeera*, 10 May. Available from: http://www.aljazeera.com/news/2015/05/150509084945317.html.

Sattar, O. (2017) Islamic Supreme Council of Iraq at risk of fragmentation. *Al-Monitor*, 9 July. Available from: http://www.al-monitor.com/pulse/originals/2017/07/iraq-islamic-supreme-council-ammar-hakim.html.

Saudi Embassy (2006) Ministry of Hajj refutes allegation by outgoing Iraqi PM. 1 June. Available from: https://www.saudiembassy.net/archive/2006/news/page935.aspx.

Schmidt, M. S. and E. Schmitt (2012) Flexing muscle, Baghdad detains U.S. contractors. *New York Times*, 15 January. Available from: http://www.nytimes.com/2012/01/16/world/middleeast/asserting-its-sovereignty-iraq-detains-american-contractors.html.

Sdqian, M. S. (2014) Drawing new foreign policy and activating the Council of Representatives. *Al-Hayat*, 15 November. Available from: http://www.alhayat.com/Articles/5701815/إلغاء-قانون--اجتثاث-البعث--ورسم-سياسة-خارجية-جديدة-وتفعيل-مجلس-النواب.

Security Council Report (2009) Middle East, Iraq: Key recent developments. 1 December. Available from: http://www.securitycouncilreport.org/monthly-forecast/2009-12/lookup_c_glKWLeMTIsG_b_5614715.php.

Security Council Report (2016) Chronology of events. Available from: http://www.securitycouncilreport.org/chronology/iraq.php?page=all&print=true.

Semple, K. (2007) US and Iranian officials meet in Baghdad, but talks yield no breakthrough. *New York Times*, 29 May. Available from: http://www.nytimes.com/2007/05/29/world/middleeast/29iraq.html.

Shafaaq (2019) Al-Nujafi: Iraq began to thwart the empire of ran in the region. 3 December. Available from: https://www.shafaaq.com/en/iraq-news/al-nujaifi-iraq-began-to-thwart-the-empire-of-iran-in-the-region/.

Sistani, A. (2006) Book register: Sistani's position since the invasion. Sistani's official website, 23 December. Available from: http://www.sistani.org/arabic/in-news/1014/.

Sistani, A. (2014) Grand Ayatollah Al-Sayyid Ali al-Husseini al-Sistani called upon all able bodied Iraqis to defend country. Sistani's website, 13 June. Available from: http://www.sistani.org/arabic/in-news/24908/.

Sistani, A. (2015) Sistani reject the US congress bill proposal. Sistani's official website, 1 May. Available from: http://www.sistani.org/arabic/in-news/25083/.

Sky News Arabia (2014) Abadi: We will give more importance to foreign policy. 9 September. Available from: http://www.skynewsarabia.com/web/video/686924/العبادي-سنولي-السياسة-الخارجية-أهمية-أكبر.

Sky News Arabia (2015a) Oil and gas in Iraq. 3 November. Available from: https://www.youtube.com/watch?v=Is4opDvZznk&feature=youtu.be.

Sky News Arabia (2015b) Dr. Barham Salih interviewed by Sky news Arabic program – Besaraha. Available from: https://www.youtube.com/watch?v=-u4tmz_Siv8.

Smith, H. L. (2017) Turkey and Iraq team up for military drills on Kurdish border. *Times*, 26 September. Available from: https://www.thetimes.co.uk/article/turkey-and-iraq-team-up-for-military-drills-on-kurdish-border-bflbkvxf3.

Sneed, W. A. (2014) Iraqi governor hires Chartwell out of pocket in ISIS fight-The British are coming. Politico, 3 October. Available from: http://www.politico.com/tipsheets/politico-influence/2014/10/iraqi-governor-hires-chartwell-out-of-pocket-in-isis-fight-the-british-are-coming-212543.

SOMO Oil (2013) About: SOMO Oil marking company. 12 May. Available from: http://somooil.gov.iq/en/index.php/2015-11-14-05-53-22.

Steele, J. (2015) Analysis: Inside the minds of Iraq's grand ayatollahs. Middle East Eye, 3 December. Available from: http://www.middleeasteye.net/news/najaf-iraq-shia-sistani-1775384129.

Stein, J. (2014) Maliki compromised CIA spies in Iraq for years. *News Week*, 26 June. Available from: http://www.newsweek.com/maliki-government-seriously-compromised-cia-operations-iraq-years-256353.

Sulaivany, K. (2016) Watch: World Bank in discussions to provide to provide loan to Iraq, KRG. Kurdistan 24, 30 November. Available from: http://www.kurdistan24.net/en/feature/f709237f-71d7-4653-8f16-3ca7c43bc7eb.

Symonds, P. (2004) Long time CIA 'asset' installed as interim Iraqi prime minister. International Committee of the Fourth International, 31 May. Available from: http://www.wsws.org/en/articles/2004/05/iraq-m31.html.

*Today's Zaman* (2008) Iraqi ambassador: Further steps to follow President Talabani's visit. Available from: http://www.todayszaman.com/_iraqi-ambassador-further-steps-to-follow-president-talabanis-visit_136573.html.

Tohme, A. W. (2016) Former Iraqi Vice President Osama al-Nujaifi speaks out. *Al-Monitor*, 3 March. Available from: http://www.al-monitor.com/pulse/politics/2016/03/iraq-nujaifi-abadi-turkey-forces-interview-hayat-mosul.html.

Trade Arabia (2015) Iraq oil overtakes Saudi in Europe as OPEC battles rage on. 13 November. Available from: http://www.tradearabia.com/news/OGN_294586.html.

Trading Economics (2016) Iraq GDP annual growth rate. Available from: http://www.tradingeconomics.com/iraq/gdp-growth-annual.

Trend News Agency (2014) Iranian spends some $16 million for holy shrines reconstruction in Iraq. 19 August. Available from: http://en.trend.az/iran/2303930.html.

Tripp, C. (2008) Iraq: The politics of local. Open Democracy, 25 January. Available from: https://www.opendemocracy.net/article/middle_east/iraq_the_politics_of_the_local.

UN Meetings Coverage and Press Releases (2014) Security Council, in statement, expresses deep outrage at 'ISIL', urging expanded support for New Iraqi government to defeat it. United Nations, 19 September. Available from: http://www.un.org/press/en/2014/sc11571.doc.htm.

UNCTAD (2016) Strengthen Iraqi trade policy and WTO negotiations. 18 February. Available from: http://unctad.org/en/pages/newsdetails.aspx?OriginalVersionID=405.

United Nations (2012) General Assembly, in resolution, demands all in Syria 'immediately and visibly' commit to ending violence that secretary-general says is ripping country apart. 3 August. Available from: https://www.un.org/press/en/2012/ga11266Rev1.doc.htm.

United States of America Department of Commerce (2013) Doing business in Iraq: 2012 country commercial guide for US. Available from: http://photos.state.gov/libraries/iraq/216651/Dossiers/Doing_Business_in_Iraq_CCG_2012.pdf.

United States of American Department of State (2013) Remarks with Iraqi foreign minister Hoshyar Zebari. 15 August. Available from: https://statedept.brightcovegallery.com/detail/video/2608761506001/remarks-with-iraqi-foreign-minister-hoshyar-zebari.

US Department of State Archive (2007) US–Iraq Declaration of Principles for Friendship and Cooperation. 26 November. Available from: https://2001-2009.state.gov/p/nea/rls/95640.htm.

US State Department: Diplomacy In Action (2014) Jeddah Communiqué. US Department of State Archive, 11 September. Available from: http://2001-2009.state.gov/p/nea/rls/rm/2007/95717.htm.

US EIA (2015) Turkey: International energy and analysis. Available from: https://www.eia.gov/beta/international/analysis.cfm?iso=TUR.

US EIA (2016) Country analysis brief: Iraq. 28 April. Available from: https://www.eia.gov/beta/international/analysis_includes/countries_long/Iraq/iraq.pdf.

Usama, M. (2015) Religious reference: Iranian and Russian intervention in Iraq and Syria is to suppress the Sunnis'. Elaph, 13 October. Available from: http://elaph.com/Web/News/2015/10/1045818.html.

Uyanik, M. (2017) Turkey and the KRG after the referendum: Blocking the path to independence. *Center for Strategic and International Studies*, 22 November. Available from: https://www.csis.org/analysis/turkey-and-krg-after-referendum-blocking-path-independence.

Wales Summit Declaration (2014) NATO's Wales Summit Declaration. Available from: https://www.gov.uk/government/uploads/system/uploads/attachment_data/file/351406/Wales_Summit_Declaration.pdf.

Whitcomb, A. (2014) Kurdish oil sold to buyers in Austria, India. Rudaw, 14 June. Available from: http://www.rudaw.net/english/business/14062014.

White House (2011) Remarks by President Obama and PM al-Maliki of Iraq in a joint press conference. 12 December. Available from: https://www.whitehouse.gov/the-press-office/2011/12/12/remarks-president-obama-and-prime-minister-al-maliki-iraq-joint-press-co.

White House (2014) The Strategic Framework Agreement and the security agreement with Iraq. White House Archives Government. Available from: http://georgewbush-whitehouse.archives.gov/infocus/iraq/.

Wikileaks (2006) Iraqi prime minister visits kingdom on first trip abroad. 5 July. Available from: https://wikileaks.org/plusd/cables/06RIYADH5322_a.html.

Wikileaks (2007) A closer look at the Iraqi Islamic Party. 28 March. Available from: https://www.wikileaks.org/plusd/cables/07BAGHDAD1075_a.html.

*World Affairs Journal* (2013) Energy: Jordan, Iraq and Egypt sign oil, gas agreement. 5 March. Available from: http://www.worldaffairsjournal.org/content/jordan-iraq-and-egypt-sign-oil-gas-agreement.

World Bank (2015) Oil revenue, economic growth and decreased violence has little impact on Iraq's poor. World Bank Press Release, 28 January. Available from: http://www.worldbank.org/en/news/press-release/2015/01/28/oil-revenues-economic-growth-decreased-violence-little-impact-iraq-poor.

Yaphe, J. (2012) Maliki's maneuvering in Iraq. *Foreign Policy*, 6 June. Available from: http://foreignpolicy.com/2012/06/06/malikis-manuevering-in-iraq/.

Younis, N. (2014) Nouri al-Maliki's return would damage Iraq. *Guardian*, 19 October. Available from: https://www.theguardian.com/commentisfree/2010/oct/19/nouri-al-maliki-return-damage-iraq.

Zaaiter, H. (2012) Iraq seek to boost production, challenge Saudi Arabia in global oil market. *Al-Monitor*, 17 February. Available from: http://www.al-monitor.com/pulse/ar/business/2012/02/oil-reserves-of-iraq-enable-it-t.html.

Zand, B. (2014) Foreign Minister Zebari: Iraq is facing a mortal threat. *Spiegel*, 30 June. Available from: http://www.spiegel.de/international/world/spiegel-interview-with-iraqi-foreign-minister-hoshyar-zebari-a-978341.html.

Zhdannikov, D. (2017) The great Russian oil game in Iraqi Kurdistan. Reuters, 19 April. Available from: https://www.reuters.com/article/us-rosneft-iraq-insight/the-great-russian-oil-game-in-iraqi-kurdistan-idUSKBN1HQ1R3.

*Books*

Al-Ali, Z. (2014) *The Struggle for Iraq's Future: How Corruption, Incompetence and Sectarianism Have Undermined Democracy*. London: Yale University Press.

Al-Alkim, H. H. (2012) *Dynamics of Arab Foreign Policy-Making: In the Twenty-First Century*. London: SAQI Books.

al-Jumaili, G. A. (2013) *Foreign Policy*. Beirut: Iraq's Ministry of Foreign Affairs-Al-Daera al-Sahifa.

Allawi, A. A. (2007) *The Occupation of Iraq: Winning the War, Losing the Peace*. New Haven: Yale University Press.

Alshamsi, M. J. (2011) *Islam and Political Reform in Saudi Arabia: The Quest for Political Change and Reform*. New York: Routledge.

Anderson, L., and G. Stansfield (2004) *The Future of Iraq: Dictator, Democracy or Division?* 1st edn. New York: Macmillan.

Atwan, A. B. (2015) *Islamic State: The Digital Caliphate*. London: Saqi Books.

Baker, J. A., and L. H. Hamilton (2016) *The Iraq Study Group Report*. New York: Random House.

Baram, A. (1991) *Culture, History, and Ideology in the Formation of the Ba'thist Iraq, 1968–89*. London: Palgrave Macmillan.

Bhandari, S. (2014) *Self-Determination and Constitution Making in Nepal*. London: Springer.

Bobrow, D. B. (2008) *Hegemony Constrained: Evasion, Modification and Resistance to American Foreign Policy*. Pittsburgh: University of Pittsburgh Press.

Buchan, R. (2013) *International Law and the Construction of Liberal Peace*. Oxford: Hart.

Cagaptay, S. (2017) *The New Sultan: Erdogan and the Crisis of Modern Turkey*. London: I.B. Tauris.

Carcano, A. (2015) *The Transformation of Occupation Territory in International Law*. Leiden: Brill Nijhoff.

Corboz, E. (2015) *Guardians of Shi'ism*. Croydon: Edinburgh University Press.

Cordesman, A. H. (2006) *Arab–Israeli Military Forces in an Era of Asymmetric Wars*. Washington, DC: Center for Strategic and International Studies.

Cordesman, A. H. (2008) *Iraq's Insurgency and the Road to Civil Conflict*, vol. 2. Washington, DC: Centre for Strategic and International Studies.

Cordesman, A. H. (2009) *Saudi Arabia: National Security in a Troubled Region*. Washington, DC: Centre for Strategic and International Studies.

Cordesman, A. H., and S. Khazai (2014) *Iraq in Crisis*. Center for Strategic and International Studies. New York: Rowman & Littefield.

Cordesman, A. H., and N. Obaid (2005) *National Security in Saudi Arabia: Threats, Responses, and Challenges*. London: Praeger Security International

Dabashi, H. (2016) *Iran: The Rebirth of a Nation*. New York: Palgrave Macmillan.

Danilovich, A. (2014) *Iraqi Federalism and the Kurds Learning to Live Together*. London: Routledge.

Dawisha, A. (2009) *A Political History from Independence to Occupation*. Princeton, NJ: Princeton University Press.

Dodge, T. (2012) *Iraq: From War to a New Authoritarianism*. New York: Routledge.

Dougherty, B. K., and E. A. Ghareeb (2013) *Historically Dictionary of Iraq*, 2nd edn. Plymouth: Scarecrow.

Ehrenbery, J., J. P. McSherry, J. R. Sanchez and C. M. Sayei (2010) *The IRAQ Papers*. Oxford: Oxford University Press.

Gvosdev, N. K. (2016) *Communitarian Foreign Policy: Amitai Etzioni's Vision*. New Jersey: Transaction.

Habeeb, W. M. (2012) *The Middle East in Turmoil: Conflict Revolution and Change*. Santa Barbara, CA: Greenwood.

Henry, C. M. and R. Springborg (2014) *Globalization and the Politics of Development in the Middle East*, 2nd edn. Cambridge: Cambridge University Press.

Hinnebusch, R. (2003) *The International Politics of the Middle East*. Manchester: Manchester University Press.

Ishiyama, J. T. (2012) *Comparative Politics: Principles of Democracy and Democratization*. West Success: Wiley-Blackwell.

Johnson, D. W. (2017) *Democracy for Hire: A History of American Political Consulting*. New York: Oxford University Press.

Juneau, T. (2015) *Squandered Opportunity: Neoclassical Realism and Iranian Foreign Policy*. California: Stanford University Press.

Kahana, E., and M. Suwaed (2009) *The A to Z of Middle Eastern Intelligence*. Plymouth: Scarecrow.

Kumral, M. (2016) *Rethinking Turkey–Iraq Relations: The Dilemma of Partial Cooperation*. New York: Palgrave Macmillan.

Leaman, O. (2006) *The Qur'an: An Encyclopedia*, 1st edn. New York: Routledge.

Makiya, K. (1989) *Republic of Fear: The Politics of Modern Iraq*. Los Angeles: University of California Press.

Natali, D. (2010) *The Kurdish Quasi-State: Development and Dependency in Post-Gulf War Iraq*. Syracuse: Syracuse University Press.

Osman, K. (2015) *Sectarianism in Iraq: The Making of State and Nation since 1920*. Routledge: New York.

Ottaway, D. B. (2008) *The King Messenger: Prince Bandar bin Sultan and America's Tangled Relationship with Saudi Arabia*. New York: Walker.

Prados, J. (2006) *Safe for Democracy the Secret Wars of the CIA*. Chicago: Rowman & Littlefield.

Rayburn, J. (2014) *Iraq after America: Strongman, Sectarian and Resistance*. California: Hoover Institute Press.
Rosen, N. (2006) *In the Belly of the Green Bird: The Triumph of the Martyrs in Iraq*. London: Free Press.
Sassoon, J. (2009) *The Iraqi Refugees: The New Crisis in the Middle East*. London: I.B. Tauris.
Scheller, B (2013) *The Wisdom of Syria's Waiting Game: Foreign Policy under the Assad's*. London: C. Hurst.
Segell, G. (2005) *Axis of Evil and Rogue States: The Bush Administration 2000–2004*. London: Glen Segell.
Shareef, M. (2014) *The United States, Iraq and the Kurds: Shock, Awe and Aftermath*. New York: Routledge.
Sky, W. (2015) *The Unraveling: High Hopes and Missed Opportunities in Iraq*. London: Atlantic Books.
Sluglett, M. F., and P. Sluglett (2001) *Iraq since 1958: From Revolution to Dictatorship*. London: I.B. Tauris.
Stansfield, G. (2003) *Iraqi Kurdistan: Political Development and Emergent Democracy*. London: Routledge.
Stansfield, G., and L. Anderson (2009) *Crisis in Kirkuk: The Ethno-Politics of Conflict and Comprise*. Philadelphia: University of Pennsylvania Press.
Tripp, C. (2007) *A History of Iraq*, 3rd edn. Cambridge: Cambridge University Press.
Webb, B., J. Murphy and P. Nealen (2014) *The ISIS Solution: How Unconventional Thinking and Special Operation Can Eliminate Radical Islam*. New York: St. Martin's.

*Book chapters*

Alkifaey, H. J. (2015) The Arab spring and democratization: An Iraqi perspective. In L. Sadiki (ed.), *Routledge Handbook of the Arab Spring*. London: Routledge.
Baram, A. (2011) Religious extremism and ecumenical tendencies in Modern Iraqi Shi'ism. In O. Bengio and M. Litvak (eds), *The Sunna and Shi'a in History: Division and Ecumenism in the Muslim Middle East*. New York: Palgrave Macmillan, 105–25.
Dawisha, A. (2002) Footprints in the sand: The definition and redefinition of identity in Iraq's foreign policy. In S. Telhami and M. Barnett (eds), *Identity and Foreign Policy in the Middle East*. New York: Cornell University Press. 117-37
Doyle, D. (2018) Pulling and gouging: The Sadrist line's adaptable and evolving repertoire of contention. In Dara Conduit and Shahram Akbarzadeh (eds), *New Opposition in the Middle East*. London: Palgrave Macmillan, 4–69.
Eppel, M. (2011) Kurdish politics and post-Saddam Iraq. In A. Cohen and N. Efrati (eds), *Post-Saddam Iraq: New Realities, Old Identities, Changing Patterns*. Eastbourne-UK: Sussex Academic, 104–29.
Gause, F. G. (2014) The foreign policy of Saudi Arabia. In R. Hinnebusch and A. Etheshami (eds), *The Foreign Policy of Middle East States*. London: Rienner, 185–86.
Gulmohamad, Z. (2020) The evolution of Iraq's Hashd al-Sha'abi (Popular Mobilization Forces). In P. Amour (ed.), *The Regional Order in the Gulf Region and the Middle East: Regional Rivalries and Security Alliances*. Cham: Palgrave Macmillan, 259–301.
Halliday, F. (1986) Iranian foreign policy since 1979. In J. R. I. Cole and N. R. Keddie (eds), *Shi'ism and Social Protest*. New Haven: Yale University Press, 88–106.

Hinnebusch, R. (2014b) Foreign policy in the Middle East. In R. Hinnebusch and A. Ehteshami (eds), *The Foreign Policies of Middle East State*, 2nd edn. London: Lynne Rienner, 1–34.

Hinnebusch, R. (2014c) The Foreign Policy of Syria. In R. Hinnebusch and A. Ehteshami (eds), *The Foreign Policies of Middle East State*, 2nd edn. London: Lynne Rienner, 207–22.

Lukitz, L. (2011) The Shi'is in post-Saddam Iraq: A common political front but different tactics. In A. Cohen and N. Efrati (eds), *Post-Saddam Iraq: New Realities, Old Identities, Changing Patterns*. Brighton: Sussex Academic, 53–103.

Marr, P. (2010) One Iraq or many. In A. Baram, A. Rohode and R. Zeidel (eds), *Iraq between Occupations: Perspectives from 1920 to the Present*. New York: Palgrave Macmillan, 15–41.

Marr, P., and S. Parker (2011) The new Iraq. In P. Marr, S. B. Lasensky and H. J. Barkey (eds), *Iraq, Its Neighbors, and the United States: Competition, Crisis and Reordering of Power*. Washington, DC: Endowment of the United States Institute of Peace, 13–35.

Nazim, H. A. (2008) The rise of Islamists after the US invasion of Iraq-2003. In R. M. Abhyankar (ed.) *West Asia and the Region*. New Delhi: Academic Foundation.

Riggs, R. J. (2012) Shia actors in post-Saddam Iraq: Partisan historiography. In J. Tejet et al. (eds), *Writing the Modern History of Iraq Historiographical and Political Challenges*, 287–303.

Romano, D. (2010b) The struggle for autonomy and decentralization. In M. Lamani and B. Momani (eds), *From Desolation to Reconstruction: Iraq's Trouble Journey*. Canada: Wilfrid Laureir University Press, 53–75.

Sabir, F. B. (2012) The caliphate as nostalgia: The case of the Iraqi Muslim Brotherhood. In M. Al-Rasheed, C. Kersten and M. Shterin (eds), *Demystifying the Caliphate: Historical Memory Contemporary Contexts*. Oxford: Oxford University Press, 135–46.

Soffar, M. (2010) Foreign policy under occupation: Does Iraq need a foreign policy. In B. Korany and H. Dessouki (eds), *The Foreign Policies of the Arab States: The Challenge of Globalization*. Cairo: American University of Cairo Press, 253–83.

Stansfield, G., and N. Caspersen (2011) Introduction unrecognized states in the international system. In G. Stansfield and N. Caspersen (eds), *Unrecognized States in the International System*. London: Routledge.

Tonini, A. (2005) Iraqi foreign policy under Qasim, 1958–1963. In G. Nonneman (ed.), Analysing *Middle East Foreign Policies*. London: Routledge, 123–44.

Tripp, C. (2002) The foreign policy of Iraq. In R. Hinnebusch and A. Ehteshami (eds), *The Foreign Policies of Middle East States*. London: Lynne Reinner, 167–92.

Visser, R. (2012) Trends and patterns in the Shii Heartland and Beyond. In A. Moghadam (ed.), *Militancy and Political Violence in Shiism*. London: Routledge, 59–112.

Yacoubian, M. (2011) Syria and the new Iraq: Between rivalry and rapprochement. In H. J. Barkey, S. B. Lasensky and P. Marr (eds), *Iraq, Its Neighbors and the United States: Competition, Crisis, and the Reordering of Power*. Washington DC: United States Institute of Peace, 145–63.

Yaphe, J. S. (2011a) The United States and Iran in Iraq: Risks and opportunities. In A. Etheshami and M. Zweiri (eds), *Iran's Foreign Policy: From Khatami to Ahmadinejad*. Reading: Ithaca, 37–55.

Yaphe, J. S. (2011b) Iraq and its Gulf Arab neighbors. In H. J. Barkey, S. B. Lasensky and P. Marr (eds), *Iraq, Its Neighbors and the United States: Competition, Crisis, and the Reordering of Power*. Washington, DC: United States Institute of Peace, 119–42.

Younis, N. (2017) The rise if ISIS: Iraq and Persian Gulf security. In K. Ulrichsen (ed.), *The Changing Security Dynamics of the Persian Gulf*. Oxford: Oxford University Press, 113–26.

# INDEX

Abbawi, Labeed (Iraq's former undersecretary) 9
ABC News (2007) 26
Abd al-Mahdi, Adil 51–2
Abdullah (King) 124
Ahmad, H. 36
Ahrar Alliance 15
al-Abadi, Haider (Prime Minister) 10, 13, 14, 19, 25, 27–8, 48–52, 112, 113, 124, 129
*al-A'malia al-Syasiya* 37
Al-Arabiya News (2015) 127
al-A'skari, Sami 56
al-Bayati, Abbas 37–8
*al-Bina* (Shia factions' coalition) 68
al-Faisal, Saud 49
al-Fayad, Falah 44
al-Gaylani, Rashid Ali 4
al-Hakim, Mahdi 11
al-Hakim, Mohammed Ali 61
*al-Hal* (Arab Sunni political faction) 68
al-Halbousi, Mohammad 37
al-Hashimi, Tariq 44
*al-Iraqiya* 26–7, 43
al-Issawi, Rafe 45
al-Jaafari, Ibrahim (Prime Minister) 10, 25, 40–1, 54, 57–61, 72, 110, 152
al-Jabouri, Salem 49, 68
Al-Jazeera Arabic (2009) 116
al-Jubouri, Salim 31
al-Jumaily, Ghanim Alwan 53
*al-Khatt al-Sadri* 14
al-Khozaei, Khodair 65
Allawi, Ayad 35, 38–40, 45, 56
Allawi, Mohamad 45
All-Party Parliamentary Group (APPG) 99
al-Mahdi, Jaish (Prime Minister) 14, 15, 40, 52, 112
al-Maliki, Nouri (Prime Minister) 1, 10, 41–8, 52, 57, 108, 116, 120, 124

al-Maliki's group 11–12
*Al-Manasib al-Siyadiyyah* 35
al-Mashadani, Mahmoud (speaker) 67–8, 126–7
*al-Muhasasa or al-Muhasasa al-Hizbiya wa al-taifyya* 35, 73
*al-Muhasasa* (quota system) 106
al-Mutlaq, Saleh 44
al-Naqib, Falah Hassan (Iraqi interior minister) 25–6
al-Nujaifi brothers 28–30
al-Nujaifi, Usama 50, 68
al-Qaeda in Iraq (AQI) 144, 145
*al-Quwa al-A'rabia al-Mushtaraka* 59
*al-Riasat al-Talatha* 62
al-Rikabi, Sadiq 11
al-Sadr, Muqtada 40, 48
al-Sadr's movement 118
al-Said, Nuri (Prime Minister) 4
al-Sammarai, Iyad 31
al-Shabibi, Sinan 44
al-Shawani, Mohammed 128
al-Sistani 21–3
*al-Tahalf al-Kurdistani* 78
*al-Tawafuq al-Siyasi* (political accord) 36, 58, 73, 106
*Al-Wataniya*'s programme 27, 28
*al-Wazara al-Kharyiah al-Iraqiya* 52
al-Wazara, Rais Majlis 38
al-Yawer, Ghazi Mashal (President) 62–3
Ambassador Faily 53
ammunitions 111
Annan, Kofi 39
anti-Daesh coalitions 113
anti-Iranian rhetoric 40
Arab Gulf States 22, 108
Arab League 107
Arab League's Operation Decisive Storm (*A'sifat al-Hazm*) 60
Arab League summit 56, 60, 71

Arab Middle East 4
Arab Project Party 29
Arab Sunni factions 35, 39, 50, 54, 63, 72–3, 124, 131–2, 153
Arms Control Association (2016) 108
Asa'ib Ahl al-Haq (AAH) 15, 43, 128, 153
*Ashraq Al-Awsat* (2010) 63, 140
A'tabat al-A'basya 22
A'taba al-Alawiyya al-Muqadasa 22
A'taba al-Hussaniya al-Muqadasa 22
Atlantic Council (2016) 125–6
Aziz, Abdullah (King) 19

Ba'athist's foreign policy approach 7
Badr Brigade (1981) 125
Badr Organization 15, 23, 128, 152–3
Babiker, Khairalla Hassan 57
Baghdad 75, 76, 96–7
Baghdad's foreign policy 35, 40, 105
Barzani, Masoud 45, 56, 64, 82–3
Barzani, Nechervan 77–8, 81
Barzanji, Sheikh Muhammad 76
Basra 114
BBC News (2006) 32
*BraKuji* 77
Brennan, John 42
Bush, George W. (US President) 8, 18, 32, 65, 107

Cairo 60
Cavusoglu, Mevlut 60
Center for Strategic and International Studies (2013) 111, 115, 124
centrist Shia 153
Chalabi, Ahmad 40, 45
Chatham House (2013) 12
Chevron 117
China 111, 115
clandestine 'intelligence' and counter-terrorism agencies 111
CNN (2007) 26
Coalition Provisional Authority (CPA) 21, 52, 109, 125
contentious bedfellows 112
core executive bodies 71–2
   *see also* federal government's executive bodies
Council of Ministers 36, 38, 61, 62, 69
critical bilateral agreements 112

Crocker, Ryan 65
Czech Republic, the 111

*Daily News* (2018) 134
*Daily Sabah* (2018) 134
Dai, Y. 11
Davis, Lincoln 99
Da'wa party, islamic 11–13
   post-Saddam era 10
   2005 to 2018, 10
decision-makers 75
Democratic Patriotic Alliance of Kurdistan (DPAK) 78
department of foreign relations (DFR) 75, 153
   administrative body 87
   events 87
   and I-MOFA 87–8
   Iraqi embassies 88
   purpose and activities of 88–90
diplomacy and balanced bilateral relationships 114
diplomacy and economy 106, 107
diplomacy priority 154
draft constitution Article 60/2 82, 83

Eastern Europe 112
economic penetration 130
economic priority 155
economic ties 131
Egypt 5–7, 11, 13, 28, 32, 33, 51, 63, 92, 119
*EKurd Daily* (2010) 140
elites gathering 15
Emir Sheikh Sabah al-Sabah 46
Energy Daily (2013) 116
environmental catastrophe 105
Erbil 77, 80, 96–7, 107, 108, 116–18, 123, 137, 151, 154
Erdogan, Recep Tayyip 47
ethnic/sectarian tendencies 106
Europe 2
European Commission (2016) 117
external actors 124
Exxon Mobil 117

Faily, Lukman 9, 71, 123
Fars News Agency (2015) 29
Fatah, Baker 38, 131

*fatwa Wajib Jihad al-Kafai* 24
federal government's executive bodies
   al-Jaafari, Ibrahim 72
   *al-Muhasasa*, or *al-Muhasasa al-Hizbiya wa al-taifyya* 35
   Arab League 71
   Arab Sunnis 72–3
   core executive bodies 71–2
   foreign policy 36–8
   FRC and a specific committee 69–70
   ICR's Rules of Procedures 67–8
   Interim Transitional Government (ITG) 35
   Iraqi Interim Government (IIG) 35
   parliament 35
   speaker 67, 68
   time of interview (Salih) 36
financial aid 10
*Financial Times* (2011) 114
*Financial Tribune* (2015) 130
Foreign Agents Registration Act (FARA) 98
foreign direct investment (FDI) 78, 117
foreign minister
   al-Hakim, Mohammed Ali (since October 2018) 61
   *al-Wazara al-Kharyiah al-Iraqiya* 52
   Ambassador Faily 53
   Arab Sunnis 54
   Foreign Service Institute 52
   I-MOFA 52–4
   Iraqi constitution 54
   undersecretaries *(Wakala al-Wuzara)* 52
   Zebari, Hoshyar (2003–14) 54–7
foreign relations 2, 3, 9, 7, 12–14, 18–20, 24, 31, 32, 37–9, 41–8, 51, 55, 61, 65–70, 72, 84–6, 107–8, 111, 112, 118, 146, 147, 152–5
   *see also* Iraqi Kurdish political parties; Kurdistan Regional Government (KRG)
Foreign Relations Committee (FRC) 10, 35, 67–70, 151
Foreign Service Institute 52
14 July Revolution *(Thawrat/Harakat 14 Tammuz)* 4–5

Gazprom 117
General Secretariat for the Council of Ministers 38

Geneva Center for the Democratic Control of Armed Forces (2009) 21
Geneva II conference, the 108
geography 131
Ghahban, Tamir 46
*Grand Ayatollah al-Sayyid al-Husseini Ali al-Sistani* 20–3
grassroots supporters and/or government networks 152
Greece 115
Great Britain 3
'Guardianship of Islamic Jurists' 126
Gulf Cooperation Council (GCC) 59
Gulf of Aqaba on the Red Sea 115

Haider al-Abadi's government 152
*Hajj* 41
Hammoud, M. A. 36, 49
*Hashd al-Watani/Haras Nineveh* 29
Hashemite Kingdom 3, 4
*Hezb I'raqyoon* 62
historians and political analysts 3
Holy Shia Shrines militias/A'tabat Forces 129
House Foreign Affairs Committee 46
humanitarian aid 105
Human Rights Watch (2011, 2018) 136
Hungary 98
Hussein, Fuad 76

ICR's Kurdistan Coalition 69
ICR's Rules of Procedures, article 33 67–8
improvised explosive devices (IEDs) 111
independence 75
India 115
institution building 78
interference and influence 123–4
intergovernmental organizations (IGOs) 107, 117
Interim Transitional Government (ITG) 35
internal actors 124
internally displaced persons (IDPs) 91
international aid organizations 77
international conventions 19
International Crisis Group 110
International Energy Agency (IEA) 142
International Monetary Fund (IMF) 100, 114, 118

Iran 2, 79, 92, 108, 111, 112, 116, 123, 126, 131, 152
Iranian interference in Iraq
    ISCI 125
    1980-8 Iran-Iraq War 125
    stages between 2003 and 2016 125
    Tehran's security, economic and political interests 124
Iranian Revolutionary Guard Corps (IRGC) 15, 17
Iraq 1, 105, 106, 116
    see also Saudi Arabia; Syria
Iraq Business News (2010) 116
Iraqi Accord Front (IAF) 31
Iraqi actors 155
Iraqi Arab Shia 124
Iraqi-Arab/Turkish rapprochement 59
Iraqi Army (IA) 110
Iraqi constitution 3, 16, 36, 37-8, 40, 44, 53-4, 61, 69, 71-2, 78-9, 83, 86-9, 93-7, 103-4, 118, 134, 154
    article 67 61
    article 78 38, 44
    Iraqi elites and factions 40
Iraqi Council of Representatives (ICR) 1, 10, 35, 67-70, 113, 126, 151
Iraqi Counter Terrorism Service (I-CTS) 111
Iraqi Governing Council (IGC) 38, 78
Iraqi Interim Government (IIG) 35, 107, 125
Iraqi Islamic Party (IIP) 30-3, 68
Iraqi Judiciary 44
Iraqi-Kurdish Civil War (1994-8) 77
Iraqi Kurdish political parties
    KDP 91
    leaders 90-1
    Mustafa, Falah 92
    post 2003 91
    PYD and KNC 91
    territorial control 91
Iraqi Ministry of Foreign Affairs (I-MOFA) 9, 52-4, 78, 109, 151
    Zebari (Foreign Minister) 56
    Iraqi political system 58
    Law 2013 /36, article 1 55
    PMF's relationship 60
Iraqi Ministry of Trade (2016) 117
Iraqi National Accord (INA) 25-8, 38

Iraqi National Intelligence Service (INIS) 110-11, 128
Iraqi National List (INL) 28
Iraqi National Oil Company (INOC) 7
Iraqi National Security Advisory (*Mustasharia al-Amn al-Watani al-Iraqi*) 110
Iraqi parliamentary summit 68
Iraqi Petroleum Company (IPC) 7
Iraq-Iran bilateral relationship 112
Iraqi Revolutionary Guards Corps–Quds Force (IRGC-QF) 127-8
Iraqi Security Forces (ISF) 22, 43, 109, 126
Iraqi Shia alliance (UIA) 18
Iraqi Shia islamists 39
Iraqis Party 62
Iraq's economy 114-19
Iraq's foreign relations 107-8
Iraq's military and security apparatus 127-9
Iraq's National Security Agency *(Jihaz al-Amn al-Watani al-Iraqi)* 110
Iraq's security 109-14
Islamic Da'wa Party 35, 40, 41, 44, 46, 48, 51, 65, 71, 110
Islamic State (IS) 1
Islamic State of Iraq and Syria (ISIS) 131
Islamic Supreme Council of Iraq (ISCI) 11, 17-20, 51, 125, 152
Ismail, Mohammad Sabir 37, 38, 123
Israel 7
Italy 115

Jeddah Communiqué 59
Jeffery (US ambassador) 125-6
Joint Analysis Policy Unit (2013) 111
Joint Comprehensive Plan of Action (JCPOA) 130
Joint Forces Land Component Command (JFLCC) 110
Jordan 7, 17, 111, 115

Karadaghi, Kamaran 61, 127
Kataib Hezbollah (KH) 43
Kerry, John 49
Khalilzad, Zalmay 41
Khedery, Ali 41
Khomeini, Ayatollah Ruhollah 126
Khomeini's doctrine 18, 21

Kingdom of Saudi Arabia (KSA) 2, 16, 82, 108, 123, 152
Kirkuk-Ceyhan (Turkey) pipelines 115
KRG Liaison Office 98
KRG's foreign policy
 Baghdad-based federal government 80
 Erbil-based regional government 80
 from 1991/1992 to 2003 79–80
 Hussein, Fuad 76
 interconnected phases 76
 Iraqi Kurds' external relationships 77
 post 2003 80
KRG's prime minister, The 84–6
Kurdish Democratic Party of Iran (KDP-I) 131
Kurdish policy 36
Kurdish senior 76
Kurdish Workers Party (PKK) 115
Kurdistan Alliance (KA) 57, 78
Kurdistan Democratic Party (KDP) 28, 40, 76, 131, 153
Kurdistan Regional Government (KRG) 1, 29, 42, 106, 151
 approaches 79
 emerging nature of 97–100
 external agenda, priorities and alliances 75
 federal constitution 76
 mixed or hybrid presidential-parliamentary system 75
 sociopolitical and economic evolution 75
 *see also* KRG's foreign policy; Kurdistan Region of Iraq (KR-I)
Kurdistan Region of Iraq (KR-I) 2, 131, 153
 Barzani, Nechervan 77–8
 sociopolitical development 75–6
Kurdistan Region Presidency (KRP) 82–4
Kurdistan Region Security Council (KRSC) 153
Kuwait 17, 108, 115

land desertification 105
Latif, Wael Abdul (pro-Shia Iraqi politician and minister) 138
League of Nations 4
Lebanon 21, 22, 24, 27, 50, 59, 60, 115, 127, 129, 147

Macron, Emmanuel 79
*Makatab* 38
Mashroo' al-Qanoon 69
Ma'sum, Fuad 49, 65–7
May, Theresa 79
McGarry, J. 36
Middle East 2, 6, 31
Middle East Brief (2015) 126
Middle East Eye (2015) 113
Ministerial Committee of National Security (MCNS) 110
Ministry of Foreign Affairs 54, 128
Ministry of Humanitarian Aid and Cooperation 77
Ministry of Intelligence and Security 128
Ministry of Oil 115
Mitsubishi 114
*Mubadarat al-Hiwar* 67
Multi-National Security Transition Command (MNSTC-I) 109–10
Munich Security Conferences 50
Muqtada's militia 43
Murad, Adel 45
Muslim Brotherhood 11, 31
*Muttahidum* 28–30
'My Vision for Iraq' (al-Jaafari) 40

Najem, Tareq 46
Nasrallah, Hassan 60, 129
Nasser, Gamal Abdel (Egyptian president) 4–6
National Partnership Gathering 15
National Reform Trend 58
National Security Advisory and Agency 38
NATO (2014) 110
New Generation, The 92
Ninewa Governorate 28
non-Arab population 4
non-governmental organizations (NGOs) 77
non-pro-Iran Iraqis 127

Observatory of Economic Complexity (2016) 115
Oil and Gas Committee (2015) 115–16
Oil Price (2013) 115
Oil Price (2015) 142
oil revenues 114
O'Leary, B. 36

Omran, Sabah 65
Operation Provide Comfort in 1991 77
Organization of the Petroleum Exporting Countries (OPEC) 115

Palestine Liberation Organisation 7
pan-Arabism 4
parliament 35
Pasha, Sharif 76
Patriotic Union of Kurdistan (PUK) 37, 76, 131, 153
PL Article 12 82
Poland 111
Popular Mobilization Forces (PMF) 22, 47, 109, 126, 155
post-2003 foreign policy priorities
    Iraqi decision-makers 106
    Iraq's security 109–14
Presidency Council 62, 63
Prime Minister Press Office (2017) 113
pro-Iran Iraqi Shia militias 50, 125, 128
proportional representative (PR) 36
pro-Sistani and pro-Sadr armed groups 128, 129

Qadir, Mustafa Said (Peshmerga) 82–3, 113

*Rais Majlis al-Wazara* (Prime Minister) 38
Ramazan Corps 128
*Rapareen* 77
Rosneft, a state-owned petroleum company 116
Royal Dutch Shell 114
Russia 20, 108, 111, 112, 116

Sabi, S. M. 36
Saddam's regime 112
*Sadrist Movement (al-Tayyar al-Sadri) and Muqtada al-Sadr* 14–17
*Sahwat* 43
Salih, Barham (Prime Minister) 9, 36, 37, 61, 67, 80
*Saraya al-Salam* (Peace Brigades) 16
Saudi Arabia 111, 124
    MBS's foreign policy 137
    'a Muslim international force' 137
    Saudi rulers 137
    Sunni insurgents 138

Sdqian, M. S. 42
sectarian violence 97–8
security challenges and needs 114
Security Council Report (2009) 143
Security Council Report (2016) 144
security priority 154
self-determination 75
self-justification 97
17 July Revolution (*Thawrat 17 Tammuz*) 6
Sha'alan, Hazem (defence minister) 25–6
Sharm el-Sheikh 39
Shaways, Rosh 63
Shawis, Rosh 40
Sheikh Hamad bin Jassem al-Tani 46
Shia elites and factions 155
Shia Islamic Da'wa Party 152
Shia militias 23–5, 47
    Iranian proxies, role of 108, 112
Shia policy 36
Shia religious literature 130
Shubbar, Hasan 11
Sinjari, Hussein 9–10
Sky News Arabia (2015a) 116
slow progress, fragile diplomacy 140–2
SOFA agreement 55
soft power, Iranian 129–31
Soleimani, Qasem 128
Sunni and Kurdish factions 138–40
South Korea 115
Speaker 67, 68
Specific, Measurable, Agreed upon, Realistic, Time-based (SMART) goals 106
Strait of Hormuz 114–15
State of Law Coalition (SLC) 12–13, 37
State Organization for Marketing of Oil (SOMO) 115
Status of Force Agreement (SOFA) 16, 42, 112
Strait of Hormuz 114–15
Strategic Framework Agreement (SFA) 42, 127
Sulaymaniyah 77
Sulaymaniyah International Airport 137
Sulta al-Tashria'ya 69
Sunni jihadists 43
Sunni policy 36
Supreme National Council 128

Symonds, P. 39
Syria 80–1, 105, 108, 112, 115, 116, 123
  Damascus 142
  and Iraq during the Syrian Civil
    War 144–5
  and Iraq post Saddam 143–4
  regional leadership 142
Syrian Civil War 19, 47, 49, 133

Talabani, Jalal 38, 40, 41, 61, 63–5
Talabani, Qubad 100
Tillerson, Rex 79
*Time* magazine 14
time of interview (Salih) 36
*Today's Zaman* (2008) 65
Total, transnational energy
  corporation 117
Trading Economics (2016) 114
Transitional Administrative Law (TAL) 39
Transitional National Assembly 63
Trump, Donald (President) 112, 126
Turkey 2, 42, 45, 63, 65, 79, 92, 99, 105,
    108, 111, 115, 123, 124, 131, 154
  accusations 133
  Atheel (former Mosul governor) 133
  Baghdad and Ankara 134
  Baghdad's and Ankara's regional
    policies 133
  'enemy state' 133
  and the Kurdistan Regional
    Government 134–7
  Usama al-Nujaifi (former vice
    president) 133

UK 16, 26, 49, 67, 79–81, 90, 91, 93, 99,
    111, 118
'unacceptable violations of its
  sovereignty' 65
UNCTAD (2016) 117
Union of Soviet Socialist Republic
  (USSR) 4
United Arab Emirates (UAE) 17
United Iraqi Alliance (UIA) 12–13, 40
United Nations Assistance Mission in Iraq
  (UNAMI) 90
United Nations Charter 52

United Nations Office at Geneva 37
United Nations (2012) 144
United States 1, 43, 54, 58, 63, 71–2,
    80–1, 92, 101, 106, 111, 115, 126, 127,
    129, 131
United States Kurdistan Business Council
  (USKBC) 99
United States of America Department of
  Commerce (2016) 117–18
UN's sanctions and US-led invasion 114
UN's Charter Chapter VII 56
UN Security Council 42, 59
US EIA (2016) 115–116
US-Iraqi Strategic Framework Agreement
  (SFA) 112
US-Iraq SOFA agreement 67–8
US-led anti–Islamic State (IS)
  coalition 126

victory *(Itilaf al-Nasr)* 13
volatile transformation and foreign policy
  (1958) 5–8

*Wakala al-Wuzara* 52
Washington, DC (2004) 107
*Washington Post* (newspaper) 40, 47
water competition 105–6
weapons of mass destruction (WMD) 8
weapons smuggling 111
White House 107
*Wilayat al-Faqih* doctrine 129
*Wilayat al-Ummah* doctrine 10–11, 20
Wilson, Joe 99
*World Affairs Journal* (2013) 115
World Bank (2015) 118
World Economic Forum in Davos 50, 83
World Trade Organization (WTO)
  107, 117

Yasseen, Fareed 53
Younesi, Ali (President) 127

Zarif, Javad 60
Zebari, Hoshyar (foreign minister) 54–7,
  107–10, 124

www.ingramcontent.com/pod-product-compliance
Lightning Source LLC
Chambersburg PA
CBHW070636300426
44111CB00013B/2134